EUROPEAN TEXTILE DESIGN OF THE 1920s

Kunstsammlungen Chemnitz
Catalogue of the Collection IV

EUROPEAN TEXTILE DESIGN OF THE 1920s

Texts by
Katharina Metz
Ingrid Mössinger
Wieland Poser

EDITION STEMMLE

Zurich   New York

| CONTENTS |

Chemnitz looks back upon a proud history of 700 years of textile production. The city was granted market rights in 1143, and commerce rapidly expanded to the extent that a town wall had to be built to secure the weekly markets and annual fairs. Chemnitz had received its charter as a free *Reichsstadt* by the end of the 14th century. Flourishing trade in linens, yarn and flax made it the center of the linen industry in Saxony. The city's importance was derived in part from its position at the crossroads of the major road connecting Hamburg, Leipzig, Chemnitz, Prague and Vienna along the north-to-south axis and the west-to-east route from Frankfurt to Nuremberg, Chemnitz, Dresden and Breslau. Cloth weaving replaced linen processing in the 15th century. Satin yarn spinning operations and new dying processes followed somewhat later. Significant economic progress was virtually nullified during the Thirty-Years' War, and it was not until the early 18th century that cotton and wool weaving fueled a long-awaited recovery. Major trading companies developed. The arrival of the railroad in 1852 played a decisive role in the city's rise to prosperity during the 19th century. In the years that followed, the textile factories of Chemnitz – most notably the producers of upholstery fabrics – achieved considerable economic success.

Drawing from locally available raw materials and beginning with the simplest of technologies, regional textile production had spawned a high-tech industry with a worldwide reputation by end of the First World War. Major industrial enterprises, including those run by the Esche and Vogel families, contributed significantly to this growth. This industrialist class was actively involved in the spheres of both business and culture at the international level. Commissions went to such artists as Henry van de Velde, Edvard Munch and Max Klinger, and generous donations were made on behalf of the newly established museum. Among these irreplaceable donations were many of the fabrics comprised within the model collections that now represent some of the museum's most valuable treasures. The realization that the future belonged to mechanized industry came sooner here than in many other places, and with it the understanding that industrial growth could not be accomplished without esthetic standards. Even then it was clear that quality, and not quantity, would be the crucial factor in determining the region's competitive standing in the international market. And thus efforts were made to bring internationally renowned artists and works of both independent and applied art to Chemnitz. A free public library was established as part of the museum. The goal articulated and pursued in Chemnitz around the turn of the century – to produce technically so-

phisticated goods in keeping with the highest esthetic standards while forging a link between art and life – is still worth striving for today.

The roughly 200 objects presented in the *Kunstsammlungen Chemnitz* at the exhibition "European Textile Design in the 1920s," which commemorates the 100th anniversary of the founding of the Textile and Handicrafts Collection, and documented in the catalogue offer indisputable proof that quality hand-crafted and industrial products, like great works of art, are not subject to the changing moods of fashion. Honoring the Textile and Handicrafts Collection in an appropriate manner required extraordinary efforts on the part of many people. My thanks are due first and foremost to Katharina Metz, curator of the exhibition and editor of the catalogue, for her commitment and outstanding scholarly contribution. I wish to express my gratitude as well to her assistant Liane Sachs and to the textile restorationist Eva-Maria Gawron. I thank Wieland Poser for the broad-based catalogue essay written specifically for this occasion. A special word of thanks is due to Martin Rupprecht. Mr. Rupprecht, a well-known designer of stage sets for major musical and theatrical events, responded with great enthusiasm to the idea of presenting these beautiful fabrics in a worthy setting. As expected, he and his assistant Christoph Melching succeeded in turning the opening of the exhibition into a truly festive occasion.

A project of the complexity and magnitude of the "European Textile Design in the 1920s" exhibition requires not only considerable scholarly input but also places a considerable strain upon funding capacities as well. I am very grateful to the *Kulturstiftung des Freistaates Sachsen* and its director Dr. Jürgen Uwe Ohlau for providing generous financial support for the physical presentation of the exhibition. I also wish to thank Dr. Joachim Voigtmann, Director of the *Sächsische Landesstelle für Museumswesen,* for assistance in funding the catalogue. As is so often the case today, available public funding resources would not have sufficed to cover all the needs of this ambitious project. I therefore wish to thank Petra Borges, Director of the Culture Department of the City of Chemnitz, for arranging contacts with representatives of the textile industry. A special word of thanks is due as well to Herbert Riedel of *Riedel und Tietz* in Limbach-Oberfrohna for providing both enthusiastic moral support and generous financial assistance. Mr. Riedel was also instrumental in recruiting support for the project from textile companies located not only in Saxony but in other parts of Germany as well. In this context I wish to thank Roland

Schönfelder of *Brückner Trockentechnik GmbH & Co. KG*, Leonberg; Mr. Bitzer of *Jernberg*, Albstadt; Mr. Burr of the *Sächsische Baumwollspinnerei*, Mittweida; Mr. Böhringer, *Terrott*. Stuttgart-Bad Cannstatt and Mr. Dobler of *TWD*, Deggendorf. They and all the other persons and organizations listed in the catalogue deserve special thanks for their generous financial contributions.

Western history clearly shows us that culture cannot be left in the hands of government institutions alone. It needs the dedicated involvement of entrepreneurial personalities from the private sector as well. Textiles and woven goods have relied for centuries upon international exchange with respect to inventions, esthetics, production, distribution and trade. Thus only very few industrial and esthetic objects are capable of offering as convincing an illustration of the idea of a United States of Europe from a historical perspective as textiles.

Ingrid Mössinger

The catalogue *European Textile Design in the 1920s* is the first published presentation of the extensive collection of textiles from this period comprised within the Textil- und Kunstgewerbesammlung Chemnitz. The book appears on the occasion of the 100th anniversary of the founding of the Chemnitz collections and in conjunction with the major commemorative exhibition associated with the anniversary celebration. Offered as a basic survey and a supplement to existing publications on textile collections, this volume presents some 200 European textiles, decorative and upholstery fabrics and wall hangings from the decade of the twenties. It contains a broad sampling of the spectrum of forms created during the period as well as an abundant range of designs, which in its entirety is well suited to a critical reassessment of existing ideas and opinions about the textiles of this first decade in the interim between World Wars. Manifestations of coincidence and subjective preferences in the selection cannot be ruled out, of course, as all of the fabrics and decorative materials shown here were also purchased in their time on the basis of considerations that were unaffected by later reappraisals.

It has been difficult to establish exact dates for many of these objects. In cases where no pertinent information could be found in the literature or in publications from the period, the year of purchase has been indicated as a guide to the approximate year of origin. Such an approach appears legitimate and sensible in this case, as a close correspondence between the dates of production and acquisition is typical of collection activity during this particular decade. The period designated as "the 1920s" has been broadly defined to include a number of pieces produced in the early 1930s as well, since these clearly belong in a substantive sense to this phase of development, which did not begin to unfold in Great Britain and France until somewhat later.

No distinction was made in the process of selection between wall hangings as one-of-a-kind articles and decorative or upholstery fabrics produced serially. The period under scrutiny here is characterized in particular by a close and fruitful interaction between art and design, between the one-of-a-kind piece and serial production during the first half of the 20th century. This productive tension is illustrated by the example of the weaving workshop at the Bauhaus in Weimar and Dessau.

The Bauhaus undoubtedly exercised significant influence, both directly and indirectly, upon the development of 20th century surface design. Yet the diversity of textiles in the Chemnitz collection makes it possible to present modifications and digressions from main currents in textile design or to highlight developments

associated only with a single artist, as in the case of the Italian designer Mario Fortuny, for example. It also enables us to illustrate the different ways in which specific aesthetic concepts were taken up in other European countries. Although several artists who played important roles in the development of art during the period are missing from the collection, it is possible to present a broad survey of European textile design covering not only the dominant tendencies of the decade but the diversions and byways of surface design as well – secondary currents that enriched the life of the period and contribute to our understanding of it today.

The book concludes with an extensive appendix consisting of a glossary, biographical sketches of individual artists and an index of schools, workshops and companies. Although a number of publications on the subject in question have appeared in recent years, we should note as well that research on textiles of the 19th and 20th centuries is still in its infancy as we near the end of our millennium and that our knowledge is clearly deficient in many specific areas.

History of the Collection

The founding of the *Vorbildersammlung* (Model Collection), as the Textil- und Kunstgewerbesammlung Chemnitz was originally named in 1898, the year of its origin, came during a highly productive period marked by significant change, an era that is only roughly characterized by reference to the reform movement and Art Nouveau. The city of Chemnitz was shaped to an appreciable extent during these years by the textile and textile-machine industry, whose imprint it still bears today and was indeed one of the most important industrial centers in Germany. Thus the presence of a textile collection of this scope and quality, whose reputation has spread far beyond regional boundaries and which is now recognized as one of the truly great textile collections of Germany and Europe as well, should come as no surprise. The purpose of such collections of textile models was clearly defined. Artists, architects and designers were to be offered an opportunity to learn about the diverse contemporary currents in art first hand. These model collections of articles from widely ranging fields of collection were conceived as information centers at which so-called "models," or examples of modern design, could be introduced to industrial producers, artisans and artists alike.

The unrivaled leaders of the new reform movement were the newly established museums of arts and crafts. Founded between 1870 and 1890, these institutions engaged in an extensive program of art education, which originally propagated the forms and techniques of Renaissance art as style-shaping models for all areas of the art and the arts-and-crafts industries. This activity was encouraged by the hope that imitation and mastery of the formal vocabulary and techniques of the Renaissance, the heyday of the arts, would lead to the growth of an original 19th-century style.

By the end of the century it was clear, however, that the quest for renewal had deteriorated into mere stylistic imitation of historical models and that reality as it affected the design of the human environment and of the utilitarian goods of everyday life was determined only by commercial interests in eclectic forms. It was not long before counter-movements led primarily by groups of young, socially committed artists began to emerge in cities all over Europe. This avant-garde saw itself challenged to seek new goals. Its advocates were convinced of the need to abandon traditional paths in order to be able to shape the art of their time and to give expression, as artists, to the perception of art prevailing in the immediate present. They appealed for a change in the creative process itself. This demand was realized through the formation of the various artists' associations and splinter groups known as the *Secessions*.

Museum directors like Justus Brinkmann in Hamburg and Friedrich Deneken in Krefeld began to build model collections of especially high-quality objects of modern contemporary arts and crafts in order to introduce and promote these international developments in Germany and at the same time to establish standards of quality for German designers. While art museums concentrated primarily upon the collection of historical art of past eras, the arts and crafts collections pursued with their "models" the express goal of providing new impulses to contemporary design and thereby elevating it to a new level of quality.

The *Vorbildersammlung Chemnitz* was conceived as a research collection from the very beginning. Furnished with a large and valuable reference library donated by the Kunstgewerbeverein as well as a reading room, the collection was to serve as a training center for young textile artists and designers, providing them the opportunity to work with these textile models in the model studios. Textiles from all regions and periods were acquired for the *Vorbildersammlung* from the outset, and no restrictions were imposed with respect to the types of material selected. The objective was to collect a wide range of representative textiles in order to present as broad a spectrum as possible. Thus only few large, older pieces are found in the Chemnitz collection, as individual examples and the availability of a large number of different objects were more important criteria for a research collection. Founded during the era of Art Nouveau, the collection quite naturally contains a rich selection of textiles from that period, in which the then most important centers of production in England, France, Austria, Germany and Italy are extensively represented. Decorative and upholstery fabrics were a focal point of collection efforts. Impossible to overlook, the preponderance of interior textiles reflects the

city's industrial potential at the time, with its many textile machine factories and plush upholstery weaving mills. Many of the designers of these textiles were well-known architects, painters and graphic artists such as William Morris, Charles Francis Annesley Voysey, Kolo Moser, Josef Hoffmann, Richard Riemerschmid, Henry van de Velde, Otto Eckmann, Emil Rudolf Weiss and many others. For most of these artists, textile design represented only one of their creative fields, and the designs themselves often originated within the context of complete interiors. Other designers are relatively little-known today. Such figures as Arthur Silver, J. Bohl, Lewis Foreman Day were first and foremost textile artists or designers whose best work was done in the field of textile design. Given the character of the collection profile and the intended purpose of the *Vorbildersammlung,* it comes as no surprise that only a very few textiles from Chemnitz and Sachsen are found in the collection. Local products were familiar to everyone. This is all the more regrettable in view of the fact that the well-known Wilhelm Vogel company of Chemnitz produced textiles designed by Henry van de Velde as early as 1904.

Thanks to the modern and far-sighted collection concept developed for the *Vorbildersammlung* at the time of its founding, the extraordinarily extensive inventory of textiles comprised by the collection today provides a revealing survey of developments in textile design in England, France, Austria and Germany. It was deemed appropriate from the outset to collect textiles from all periods and from a wide range of different countries. Some 20,000 items were acquired for the research collection, which was conceived as a training institute and a public exhibit. Significant gifts and bequests have been added from time to time. The collection of 19th and 20th-century textiles was augmented even in its early years by the acquisition of much older textile objects. On the occasion of its founding, for example, the Chemnitz collection obtained a large collection of historical silks, white embroidered items and lace from the 16th, 17th and 19th centuries – known as the "Dresdener Doubletten," from the Kunstgewerbemuseum Dresden. The purchase of the Sammlung Schütz of Dresden expanded and complemented the collection through the addition of silk damasks and brocades from the preceding four centuries. Non-European textiles were also purchased and received as gifts, among them items from Indonesia, China, Japan and the Near East. The *Vorbildersammlung* was renamed as the *Textil- und Kunstgewerbesammlung* (Collection of Textiles, Arts and Crafts) in 1928 and further expanded to incorporate fields of collection such as wood, metal, glass, ceramics and porcelain. In view of the dominance of the textile holdings, these collections remained relatively small, yet they represent a significant qualitative enhancement of the collection as a whole.

Textile Design between the World Wars
Many of the influences that would affect the development of textile design during the 1920s and 1930s were already present in rudimentary form before World War I. Major currents in art in the years preceding the First World War were driven primarily by

artists from the new arts and crafts movement. Worthy of particular note in this context are the activities of the Artists' Colony in Darmstadt and the work of Henry van de Velde in Weimar, to name only two examples. Important centers emerged in Munich, with the Vereinigte Werkstätten für Kunst im Handwerk, and in Dresden, with the Dresdner, later the Deutsche Werkstätten. Richard Riemerschmid and his designs were of considerable importance to both of these enterprises. Founded in 1898 as an association of several artists, the Vereinigte Werkstätten München referred both in name and in conceptual orientation to the English *Arts and Crafts* movement. Besides Emil Rudolf Weiß, also Fritz August Breuhaus de Groot, Bruno Paul and the previously mentioned Richard Riemerschmid supplied designs for the Vereinigte Werkstätten. Riemerschmid's tightly structured, simple designs in small pattern units derived from floral imagery would serve as a signpost for significant developments in 20th-century design.

Even as early as the pre-war years, a shift away from representational motifs became evident in textile patterns, which showed signs of an approach towards abstraction under the influence of interaction with free art. The principle of background and pattern began to change as pattern units became smaller. The Wiener Werkstätte provided seminal impulses for this development with its striving for a total work of art in which furniture and carpets, fabrics and utilitarian objects, including the owner's clothing as well, were to form a unity of mutually complementary parts. This objective was achieved through reduction and rationalization of the vocabulary of forms as practiced most notably by Josef Hoffmann.

The Wiener Werkstätte

The founding of the Wiener Secession in 1897 laid the cornerstone for the growth of a new style that represented a turning point in the development of surface design in the 20th century. Kolo Moser was one of the leading figures in this movement. Moser drew upon floral motifs from nature for his textile designs, in which they appeared in marked abstraction, arranged in small pattern units. Tending towards an abstract vocabulary, he found one of his most important sources of inspiration in the Japanese dying templates known as *katagamis*. In contrast to Kolo Moser, Josef Hoffmann pursued entirely new directions with his textile designs. Typical of his work is a strong tendency towards geometric patterns. It was in these textiles that Hoffmann first developed the surface style that would become synonymous for his textile designs during the first years of the Wiener Werkstätte. "Notschrei" (Cry for Help), with the grid motifs and vertical lines that are so typical of Hoffmann, is highly characteristic of his early approach to textile design, in which surface area is structured through intricate grid patterns which in turn provide an ordering structure for his abstract or abstracted interior forms. Designed by Hoffmann in 1904 and produced by Backhausen in the same year, "Notschrei" became one of the most popular deco-

rative fabrics. It was used in a variety of settings, including the Purkersdorf sanatorium, the only utilitarian building associated with Hoffmann during his early creative period and the first modern functional structure erected in Austria.

In contrast to his woven decorative fabrics, Hoffman used more or less radically abstracted natural forms in fresh, clear colors in his printed fabrics. A classical example of the printed fabrics designed by Hoffmann for the Wiener Werkstätte before World War I is "Jagdfalke" (Hunting Falcon). These striking patterned textiles with their clear, rational decorative style and their intricate patterns were ideally suited for integration into the interiors of the Wiener Werkstätte. The decorative style conceived by Josef Hoffmann played a pioneering role in the development of textile design in the 20th century. The Wiener Werkstätte is represented in this volume by fabrics designed by Maria Likarz (Nos. 112, 113), Felice Rix (Nos. 114, 115) and Dagobert Peche (Nos. 109, 110, 111). The artists of the Wiener Werkstätte had abandoned stylized floral patterns and characteristic sweeping lines long before the outbreak of World War I. The influence of Futurist, Cubist and Constructivist currents in art during these years on textile design is impossible to overlook. Maria Likarz occupies a prominent position in this context. Her famous "Irland" (Ireland) fabric, a totally abstract pattern design, was created in 1910 and produced until the late 1920s. Today, it still appears timeless and modern; its expansive pattern and impressive effects have no equal among the designs created by artists of the Wiener Werkstätte during the same period. Likarz did not begin her intensive design work for the fabrics department of the Wiener Werkstätte until after 1918. In the course of the many years of her association with the Wiener Werkstätte, she became one of its most creative and productive artists, having provided designs for the WW even as a young student of Josef Hoffmann's at the Kunstgewerbeschule. Maria Likarz went to Halle in 1915, where she became director of the "Fachklasse für Kunstgewerbliche Frauenarbeit" (Special Course for Women's Arts and Crafts) and was entrusted with the development of an enameling workshop at the Handwerker- und Kunstgewerbeschule in Halle/Saale in 1916. She returned to Vienna and the WW in 1920 and worked in the fashion and textiles department there until the company folded in 1931. Maria Likarz's pattern designs (Nos. 112, 113) bear witness to the creativity and the independence with which she incorporated international tendencies into her work, which explains at least in part the impression of modernity and timelessness her works continue to evoke today.

Dagobert Peche presents a different case entirely. His characteristic surface patterns for wallpaper and fabrics show the unmistakable influence of the period in which they originated and of the tendencies associated with international Art Déco. Alongside Kolo Moser and Josef Hoffmann, Dagobert Peche was the third prominent artist in the great triple star constellation at the WW.

Like Hoffmann, Peche was an extraordinarily creative artist active in all areas of applied art. His interests included architecture, interior design, furniture, graphic art, fashion, silver-crafting, lace, wallpaper and fabric patterns. During his relatively short association with the WW, which ended with his untimely death in 1923, Peche designed some 113 fabric patterns characterized by a consistent stylistic unity in keeping with his own esthetic principles. A typical feature of Peche's works is his preference for stylized objective forms, based upon drawings, in which lines played a particularly important role. As in "Pan" (No. 109) and "Tulpen" (Tulips, No. 110), flowers, winding vines and bouquets (No. 111) are among his most frequently used motifs; designs with abstract patterns are relatively rare in his work. Peche greatly influenced other artists at the WW, and his innovative ideas affected and stimulated virtually every department. Indeed, his holistic concept of form left an indelible imprint upon an entire line of development in art for a certain period of time. His love of extraordinary ornamental forms stood in stark contrast to modern objectivism, the conceptual scheme of which was clearly dominated by functionality, reduction of the ornamental and the importance of material qualities. "Even more important (…) it would seem, was the fact that Peche effected a significant change in the general tendency pursued at the Wiener Werkstätte, diverting it towards principles of form and craftsmanship which ultimately, years after Peche's death, when such values came to be viewed negatively, left the works of many WW artists looking so insignificant and out of tune with the times. (…) Peche was a declared opponent of industrial forms of production and argued accordingly, in keeping with the 1905 work program issued by the Wiener Werkstätte. With the active support of Hoffmann, he stubbornly defended an approach devoted to the production of luxurious decoration in perfectly hand-crafted single pieces. (…) With his esthetic principles, Peche ultimately paved the way for the failure of the Wiener Werkstätte, whose products gradually deteriorated into the negative realm of 'arts and crafts.'"[1] Austria was represented primarily by products from the Wiener Werkstätte at the Paris Art Déco exhibition. The textiles exhibited in Paris, appealing light and light-colored printed fabrics with attractive patterns and figures, had little in common with the emphatic opulence and luxury of the Art Déco style that dominated the show. It should be noted at this point that the fabric designs of the Wiener Werkstätte in particular reflect an intense involvement with developments in art during the period – with such movements as Futurism and Russian Constructivism or the influences of the Bauhaus. Artists like Maria Likarz and Felice Rix responded to these new creative influences and the associated tendencies towards objectivity, abstraction and a geometrical language of forms in their work.

In general, we note a change in the use and functions of interior textiles during the 1920s. Whereas decorative and upholstery fabrics accounted for well over half of the total textile production before World War I, a marked proportional shift in favor of clothing fabrics took place during the twenties. One of the

underlying causes was rapid growth in the fashion industry and a corresponding rise in the production of ready-to-wear articles, which enabled an increasingly broad segment of the public to keep pace with "fashion trends." In addition, textiles no longer played a central role in the design of modern interiors. Sufficient evidence for this change can be found in Gropius' study at the Weimar Bauhaus or the *Meisterhäuser* in Dessau, where the dominance of stone, concrete, glass and metal is obvious. The use of textiles was limited for the most part to wall hangings, carpets and curtain fabrics.

Staatliches Bauhaus in Weimar 1919–1923, cover:
Herbert Bayer; Bauhausverlag Weimar-München, undated

The Bauhaus
It is virtually certain that no other institution devoted to art education achieved a worldwide impact even remotely equivalent to that of the Bauhaus, an establishment that existed for only fourteen years (1919–1933). The Bauhaus is held in great esteem today and associated primarily with the style of design to which it gave birth. The Bauhaus teachers, including such figures as Wassily Kandinsky, Lyonel Feininger, Paul Klee, Oskar Schlemmer, were among the leading artists of their time. The training methods and educational reform concepts practiced at the Bauhaus, approaches developed most notably by Johannes Itten, Josef Albers and László Moholy-Nagy, are still regarded as exemplary today and have since been incorporated into the educational programs of many schools of art and design all over the world.

The goal of the Bauhaus movement was to overcome the subdivision of the arts into separate disciplines and to promote close cooperation among all fields. "Thus the Bauhaus once again took up ideas of the English reform movements, of the Werkbund and of the Viennese *Gesamtkunstwerk*, albeit at a different level of consciousness. Influenced largely at first by Abstract Expressionism and Constructivism, the Bauhaus vision very quickly came under the influence of the Dutch De Stijl Group and the Russian Constructivists and turned towards an exclusive form of functionalism, which was practiced in pure form only verbally, however. Functionalism itself rejects both the ornament and all forms of decoration subsumed within it."[2] The confrontation with decor engendered a discussion about function and functionalism, about technical form, construction and Constructivism.

Whereas Gropius had still defended the concept of "Art and handicraft – a new unity" in 1919, work at the Bauhaus began to move in new directions during the early 1920s, and a more pronounced orientation towards technology and industry became evident. "This change, towards which Gropius deliberately set his sights early on and which he soon began to carry out step by step, played an essential role in the history of the Bauhaus. In pursuing it, the Bauhaus focused its attention on a single field of endeavor: contemporary design for the industrial age, an area that had interested virtually no one before. The word 'design,' in fact, did not find its way into use in Germany until after 1945. In the eyes of those concerned with the 'Age of the Machine,' the term 'Bauhaus' soon stood for the very opposite of handicraft and activities in the field of arts and crafts."[3] The development that led from "Bauhaus-Textil Weimar" to "Bauhaus-Textil Dessau" can be traced in the two works by Benita Koch-Otte and Ruth Hollos-Consemüller. The weaving section was one of the first workshops established at the Bauhaus in Weimar. Walter Gropius appointed Georg Muche as form master of the weaving workshop in 1920. Among the successful students of the weaving department were Gunta Stölzl and Benita Koch-Otte, whose famous wall hanging is shown in Illustration No. 1. The narrative motif carpet of the type that experienced renewed popularity during the Art Nouveau period was replaced by a surface-oriented, constructive style closely resembling the new abstract art. Important stimulus for these stylistic innovations came from instruction at the hands of the visual artists. The influence of Johannes Itten's teaching during the years up to 1921 cannot be overestimated; and the same applies to Paul Klee in the ensuing years. Basic forms such as circles, squares and triangles were transferred by students into their woven and hooked textiles; wall hangings and carpets were composed in the manner of non-representational pictures. At the initial center of attention was the "individual work of art," which has no place in industrial production. Yet by the end of the Weimar period the groundwork had been laid for industrially reproduced model utilitarian textiles such as tablecloths, curtains, wall coverings of the kind produced during the Dessau phase of the Bauhaus after 1926. Gunta Stölzl, who assumed the position of director of the weaving workshop during this time, deserves the lion's share of credit for the development of the "Bauhaus

fabrics." Anni Albers and later Otti Berger were actively involved in the changeover to a new program featuring machine-produced structured woven fabrics around 1930. Typical of the textiles of these years are the use of new artificial fibers made of aluminum, light-metal alloys and cellophane and experimentation with the fruits of new scientific discoveries in the field of mechanical processing. A work from this period is Ruth Hollós-Consemüller's "Flügeldecke" (Winged Tablecloth, No. 3). The piece features the new synthetic silk fiber. As a technically complex double-woven product, it also bears witness to experience in manual craftsmanship.

Burg Giebichenstein

Most educational institutions concerned with creative arts and crafts found themselves concerned with the methodology and accomplishments of the Bauhaus. This influence was especially strong at Burg Giebichenstein in Halle, a school that played an outstanding role in the period in question and to which a number of teachers transferred following the closing of the Bauhaus in Weimar. The school's director Paul Thiersch was able to recruit, among others, Gerhard Marcks (as director of the sculpture workshop) and the ceramic artist Marguerite Friedlaender to service in Halle. Benita Otte also went to Halle, where she took over the textiles program as successor to Johanna Schütz-Wolff. "During her years there, from 1925 to 1933, Benita Otte built the weaving department at Burg Giebichenstein into a production facility for modern woven interior textiles operating in productive competition with the Bauhaus weaving workshop."[4]

The workshops of Burg Giebichenstein were constantly compared with those of the Bauhaus even by contemporaries, and Thiersch feared that the geographic proximity and the similarities in structure shared by the two schools would encourage transfers of students and teachers. Actually, however, the Halle school was comparable at best with the Weimar Bauhaus. It remained true to the workshop program developed in the early 1920s and its emphasis upon manual crafts and thus had little to do with the principles of industrial design developed at the Bauhaus Dessau. This trend towards technology, along with the incessant, fruitless didactic discussions, discouraged a number of Bauhaus teachers from making the move to Dessau. The work of the Halle school appeared much more compatible with their personal esthetic concepts. "It was mainly the artistic freedom that fascinated the Bauhaus people in Halle, along with the workshop program, which was indeed oriented towards the objectives of modern design, although it preserved a traditional respect for handicraft. There was no intention at the Burg to use the artisan's workshop for the exclusive purpose of creating models for industry. Instead, the idea was to provide industry with technically and formally superior designs in keeping with quality standards derived from handicraft, and thus to exercise an enhancing influence upon taste. The creative process was consistently emphasized in all aspects of work, and this often

WERKBUNDAUSSTELLUNG
DIE WOHNUNG
STUTTGART
23. Juli bis 23. Oktober 1927

Catalogue for the Werkbund exhibition "Die Wohnung," Stuttgart, 1927

led to a co-mingling of art and handicraft."[5] Thiersch and the school took the opportunity to present and realize their original ideas at the 1927 Werkbundausstellung "Die Wohnung" (Apartment Interiors) in Stuttgart by furnishing and decorating two four-room flats in the apartment house designed by Peter Behrens. Nearly all of the workshops at Burg Giebichenstein were involved in the project. The cabinet-making shop produced furniture designed by Thiersch. Despite its simplified geometric forms, Thiersch's furniture was not intended to represent models for serial production. With its solidity, its showpiece character and the use of fine veneers, traditional upholstery and hand-woven coverings, it was still meant for the individual consumer. The textile workshops were represented by the familiar high-quality interior fabrics and the large hanging shown in the Chemnitz collection (No. 6). Even the inadequate historical illustration shows something of the monumentality of this weaving style – a grandiose quality derived from an exceptionally frugal color contrast between dove-gray and purple, a convincing composition and the variations in structure achieved through alternation of the weave. The different-sized

squares and rectangles interrupt a rhythmic stripe pattern in a piece that demonstrates the mastery of modern surface structure achieved by the weavers of Halle. The identity of the artist who authored the design is a matter of conjecture, as workshop regulations required that products be exhibited anonymously at trade fairs or exhibitions and sold without reference to the designer. The only clue to their origin was a tag identifying them as a "Product of the Kunstwerkstätten Halle." Nevertheless, the importance attached to the furnishing and decoration of the flats for presentation at the Stuttgart exhibition suggests that Benita Otte, director of the textile class, was intensively involved in the production of this hanging. Even the yard goods, the interior fabrics produced by the Burg, can be seen as innovations in their time, as the school had deliberately embraced the goal of contributing to a revitalizing of neglected handicraft traditions. The light curtain material (Nos. 9, 10), produced as a so-called turner weave, represent a cross between curtain and drapery. By virtue of their physical properties and functional characteristics they were well suited for use in the new living environments.

Werkbund exhibition "Die Wohnung," Stuttgart, 1927: Furnishing and decoration of a flat in a house of Peter Behrens, designed and produced by the Werkstätten der Stadt Halle – Burg Giebichenstein, in: *75 Jahre Burg Giebichenstein,* 1915–1990, Halle, 1990

Hand-Weaving and Industrial Production

As has already been pointed out, the Bauhaus weaving workshop received new impulses under the direction of Gunta Stölzl and developed textile designs as prototypes for industrial production during the Dessau phase from 1926 to 1931. The uneasy relationship between the one-of-a-kind creation and serial, industrial production provided a constant stimulus to inquiry and experimentation and is exemplified in efforts to clarify the position of the weaving workshop. Following the move from Weimar to Dessau it became necessary to purchase looms. A long and often bitter controversy ensued with respect to the way in which the new workshop should be equipped. As form master, Georg Muche was responsible for the weaving workshop and the purchase of Jacquard looms, which the students, as hand-weavers, initially rejected but eventually came to accept.

"The move from Weimar to Dessau resulted in a number of changes in the weaving workshop, changes initiated and promoted to a considerable extent by Gunta Stölzl. 'through the move to dessau, the weaving workshop, like all other workshops and departments, acquired new, healthier operating conditions; it purchased a variety of loom systems – counter-march – shaft looms – jacquard looms – carpet hooking looms – and all of the apparatuses needed to set up the looms – its own dying facility. rigorous technical and theoretical training (journeyman's training) was established.' (Gunta Stölzl) The curriculum was also expanded: 'weaving theory, material theory, fabric analysis, dying … the student becomes familiar in the course of training with the basic tools of the weaver's trade. it remains his task to learn to use them properly … weaving is building, constructing ordered patterns from disorderly threads.'"[6]

During her tenure at the Bauhaus and in later years as well, Gunta Stölzl – unlike Georg Muche – consistently contended that, despite the strong trend towards industrialization in weaving, training should be based upon hand-weaving skills and not, as others frequently demanded, upon work with the power looms used in industrial mills. Even today, training at most institutions of higher learning takes place on the hand loom. This issue was of great importance to Gunta Stölzl, and she published her thoughts on the matter in a number of articles. In a manuscript written in 1937 she recalls: "Our goal was to train young people through practice in manual crafts to develop their technical skills and artistic talents. We kept the hand-weaving workshop not out of nostalgic romanticism or as a protest against mechanical weaving but in order to be able to develop the widest possible range of fabrics using the simplest and clearest means possible and thus to provide students with a basis from which to realize their ideas."[7] At another point she adds that "the hand loom offers many more possibilities than the power loom. we believe that it is better to begin with abundance and proceed to selection rather than the other way around… our goal: not hand-woven fabric but only the pattern for mechanical production."[8]

Like Anni Albers and Otti Berger, her most gifted students, Gunta Stölzl never rejected industrial weaving. Yet she consistently emphasized the importance of the hand loom in her own work: "Like Otti Berger, Anni Albers also believed that the creative artisan could become a pioneer once again: as an experimenting outpost of an industry that is itself engaged in selective and increasingly specialized experimentation. Neither Berger nor Albers had a sentimental attachment to hand-weaving. 'Machines are a blessing for me,' wrote Albers, 'and my own experience shows that the often cited difference in quality vis-à-vis hand-weaving does not exist, provided we make the appropriate adjustments to the power loom and its own particular productive possibilities, as we would do with any other tool as well.'"[9] The debate about the individual work of art versus the mass-produced industrial product is typical of the time and of the efforts to determine the role of hand-weaving in an industrial society. And it is particularly remarkable in light of the fact that this recognition of the specific

Company catalogue issued by Polytextil Gmbh, Berlin, undated

accomplishments of hand-weaving and industrial production, respectively, produced very fruitful effects for both, as each form influenced and profited from the other.

This is quite evident in the work of Sigmund von Weech. The two upholstery fabrics illustrated here (Nos. 19, 20) were produced on hand looms in his hand-weaving workshop in Schaftlach (Tegernsee). On the basis of its size alone (60 looms), the operation resembled rather a manufacturing plant than a traditional workshop. Influenced by Bauhaus design principles, his fabrics for steel-tube chairs by *Junkers* were designed and produced on hand looms. Like Gunta Stölzl, von Weech himself emphasized the importance of hand-weaving to the process of developing prototypes of textiles according to their specific interior function. He was able to integrate his textiles into interior space in such a way that they became a part of the architecture yet retained their own formal language. The opposition between serial production and individual aura is eliminated and turned to productive use in his fabrics. Considerable emphasis is placed upon the material qualities of the textile fibers, which are underscored through the weaving process. Chenille plays a dominant role in establishing the character of von Weech's upholstery fabrics. Due to its particular properties, this special material was

extraordinarily popular during the period and was used by many designers and weaving operations.

Polytex fabrics

One of these was the Polytex Textilgesellschaft mbH of Berlin. The consistent use of viscose rayon as warp material and cotton chenille as a filling almost takes on the character of a trademark in fabrics produced by this firm. The lively, richly varied fabric surface is designed using a sophisticated and quite complicated weaving technique in which the surface structure is configured at once by the chenille filling and the viscose rayon warp (Nos. 25, 26). The formally abstract, sensitively colored yet vigorously contrasted Polytex fabrics would have been inconceivable in the absence of the Bauhaus influence. At the same time, however, they represent an autonomous and relatively self-sufficient variation on the textile design style of the period. This is further underscored by the fact that Polytex had no hesitation in signing a contract with Polytex in 1930 granting a license to the company to produce upholstery and drapery fabrics from hand-woven Bauhaus patterns. The company brochure shown in the illustration contains a reference to a special catalogue featuring Bauhaus Dessau fabrics. Polytex produced only upholstery fabrics. The company brochure makes it possible to correlate these rather heavy textiles with the corresponding seating furniture. But for a single exception, all of these fabrics were produced as yard goods. The exception, referred to as a wall material, shows no recurring pattern unit (No. 24). In the style of a wall hanging, the entire surface area was designed as a whole and was intended to serve as a wall decoration. The choice of the rather obvious word "wall material" points beyond its purely decorative function and suggests its suitability for purposes of individualized heat regulation and protection for wall paint or paper.

Unfortunately, these textiles cannot be attributed to specific artists or designers. Bruno Paul is named in the company brochure as art and technical director of the weaving department; Bernhard Jentsch and Paul's assistant Tillie Prill-Schloemann are also mentioned. Yet Bruno Paul's influence on the design of Polytex fabrics should not be underestimated, as they show a great deal of stylistic unity and a strong degree of compatibility with his interiors and interior architectural plans.

Fireside setting in the residential hall of Haus Traub, Prague; architect: Bruno Paul, in: *ID,* 1935, p. 125

Bruno Paul, a co-founder of the Deutscher Werkbund, is regarded as the leading figure in the field of German interior art and architecture between Art Nouveau and Modernism. With countless designs for furniture and hand-crafted objects, which were produced by the Vereinigte Werkstätten für Kunst im Handwerk, he significantly influenced the development of interior architecture in Germany. Paul favored individualized approaches which later became prototypes for specific solutions and were then varied only in matters of detail for long periods of time. The style of furnishing and decoration advocated by Bruno Paul, which defined a position somewhere between Neoclassicism and the New Objectivity, gained widespread popularity during the first three decades of the 20th century among private consumers representing the wealthy upper middle class, in social housing pro-

grams and in the development of serially produced furniture commissioned by the Deutsche Werkstätten.

The Deutsche Werkstätten
Founded before World War I, the Deutsche Werkstätten soon overcame the setbacks suffered under the influence of war and inflation and found themselves well on the way to economic recovery in the mid-1920s. This new wave of expansion is closely associated with the name Bruno Paul, whom the company succeeded in recruiting as a permanent staff member. The Deutsche Werkstätten were involved in the previously mentioned Weißenhofsiedlung project in 1927. The firm developed a constructive furniture program regarded as suitable for social housing. The image of the Werkstätten during the 1920s was shaped above all by their contributions to extensive furnishing projects for prominent objects (hotels, resort centers, ocean liners) in the form of high-quality furniture. Within the context of this furnishing program, the Deutsche Werkstätten and their subsidiary, the Deutsche Werkstätten Textile Gesellschaft (De-We-Tex, founded in 1923), designed and produced a large number of fabrics on a par with the products of the Wiener Werkstätte during the 1920s.

Among the most important members of the art staff of the Deutsche Werkstätten during those years, Josef Hillerbrand and Ruth Geyer-Raack are represented by works in the Chemnitz collection. Josef Hillerbrand designed many fabrics characterized by lively grace and lightness for De-We-Tex. Their clear contours give them a cheerful, casual look, and many of these pieces are among the finest examples of the surface art of the period (Nos. 43, 44, 45). The Chemnitz textile collection comprises a large number of De-We-Tex fabrics, most of them printed materials. They are deliberately light-hearted fabrics that evoke a mood of delicacy and light that shares little with the highly stylized Art Déco orientation in France.

The functional shift in textiles mentioned above is evident in another tendency recognizable in the work of the Vereinigte Werkstätten and, to an even more marked extent, of the Deutsche Werkstätten. "Textiles are liberating themselves in a certain sense from architecture and focusing increasingly upon the human being. In other words, the demonstrative interior architectural function of textiles is diminishing in importance; they are becoming useful in a more subject, more private and more personal way."[10] This change in focus had a significant impact upon the textiles produced by both "Werkstätten."

The Vereinigte Werkstätten
The Vereinigte Werkstätten München cooperated with a number of excellent artists. Fritz August Breuhaus, Paul László and E. Engelbrecht, to name only a few of the most noteworthy, among

them, are represented by works – primarily luxurious upholstery fabrics – in the collection (Nos. 30 to 38). Although the often extravagant textile designs and interiors of Breuhaus and László received extensive coverage in contemporary literature, little is known of Engelbrecht's work, with the exception of a single printed fabric.

The evolution of patterns produced by the Vereinigte Werkstätten reveals a greater concentration upon tensions of color and form than that of the Deutsche Werkstätten, as examples No. 31 and No. 32 show. Surprise effects and pronounced stylization are typical of these textiles; consequently, the fabrics are showier and more sophisticated. This applies in particular to the upholstery materials produced by the F. A. Breuhaus studio. The extraordinarily splendid brocade upholstery fabrics exhibited as No. 33 and No. 34 were made for the library and the salon of the high-speed ocean liner "Bremen." The luxury liner made its maiden voyage on the Bremerhaven–New York route in 1929. With the exception of the smoking room, Fritz August Breuhaus was responsible for all of the first-class salon furnishings.

Schule Reimann

The surprise effects and marked stylization cited with reference to the Vereinigte Werkstätten are equally evident in the work of Maria May and the Schule Reimann. Maria May began teaching at the private Kunst- und Kunstgewerbeschule Reimann in Berlin in 1922. While serving as director of the special textile course she built up a separate program for design and decorative painting. In a joint undertaking with the IG-Farben-Industrie, new developments in dying technology were tested and used in producing the sprayed fabrics in Maria May's characteristic style. Her "Paris" (No. 16) is an excellent example. A contemporary critic wrote: "Paris: hints of the Eiffel Tower, Notre Dame, Sacré Cœur, the Arc de Triomphe, Café du Dôme, Montmartre, houses with small balconies and chimneys, speeding cars, animated Varieté figures, aproned waiters, advertising posters, policemen in uniform are swept together in subtle, light-hearted allusions, although recognizable enough, in Futurist or Dadaist-style; a huge tricolor unfurls, and its colors set the dominant blue-white-and-red tone."[11] Although modern viewers may criticize the apparent reproduction of formulas and clichés fostered by mass tourism, it should be noted that such a cosmopolitan view of Paris was surely typical of popular feeling in Germany with respect to France during the decade preceding the outbreak of the World War I. Such thematic pieces as "Paris," "Venedig," "Sevilla" and "New York" originated within the immediate context of the annual study tours, known as summer studios, conducted by the school in various different countries. Other printed fabrics designed by Maria May reveal a totally different side of her creative work. "Schwarz-Weiss-Grau," "Odette" and "Spitzen" (Nos. 12, 13, 17) are examples of her abstract, geometric pattern designs.

The school presented itself and the work of its staff and students in major touring exhibitions in Germany and the U.S. It was represented at the 1927 exhibition of the Textil- und Kunstgewerbesammlung Chemnitz. Maria May exhibited works on that occasion. It is likely that the first purchase of fabrics for the Chemnitz collection was made following the 1927 exhibition. Maria May also worked for the Vereinigte Werkstätten during the late 1920s.

Equally playful and fragrant, yet extremely delicate in color and totally devoid of striking effects are the printed fabrics designed by Wilhelm Marsmann and Viktor von Rauch for the Münchner Farbmöbelwerke. The material illustrated here (No. 59) calls to mind rather a vision of a distant world. Hans Wichmann's comments on the textiles of this group are quite revealing: "These are fabrics that evoke a life-affirming atmosphere while alluding as well to the vacillating mood of the time, fabrics that want to be more cheerful than reality would really permit. If one allows these mostly printed woven materials from London, Vienna, Berlin, Dresden, Munich and Hamburg to gather together before one's inner eye, one sees a colorful parade of appealing, decorative hues and shapes that passes by without dramatic gesture, revolutionary posturing or constrained pretensions to the throne of art. They are things of our own lives, which glide through our hands with a certain sense of melancholy, revealing glimpses of a more lovable side of human existence. They remind us more of wishes, hopes, joys, more of holidays, summer and peaceful rest than of reality, with its ideological dictates, its world of work and its political power plays. It is an appropriate, certainly inconsequential world, which keeps its distance but is all the more pleasant for that."[12]

The most important parallel currents of the time stand out clearly against this background: the German line of development described above, shaped by the Bauhaus and schools oriented towards similar esthetic principles (including Burg Giebichenstein), one the one hand, and the style of Art Déco with its playful distortions and its trifling refinement. Because of their more clearly esthetic orientation, only a very few textiles of this kind are represented in the Chemnitz collection, however.

There is clearly also a link between the Bauhaus textiles and the anonymous mass-produced fabrics of the decade in question. "Anonymous," in this case, simply means that materials cannot be attributed to certain artists, although their origins, i.e. their manufacture, are known. Production during this period is characterized by a high level of quality in design and the use of both superior materials and a wide variety of technical approaches to the manufacture of woven goods. The collection comprises abundant examples of textiles, so-called warp and filling gobelins, upholstery plushes, Turkish toweling, moquettes, which, regardless of the quality of their designs, show how important a role was played by the machinery available to mechanical weaving operations for the production of specific textiles. The upholstery fabrics produced by Vorwerk (Nos. 46, 49, 50) and the textiles exhibited as Nos. 57, 66, 67, 71, 72, 74, and 78 demonstrate very clearly that the industrial production of such esthetically sophisticated textiles stood in a relationship of productive competition with the products of hand-weavers during the decade in question, and that each profited from the other. Intensive theoretical investigation, a considerable amount of public reflection upon the role and function of hand-woven and industrially produced textiles and practical demonstrations conducted at trade fairs and exhibitions have made it possible to identify a clear allocation of functions and characteristics between the two types of textiles that strikes us as exemplary today. The textiles produced by the Munich company Hahn und Bach can also be viewed within this context, although with certain qualifications, as some of the pattern designs are purely decorative and expressive of response to fashion trends.

Modern Textile Art

One of the most important exhibitions of 20th-century textile art opened in Dessau in 1929: the touring exhibition "Moderne Bildwirkereien." Conceived by Ludwig Grote, Landeskonservator in Dessau, it was subsequently shown in eight other German cities: Essen, Leipzig, Berlin, Erfurt, Hamburg, Wiesbaden and Munich and at the Textil- und Kunstgewerbesammlung Chemnitz.

Ludwig Grote later reminisced about the Dessau exhibition, the basic idea for which was developed in response to a suggestion by Johanna Schütz-Wolff, Benita Otte's predecessor as director of the weaving workshop at Burg Giebichenstein Halle: "At the exhibition of knit motif textiles I organized in 1930, with which I [hoped] to liberate such works from their banishment into the realm of arts and crafts and to proclaim their value as artistic creations no less worthy than paintings or sculptures – the 'Male Nude' was the great sensation. One got the impression that the entire exhibition of motif carpets by Hans Arp, Kirchner and Schmidt-Rottluff and the woven pieces from the Bauhaus was centered around this work."[13] An illustration of the "Male Nude" to which von Grote referred was printed on the cover of the accompanying catalogue. It is regarded today as one of Schütz-Wolff's most important motif carpets, in which she took up the grand tradition of the wall hanging and developed her own modern expressive vocabulary. The index of exhibitors contains the names of all the noteworthy artists of the time, along with their major works. In addition to those of Arp, Kirchner and Schmidt-Rottluff, works by such artists as Anni Albers, Martha Breuer-Erbs, Ruth Hollós, Ida Kerkovius, Benita Koch-Otte, Alen Müller, Gunta Stölzl, Sophie H. Taeuber-Arp and Else Mögelin were presented alongside carpets by French artists, including Fernand Léger and Jean Lurcat. These names identify the poles between which textile art moved during the 1920s.

Catalogue for the exhibition "Moderne Bildwirkereien," 1930

Among the works selected for this exhibition were two pieces by Wenzel Hablik acquired from the artist by the Textil- und Kunstgewerbesammlung Chemnitz during the previous year (1928). The wall hangings entitled "Korallenbaum" (Coral Tree, No. 97) and "Bären" (Bears, No. 94) are examples of his most powerfully expressive work. They feature the dominant geometric formal vocabulary of the Cubist and abstract art of the twenties and thirties. Hablik's textile designs, produced in the Hablik-Lindemann hand-weaving workshop, had a profound impact upon weaving techniques and the weaver's art in Germany during the twenties and the early thirties. Hablik could probably not have created his diverse oeuvre or realized his ambitious plans without the contribution of his wife, Elisabeth Hablik-Lindemann, who was intensely involved in the production of his creative designs as workshop director. Wenzel Hablik used animal figures abstracted to geometric forms, as did Else Mögelin in her wall hanging "Rotes Reh" (Red Deer, No. 100). Both Hablik and Else Mögelin exhibited works at the International Exhibition of Arts and Crafts in Monza in 1927. The illustration shows an exhibition room and Mögelin's "Rotes Reh." The two artists were among the regular exhibitors at the annual Grassi expositions in Leipzig and were invited by Richard Graul, director of the Grassi Museum, to participate in "Europäisches Kunstgewerbe," a programmatical exhibition held in 1927.

The wall hanging by Valerie Jorud (No. 99) represents a chronological endpoint and an example of the intensive interaction, indeed the virtual identity in many cases, of textile art and textile design. Little is known about the Berlin artist or her work today. She took part in the Grassi exposition in Leipzig in the early 1930s, after which this work was purchased for the Chemnitz collection. Another large wall hanging went to the Grassi Museum of Leipzig. Technically speaking, these pieces are quite simple: sewn works in which red cotton strips were stitched onto canvas to form the pattern design. The colossal effect they achieve derives from the absolute precision with which the cotton strips are positioned and the sophisticated geometric surface pattern, which seems almost to anticipate Op Art.

France

The "Exposition Internationale des Arts Décoratifs et Industriels Modernes" took place in 1925, an exhibition that would become synonymous with an important current of art during the 1920s – the style known as Art Déco. The dominant position at the exhibition, Art Déco focused intensely upon decoration, decor and patterns and favored the luxurious individual work of art. Thus it stood in opposition to the tendencies of Objectivism, Functionalism and Constructivism developed in Germany at the Bauhaus and propagated by the Werkbund. The exhibition had been planned for 1916, and its opening generated heated discussions on the issues of function and Functionalism, technical form and construction. Fabrics intended for the high society milieu dominated the tone of this exhibition, printed fabrics with splendid, colorful floral patterns entirely in keeping with the concept of elegance in textiles that prevailed most notably in France at the time.

Catalogue for the exhibition "Europäisches Kunstgewerbe 1927," Leipzig, Grassi Museum

International Arts and Crafts Exhibition in Monza, 1928; textile interior in the German section, in: *DKuD,* Oct. 1927–Mar. 1928, p. 207

Also shown at the exhibition were the very different fashion designs and fabrics created by Sonia Delaunay, however. Robert Delaunay referred to the textiles designed by his wife as "Simultaneous Fabrics," which he described as follows: "The rhythm of the forms is determined by the colors alone, their arrangement, their distribution and their relationship to one another on the surface of a painting, a fabric or a piece of furniture, i.e. in space in a general sense, and these forms are developed as color fields, whose harmony is like that of a fugue."[14] The term "simultané" was the hallmark of the Delaunays' esthetics, of their art, their theory and their view of life. Their esthetic concept of "simultaneity" was based upon the idea that visual vibrations set in motion by simultaneous color contrasts represented empirical proof of the existence of cosmic rhythms. They saw these vibrations as the visible expression of the link that connects human beings with the dynamic forces of modern life. Contrasting colors in motion, they believed, presented an image of modern reality, and the artist's task was to select the right color elements with the right color qualities for a given situation.

Prior to 1924, Sonia Delaunay created articles of clothing decorated with applications or embroidery. Most of her early printed fabrics were based upon these models. Her textile patterns reveal a wide range of influences: African, oriental, ancient and archaic. Also quite obvious in her fabrics is the tremendous influence of the textiles produced by the Wiener Werkstätte, which had been adapted by the Paris fashion designer Paul Poiret in his models long before World War I. Her reinterpretation and especially the comparative juxtaposition of these different sources of inspiration engendered a universe of infinite rhythms in which the visual vibrations of simultaneous color contrasts dissolved spatial boundaries. Sonia Delaunay's compositions are frequently characterized by rhythms built in the manner of a stairway. The oblique axis, usually running from the upper left to the lower right, creates an unstable situation that is balanced by one or more dynamic opposing movements. The illustration showing fabrics by Sonia Delaunay was taken from a portfolio she presented under the title *Tapis et Tissus* (Ill.). A total of fifteen different albums were published by Editions D'Art Charles Moreau of Paris in a series entitled *L'Art International D'Aujourd'hui*. Sonia Delaunay's Album was the fifteenth and thus the last in the series. It was published with an explanatory text in 1929. Her selection is clearly indicative of the widespread popularity of the ideas of the Bauhaus and of associated abstract, geometric surface designs in France, and it also shows how far the French had moved away from the exhibition of 1925. In addition to French artists such as Francis Jourdain, Da Silva Bruhns, Fernand Léger, Jean Lurcat, Eileen Gray, Marguerite Dubuisson and Sonia Delaunay herself, German artists were also prominently represented with highly characteristic works, among them Gunta Stölzl with her wall hanging "5 Chöre" (Five Choirs) and another wall hanging done in 1923, Martha Erps, Else Mögelin ("Rotes Reh"), Anni Albers, Edith Eberhart und Wenzel Hablik ("Korallenbaum"). Artists from the Wiener Werkstätte, with whom Sonia Delaunay had become closely acquainted even before World War I, were also included in her album (M. Likarz, M. Flögl, J. Hoffmann, L. Jacker). Unfortunately, no textiles designed by Sonia Delaunay are to be found in the Chemnitz collection. However, the French fabrics acquired during the twenties and early thirties follow this modern line marked out by the Delaunays. The tendency towards geometric abstraction, combined with the opening of surface into space is clearly evident in the textiles edited by Rodier (Nos. 149, 150, 151) and in a number of other French upholstery fabrics as well (Nos. 148, 156, 157, 158, 160, 161).

Sonia Delaunay's album featuring works of the German avantgarde was not the only publication to call attention to other tendencies. Others attempted to enlighten as well. Controversy arose

Sonia Delaunay, fabrics, from the album *Tapis et Tissus,* Paris, 1928

after the 1925 Paris exhibition with respect to the tendencies of Art Déco, most prominently represented in France. Indeed, the exhibition represented rather the swan song of a style than a point of departure for a modern approach to formal design as pursued in Germany primarily in the Bauhaus movement and in the Netherlands by the De Stijl group. Among the most prominent opponents of the exhibition was Le Corbusier, who repeatedly criticized the self-indulgent anachronism of Art Déco objects and outlined his ideas about modern design in issues of the journal *L'Esprit Nouveau* published between 1920 and 1925.

A copious album entitled *The New Style in France* was published in parallel with the opening of the Paris exhibition by the Verlag Ernst Wasmuth of Berlin in 1925. Its author was Henry van de Velde, who, addressing the question of whether France had missed the opportunity to take part in the development of the new style, referred to himself as the "godfather" of that style: "One should not conclude simply because the French artists whose works are reproduced in this album took longer to see the light that France has arrived too late. This is of no significance whatsoever, and as far as I am concerned, nothing will rob me of the pleasure of serving as 'godfather' at the baptism. Nothing at all – not even the exhibition of decorative arts that is just now opening in Paris."[15] Van de Velde had selected a broad range of French artists and their works, which included examples of architecture, interior furnishings and utilitarian objects as well as such things as showcase-window and building façade designs, the deck of a mail clipper of the Compagnie Transatlantique and a lady's hairstyle by Antoine. The strikingly objective, modern photographs present a dining table and chairs by Robert Delaunay, furniture by Pierre Legrain, interiors and spatial designs by Le Corbusier and Pierre Jeanneret along with houses by André Lurcat and Robert Mallet-Stevens. It was a selection meant for German-speaking readers, a presentation that stood in diametrical opposition to the 1925 Paris exhibition of arts and crafts mentioned above. In the midst of the luxury and decorative refinement of that exhibition, Le Courbusier's simple, modern contribution, the Pavillon de l'Esprit Nouveau, pointed the way for future developments in France.

Great Britain

These movements towards modern formal design did not gain a foothold in England until later and were not genuinely accepted until the early 1930s. We know, for instance, that British artists and architects traveled to Dessau in 1931 to study the work of the Bauhaus first hand. Convinced by what they witnessed there, they attempted to promote recognition of Bauhaus ideas in Great Britain after their return. After the Bauhaus was closed in 1933, this influence became stronger in England, as a number of former Bauhaus artists emigrated to England – among them Walter Gropius, Marcel Breuer and Otti Berger. Although several important artists are missing, the British textiles in the collection of the Chemnitz Museum are quite representative of the work done in England in this area during the period in question. The influence of the arts and crafts movement had begun to wane in Great Britain even before World War I. Morris fabrics were still sold and exhibited (at the 1925 Paris exhibition, for example). The British textile industry continued to rely upon high-quality materials and superior craftsmanship. British textiles tended to be rather conservative during these years. In fact, it appeared as if a conservative look had become the trademark of the British approach to textiles and textile design. Historical print models were reintroduced in great numbers, and model designs from the 18th century were used to produce new versions of chintzes and printed fabrics. As might be expected, materials and print quality were excellent.

This can also be said without qualification of British woven fabric, although models from centuries long past continued to dominate in the area of patterns, as is evident in the upholstery material exhibited as No. 120, based upon 17th-century Mortlake carpets. Heraldic motifs (the unicorn) and a variety of animals and stylized plants presented on dark backgrounds are frequently found in British textile patterns of the period. With respect to the "Europäisches Kunstgewerbe" exhibition held at the Grassi Museum in 1927, Harry H. Peach, general curator of the British section, wrote: "The trade offers woven and printed upholstery fabrics in variations of old patterns of fine quality but with little originality – with the exception of individual items for household use or export goods. Viewed as a whole, the available commercial goods lack the character and individuality that a leading mind would produce in cooperation with artists who have something to say and are encouraged to say it. But we have no Hoffmann in England, and no Wiener Werkstätte."[16] Peach also mentioned his admiration for Foxton Fabrics, referring to them as the most experienced and modern producers of woven and printed fabrics. Foxton was represented at the Leipzig exhibition with artists' fabrics based upon designs by C. Irving, C. F. A. Voysey, D. Hutton, C. L. Fraser and M. McLeish. William Foxton regarded himself as a mediator between art and industry, and the fabrics he produced are still looked upon today as some of the most lively textiles of the period. Minnie McLeish designed the printed fabric "Old English Shop Signs" (No. 116), also produced by Foxton, which is one of the very few works that breaks away from the phalanx described above. One of the most important British designers, Minnie McLeish, reached the zenith of her creative career during the 1920s. The extraordinary quality of the color in her printed fabrics has been emphasized on many occasions.

Mariano Fortuny

Mariano Fortuny, a native of Spain who spent most of his life in Venice, saw the art of the past as his source of creative inspiration. This essay would be incomplete without a discussion of the art of the past and its transformation in Fortuny's fabric designs and

Mariano Fortuny: Staged interior setting at the "Morellina" exhibition, Naples, 1927, in: Marangoni, Guido, *Enciclopedia Delle Moderne Arti Decorative Italiane,* Milan, Casa Editrice Ceschina, 1928, p. 53

garments, as they represent a uniquely Italian or – to be more precise – Venetian version of the textile design of the 1920s. Fortuny, who was intensely involved with aspects of stage design and lighting techniques, had made a name for himself before World War I with his printed fabrics and his extravagant garments. Stimulated by the precious Venetian fabrics of the Renaissance, he created his famous pressed and printed velvets, the "Knossos" shawls and "Delphos" robes based upon ancient Greek patterns, to which the names refer. His fabrics illustrated in the catalogue give us an idea of the breadth of the range of approaches to design he developed and of the spatial effects associated with them. Photographs show his staged exhibition presentations, in which paintings of the old masters are hung against his fabrics in natural light, virtually negating the presence of the bare wall.

Fortuny's fabrics and the spatial concepts to which they relate are not to be understood as extensions of Historicism. They represent an unmistakable rejection of the "false" methods of the Gründerzeit – the use of surrogate materials, the illusory imitation of artistic techniques, slavish copying and imitation and the banish-

ment of light and air from interior spaces. Fortuny's textiles and his ideas about interior space seem timeless ("Delphos"), yet they are clearly born of the 20th century. They appear modern to us even today, thanks in great measure to his own special printing technique. His use of color and the direct application of pigments also played a very new and decisive role in his work. Fortuny was anything but a purist who remained forever loyal to forms of his own discovery. His very own technique enabled him to make use of classical pattern types at the same time.

The textiles presented in this book represent the best of the Chemnitz collection and its abundant repertoire of possibilities for the documentation of this fascinating decade on the basis of artistically superior textiles of the period. Purchases were made for the collection as late as the early 1930s and focused to an increasing degree on European developments in design, encompassing quite naturally not only German but also modern French and British textiles as well. The institution of the Nazi dictatorship in Germany effectively brought all international developments and contacts to a stop. Germany's involvement in the growth of international art ceased, and the Textil- und Kunstgewerbesammlung was appreciably affected by this as well. Thus the textile holdings of the 1940s are of little significance.

Katharina Metz

[1] Völker, Angela, *Die Stoffe der WW 1910–1932,* issued by the Österreichisches Museum für angewandte Kunst (Vienna: Brandstätter, 1990), p. 111.

[2] *Ibid.,* p. 120.

[3] Droste, Magdalena, *bauhaus 1919–1933,* issued by the Bauhaus-Archiv, Museum für Gestaltung (Berlin, Cologne: Benedikt Taschen, 1993), p. 60.

[4] Mahn, Eva, "Textil und Mode" in: *Burg Giebichenstein – Die Hallesche Kunstschule von den Anfängen bis zur Gegenwart,* issued by Staatliche Galerie Moritzburg Halle, Badisches Landesmuseum Karlsruhe and Burg Giebichenstein (Halle, 1993), p. 215.

[5] Schneider, Katja, "Zwischen Handwerksromantik und Industriedesign – Die Burg Giebichenstein von den Anfängen bis 1933" in: *Burg Giebichenstein – Die Hallesche Kunstschule von den Anfängen bis zur Gegenwart,* issued by Staatliche Galerie Moritzburg Halle, Badisches Landesmuseum Karlsruhe and Burg Giebichenstein (Halle, 1993), p. 30.

[6] Radewaldt, Ingrid, and Stadler, Monika, *"Gunta Stölzl; Biographie"* in: *Gunta Stölzl: Meisterin am Bauhaus Dessau – Textilien, Textilentwürfe und freie Arbeiten 1915–1983,* issued by the Stiftung Bauhaus Dessau (Dessau: Hatje, 1997), p. 40.

[7] *Ibid.,* p. 40.

[8] *Ibid.,* p. 40.

[9] Wortmann Weltge, Sigrid, *Bauhaus-Textilien, Kunst und Künstlerinnen der Webwerkstatt* (Schaffhausen: Edition Stemmle, 1993), p. 114.

[10] Wichmann, Hans (ed.), *Von Morris bis Memphis: Textilien der Neuen Sammlung* (Basel, Boston, Berlin: Birkhäuser, 1990), p. 18.

[11] Osborn, Max, "Neue Arbeiten von Maria May" in: *Farbe und Form: Monatsschrift für Kunst und Kunstgewerbe,* Vol. 15, Feb./Mar. 1930 (Berlin: Verlag Schule Reimann), p. 28.

[12] Wichmann, Hans (ed.), *Von Morris bis Memphis: Textilien der Neuen Sammlung* (Basel, Boston, Berlin: Birkhäuser, 1990), p. 119.

[13] Cited from Schneider, Katja, "Heiligenbilder in einer unheiligen Zeit" in: *Johanna Schütz-Wolff – Textil und Graphik,* issued by Staatliche Galerie Moritzburg Halle (Halle, 1996), p. 27.

[14] Delaunay, Robert: "Du cubisme à l'art abstrait" in: *Documents inédits publiés par Pierre Francastel* (Paris, 1957), p. 204; cited from the exhibition catalogue *Sonia Delaunay* (Zurich: Museum Bellerive, 1987), p. 24.

[15] Velde, Henry van de, *Der neue Stil in Frankreich* (Berlin: Ernst Wasmuth, 1925), S. 8.

[16] Peach, Harry H., *"Grossbritannien"* in: *Europäisches Kunstgewerbe: Berichte über die Ausstellung 1927,* issued by Städtisches Kunstgewerbe-Museum zu Leipzig (Leipzig: Seemann, 1928), S. 39.

One hundred years of the textile collection, conceived as a model collection for the benefit of local industry in Chemnitz and the surrounding regions of Saxony and Thuringia. It was established as a setting for study devoted to continuous product innovation and intended as an institution capable of playing a crucial role in the development of standards and the improvement of quality. The textile products comprised by the collection come primarily from England and France, the industry leaders of their day. They are the fruits of mechanical and industrial production.

Over the course of the past one hundred years the collection has grown along with a rapidly developing industry that has always looked to the future. Today, it serves as a companion medium for the industry, a gauge of its development, its problems, its visions and its substantive plans. The textile industry remained at the forefront of economic growth in Germany well into the 1960s. The industry still employed more than one million people in both parts of Germany as late as 1957. Among the prominent German textile centers, that of the Saxony-Thuringia region (Plauen, Zwickau, Dresden, Chemnitz, Gera, Greiz, Bautzen, Forst, Cottbus and other cities) was one of the most significant.

Unfortunately, little is known today about the achievements of industrial textile production in these regions. Random fragments of a once rich and diverse industrial culture have been preserved, yet virtually the entire history of regional textile production – of engineering and technology as well as textile design – has receded into the shadows. Thus we lack knowledge about complex interrelationships, phases of industrial development and objective results; products remain uncollected, unanalyzed and unsystematized. Consequently, no scholarly exploration of that history has been undertaken. At a time in which the search for sound approaches to the future must necessarily become an integral component of research activities on behalf of an industry, the effects of such omissions are particularly telling.

It is hardly a sign of great self-awareness and purpose in a sector of the economy when it fails to gain access to its own history, and not merely for the purpose of satisfying nostalgic urges or museum interests. Truly effective work dedicated to future development can achieve its goals only if the achievements of the present can be measured against the progressive achievements of an industry's own history. This failure to examine the industry's history cannot be explained on the basis of the many upheavals that have marked that history during the past century alone. Instead, it is apparent that the objective results have never been looked upon as worthy of collection. Since the very infancy of industrial textile production, its products have been regarded as unworthy and tended to be classified rather as disposable goods. This fact appears all the more dramatic in the light of the growth of a highly diverse, broad-based industrial landscape in these regions during the first Industrial Revolution. Almost all known textile production techniques and technologies had been implemented on an industrial scale: weaving, knitting, embroidery, the manufacture of edging and trimming, textile finishing, etc. Evidence shows that the full range of available weaving techniques was in use, from the shaft turner, Jacquard turner, damask, wire plush, double-moquette, Axminster, Royal Axminster processes to brocading, multiple warp and multiple filling techniques. Special weaving machines are required for the manufacture of products of this kind. It is likely that the rise of the textile machine industry in the region played a significant role in the growth of this constellation. As late as 1937 more than 60 companies in the region were actively producing virtually all of the technical apparatus, machines and systems required for every phase of textile manufacture.

This development began with the construction of the first German power loom by C. W. Schönherr in Niederschlema. Schönherr and his brother L. Schönherr founded a company in Chemnitz in 1852. Five years later they had built and sold a thousand looms. "The" German textile industry succeeded in raising its total output by 130 per cent between 1850 and 1873.[1] By 1861, some 23,500 power looms and 250,000 hand looms were in use. The number of mechanically driven looms rose to 84,250 by 1875, while that of hand looms in active production dwindled to 129,000 during the same period.[2] "While looms built in England played an important role in cotton weaving, 'Schönherr's Loom' was generally recognized as the best loom for the textile industry as a whole."[3]

Yet the real achievement was the development of looms for "artistic weaving," a type of weaving which, with the aid of machines and the products that could be produced with them, crossed over into the field of handicrafts. The result was mechanically reproducible art. The realization of such an intent presupposes the existence of suitable models from the realm of art. These were indeed available in large number and quite familiar to everyone. Silks from late ancient cultures, precious textiles from the High Middle Ages – from Spain and Byzantium, for example – Italian and Chinese silks from the 13th century served as models that were just as important as Italian fabrics from the 13th to the 18th century, carpets from Persia, Asia Minor and the Caucasus, lace from Venice, etc. Such original materials were widely known and regarded as precious, rare products of highly skilled artists and artisans. They were accepted as models and prompted engineers to design and build machines capable of producing fabrics with similar, if not identical features. Although no indisputable proof has been found, it is apparent that a variety of technical processes that provided an immense potential for creative use were developed within the relatively short span of ten to twenty years. Presumably, a large number of companies emerged on the basis of these developments in Saxony and Thuringia in particular. These included such firms as Louis Schönherr and Richard Hartmann in Chemnitz, the loom factories of C. A. Röscher, Thiele in Neugersdorf and the VOMAG company in Plauen. Equipped with suitable machines, companies such as Herrmann Grosse and Oskar Schleicher of Greiz or Gebr. Harnisch of Gera experienced an unparalleled upswing. Many such companies attained a worldwide reputation within just a few short years.

The development of textile products depended upon both the availability of suitable machines and the design of extensive technical aids amenable to creative use. These guaranteed the virtually identical reproduction of copiable originals by special Jacquard machines that had been refined and modified to meet the requirements of specific techniques – Günther's shuttle machine for copying damask patterns, for example. Other special Jacquard machines were developed to control patterning systems in plush, carpet, double-carpet, madras, Royal Axminster and other weaving techniques. In addition, the development of appropriate machine components made it possible to employ plastic, plastic-spatial, transparent, semi-transparent and other expressive design features as well. Multi-warped weave constructions require corresponding loom accessories that facilitate different warp-building techniques. The Schönherr company was already manufacturing looms in which as many as four warp beams could be used in 1886. The bilateral quadruple shuttle change introduced in 1880 guaranteed a range of variations comprising up to seven filling colors. The brocading batten was developed by the Hartmann company for the production of brocaded or figured fabrics.

Thus it appeared that all mechanical devices and accessories needed to ensure the production of a copy that was as close as possible to the original, could indeed be designed and built. Jacquard machines, for example, were modified in such a way that a pattern drawing four meters long and controlled by 40,000 punchcards could be processed. It is evident from our contemporary vantage point that a comparable range of diverse mechanically controlled systems suited to creative textile design has been developed at no time since. Although research in this area is by no means complete, we note that more than 75 different machine-based textile manufacturing techniques and technologies have been identified. Nearly all of them were used on an industrial scale in the Saxony-Thuringia region in particular.

It is worth noting that engineers were stimulated to design new machines primarily by models from the realm of art. Thus *Design*

came first and was followed by mechanically controlled apparatuses. This insight is significant in view of the fact that the period of rapid development thus generated has not been repeated since. With the achievement of reliable copying techniques using technical systems, however, the phase of development driven by qualitative considerations came to an end.

It was not until such machines were harnessed in service of the "art industry" that the textile industrial sector as a whole assumed its true dimension and significance. Many generations of people lived from and with this industrial complex in more than 80 towns and cities in the region for more than 100 years. It had become the leading industrial sector by the first half of the 20th century. It comprised mechanical engineering and manufacture for nearly all machines and devices required for the production of yarn and thread, for the techniques and technologies of weaving, knitting, embroidery small-machine embroidery, textile printing, Jacquard machine construction, textile finishing, textile inspection, etc. In addition, the industry also incorporated a broad and varied range of textile manufacturing processes used for the production of clothing and interior decoration. It comprised research institutes and training schools for nearly all occupations and levels of qualification, publishing houses specialized in literature in the field and the model collection in Chemnitz.

Different attitudes and standards were applied to textile goods produced in industrial machine operations. They were regarded from the outset as second-rate and of secondary interest. "A hand-made textile is always a one-of-a-kind object and is assessed solely on the basis of its fineness and beauty, whereas price is of little importance, since such goods have an ideal value. Machine-made products, on the other hand, are always mass-produced goods whose price is the most important factor, because they are intended for the general public."[4] In his assessment of the German contribution to the 1876 World Exposition in Philadelphia, F. Reuleaux remarked: "It is to be hoped that the time will come, some day, when the word 'imitation' disappears from the vocabulary of our industry."[5] This line of argumentation applies to textiles as well, for they were also exhibited at the World Exposition. Intentions were fixed so strongly on the copying of historical originals that little thought was given to the development of truly original design qualities. Imitations have always been regarded as poor copies, as reproductions or fakes – as cheap substitutes. Thus attitudes towards such products tended increasingly to degrade them. In retrospect, of course, we recognize that superb qualities were indeed achieved despite these prevailing views. Today, we can only dream of being able to produce such articles as these.

The prevalence of copyist intentions and the mechanical capacity to carry them out served to define the principles according to which design variations were sought. The styles and ornamental treasures of the whole of art history were available for whatever use could be made of them. Theories of style and ornamental works paved the way for their appropriation for the purposes of textile production. Special occupations were established to this end. Textile draftsmen and designers assumed the functions in question. In general their work focused upon the goal of creating variations of existing technical qualities through the addition of applicable ornamentation. Designing and drawing patterns was the ostensible objective. The task consisted primarily of organizing "stimuli for the renewal of commercial aesthetics" as an apparently inexhaustible reservoir for the random, illusory modification of industrial products. Changes in pattern drawings were intended to change the product as well. "The engineer and the artist had gone their separate ways. The one designed with an eye to production and function, while the other decorated reproductively as an ordinarily anonymous pattern designer... who satisfied the constantly changing demands of the German art industry for esthetic innovations."[6]

Engineers developed the technical machinery along with the potential for their creative use. Textile draftsmen and designers were forced to rely upon what the engineers offered them in terms of resources for the fulfillment of their objectives. As communication at the professional level between the "partners" was neither planned nor feasible, the relationship of dependence was defined a *priori*. The hierarchy of values that distinguished the two groups was fixed. The engineers guaranteed optimum producibility of the technically determined forms, while ensuring that desired product quantities could be produced. These parameters represent quantitatively measurable values and are always of primary importance to a manufacturing enterprise. Designers and textile draftsmen provided only such values as were assessed on the basis of changing fashion trends as possible today and impossible tomorrow. Their services were perishable, as they were impossible to measure in quantitative terms and thus hardly recognizable to many people in the products themselves.

Designers and textile draftsmen did not enter the product planning process until manufacturing techniques, machine groups, materials to be used and specifications for important quality details had already been irrevocably established. The consequence was an exclusive fixation upon drawings as designs for products. Accordingly, the contents of instruction in training centers were also predetermined. Textile draftsmen and designers, trained at institutions, universities and academies oriented to the teaching of art, were educated in keeping with these intentions. Thus it was considered important to acquire command of the artistic skills needed to identify and vary the surface forms of products. These were to be represented in a manner suitable for practical application and in keeping with existing techniques, technologies and product categories. "Artistic training is entrusted to institutes of learning which educate a large number of young people who have not even been trained in manual crafts, who, without a fee-

ling for technical invention, acquire nothing but a capacity for restructuring certain originals."[7]

The development of productive – that is, creative – relationships between designers and technical processes and technologies was never a goal of training. Engineers were educated at technical universities. There was no professional cooperation between the two types of training institutions, and the unavoidable outcome was a duality of form. The implementation of interdisciplinary work processes subject to communicative management was never a central focus of training programs.

"'Germany's industry holds with the principle of cheap and inferior.' (...) If we examine, within the present context, the hard and bitter accusation of 'cheap and inferior,' a phrase we must interpret – as I have already suggested – as 'cheap and therefore inferior,' from a higher perspective and without reservations, we discover that a certain portion of German industry is ruled by the fundamental belief that competitiveness can be achieved simply by lowering prices. Many tend to forget, or seem to have forgotten already, that the other approach – maintaining stable prices while improving quality – is equally viable and capable of leading to business success."[8]

The intellectual intentions underlying the substantive intentions regarding the production of industrial goods have apparently specified the following goals for textiles for all times to come: *to ensure an adequate supply of decoration,* and *to maintain the illusion of alien values.* There was a huge demand for decoration and imitation to be met. Yet improvements in quality go hand in hand with changes in content. No changes in these intentions have been forthcoming, neither on the domestic front nor from the industry at large. Even at the time when the Deutscher Werkbund was founded in 1906, no programs for substantive improvements in quality for textile products had been initiated by companies in Saxony or Thuringia. Nor is there any evidence to suggest that external influences brought about any appreciable changes.

"In 1907 the *Werkstätten für Wohnungseinrichtungen München* merged with the *Dresdner Werkstätten* to form the *Deutsche Werkstätten Dresden-Hellerau und München.* Behrens, Obrist, Pankok, Paul, Endell and Riemerschmidt worked for the *Dresdner Werkstätten,* which also produced furniture in cooperation with 'local' designers such as Johann Emil Schaudt. This furniture embodies a unique 'Dresden style' characterized by an unmistakable absence of pathos which strikes a balance between the popular possibilities of a strict geometric style and an opulent symbolism. As time passed, clarity and simplicity became synonymous with the work of the *Deutsche Werkstätten.*"[9] In general, it is impossible to determine the extent to which firms from the textile industry may have been involved in such programs. There is also little information available about specific designers who achieved acclaim beyond the scope of their own companies. It is entirely conceivable that accomplishments of designers, as an occupational group, were grossly underestimated due to the professional hierarchies described above. At this level – from below, so to speak – it would have been impossible to bring about substantive changes in products through independent efforts. The rebuilding of the textile sector on the basis of the level of development reached before 1937 began immediately after the end of World War II.

A second major phase was initiated in the late 1950s. Increasingly, producers began to adopt new, alternative textile manufacturing methods. The new processes proved considerably more productive than classical methods. Although productive efficiency had always been a goal of technical development since the infancy of industrial production, it was only of secondary importance at first. The primary objective was the imitation of historical originals and models with machine technologies.

With the advent of new production processes, however, the call for huge rises in production became louder. Knitting, needle-felt double-ribbing, tufting, malimo and malipol processes, etc., accounted for the lion's share of production beginning in the 1960s. The demonstrable disadvantage of such processes, however, is that the technical systems used offer little potential for the realization of extensive and necessary product variations. Many of these processes are themselves rigid, inflexible systems. The logical response to these disadvantages was to modernize technical textile printing processes as a special form of print finishing. Existing fabric printing techniques such as screen, roller and flock printing were further refined, while new technologies, including rotary screen, spray, transfer, and chromotronic printing, etc. were introduced at the same time. These new developments now made it possible to achieve a wide range of product variations through the use of printable forms.

Many classical techniques and technologies were neglected during this period and eventually eliminated from the production process over the course of about two decades. Such processes were abandoned primarily because they offered no potential for productivity enhancement. In the course of these developments, a number of creative possibilities that would have been required to achieve product diversity were also eliminated. Thus, for example, the production of wire moquettes as well as brocading, multiple warp and filling, pleating, shaft turner, Jacquard turner, madras, velvet, bobinet techniques and others were discontinued permanently. The remaining traditional technologies, such as shaft weaving, were retooled in such a way as to bring about an immense increase in productivity. This was clearly accomplished at the expense of process systems suited to qualitative applications.

The surface modification of textile products became the dominant principle of "product development." The very "simple" conclusion that "a new decoration is in itself a new product" became the sole governing principle. Thus designers in the industry were faced to an increasing degree with the task of achieving illusory product modifications. And once again, imitation was held up as the primary creative principle. Goods had to look like woven or knitted textiles, like wood, stone or fur, like the products of the leading industry competitors and like the fashionable materials found in catalogue illustrations, etc. There appear to have been no boundaries to the realization of this objective in practice. Firms tended to avoid developing original concepts whose marketability could not be demonstrated. Work in the field of design began to become less and less meaningful as time went by. With respect to their esthetic and functional requirements, the products themselves were fixed – apparently for all times – in their roles as articles of *decoration* and *imitation*. Ultimately, the computer, equipped with a graphic design program, assumed the task realizing design functions without reference to other factors. Operators of such systems no longer required training in esthetics, art or design.

The essential features of industrially produced textiles reflect their status as anonymous, cheap, bulk, mass-produced disposable goods. Nor will that change as low-wage countries accelerate textile production and dump their products in undreamed-of quantities on European markets. They work with basically the same techniques and technologies used by manufacturers in the industrialized countries. Textile goods will be leveled *worldwide* to conform with uniform standards with respect to their substantive dispositions, their properties and their effects. Their distinctiveness will thus be reduced to considerations of cost. The long-term consequences of this trend is a condition of paralyzed stagnation affecting the entire industry. The technical advantage once enjoyed by firms in Germany and the regions of Saxony and Thuringia in particular has been eliminated entirely. The second major development is clearly to be regarded as a qualtitative one. This long-term survival of this branch of the economy can be ensured only if new, *qualitative* objectives can be articulated. Quantitative objectives have dominated as major policy accents for much too long, and they have brought the industry to the limits of its ability to survive in the European market. Emphasis in the development of qualitative goals must be placed on product development. It is only the very best products that provide evidence of a company's productive capacity. The greater the impact of a company's own intentions becomes, the greater its influence on the market will be. Thus the following goals should be pursued:

1. Bundling of all significant professional disciplines capable of contributing to a holistic product-development process. The representatives of these disciplines should be capable of working in concert without prejudice and unhampered by professional tunnel vision. Cooperative work performance needs to be the rule, rather than the exception.

2. Development of a creative approach to the market. Goals can be achieved only by those who recognize them. The market is shaped and determined by supply. Goods supplied must be original and independent, formulated and represented by business without "copyist" idealism and in an appropriate manner. Active work in the market means leadership.

3. Concentration on the development of new essential features for industrial goods. These must involve the creation of cultural values instead of everyday values, utility values instead of presentation values, collector's goods instead of throw-away goods, user-oriented values instead of non-oriented values, genuine values instead of imitative values, etc. Extensions and new definitions must be found within the functional structure of primary esthetic aspects of function in particular. The exclusive fixation upon the functions of "decoration and imitation" with respect to products is no longer enough. There have been too many such products in the market for much too long. To attempt to enhance supply in quantitative terms is an undertaking that can lead at best to short-term success. The supply of cheap, mass-produced goods currently on the market is entirely sufficient to meet the existing demand. For a high-cost country like Germany, a strategy devoted to the production of even cheaper goods can only lead to failure.

4. The creation of a working strategy based upon the principle that product forms must be developed from original requirements pertinent to the respective products. The orientation to utility value is a crucial goal of great significance. The available resources of creative design must be expanded in a variety of ways. These demands apply in particular to textile production techniques, technologies, materials, patterns and designs, colors and finishing processes and to their interactions and reciprocal effects. A fundamentally creative approach to them will ensure long-term development potential and thus competitive advantages as well.

5. Integration of the field of "design." The work objectives characterized above can only be achieved within the context of a professional discipline that thinks and acts aggressively. This occupational group should be expected to develop creative, holistic visions and the strategies needed to realize these visions. The concentration on the visual-esthetic effects upon the acceptance of functions that have always existed is actually the field of endeavor of the pattern draftsmen and designers of the 19th century. These fields of activity are no longer adequate in an industry that seeks to develop into the 21st century.

6. Development of an understanding of history as it has affected the industry. There is a crucial need today for scholarly historical research on techniques and technologies, design and the industry itself. A sound formulation of performance programs for the present and the future cannot be achieved unless it is possible to

measure them against the achievements of history. And that must include the achievements of competitors as well.

7. The goals of such work can be realized in an optimal way only if approaches to realization are tested and applied experimentally in laboratories in which a wide variety of processes and technologies are integrated. Depending upon the specified goals, it is possible to intervene creatively in these processes and technologies, and the objective must be to improve and refine them. New products require modified processes. In this way, it will be possible to modernize the principle that "*Design* determines techniques and technologies" and give it currency once again.

8. Provision of an adequate supply of properly trained personnel in all occupations and at all professional levels for the industry. This will require substantive changes in all areas of qualification. The intensification of cooperative relationships between the business community and universities and other institutions of higher learning must be given a higher priority. To an increasing extent, training and scholarship must focus upon prognostic goals and future-oriented objectives.

Change is sorely needed in the industry. To stimulate such change and equip it for survival is a worthy objective, which must first be consolidated and made feasible through the efforts of industry leaders acting in concert. The time to take up this task has long since come. Making up for lost time will be difficult, but not impossible. Ultimately, what is at stake is not merely the preservation of an industry for its own sake but the creation of fields of activity for a great many people. And that is a goal worthy of our efforts to develop new visions.

Wieland Poser

[1] *Deutsche Geschichte* (Ploetl Verlag), p. 215.
[2] Statistics cited from the *Textilkalender*, 1914.
[3] *Geschichte der Textil-Industrie* (Leipzig/Stuttgart/Zurich: Süd-Verlag GmbH).
[4] Ernst Flemming, *Textile Künste* (Berlin: Verlag für Kunstwissenschaften).
[5] F. Reuleaux, *Briefe aus Philadelphia* (Braunschweig, 1877).
[6] Gert Selle, *Geschichte des Design in Deutschland von 1870 bis heute* (Cologne: DuMont Buchverlag, 1978).
[7] Skerl, "Kunst und Industrie zwischen 1850–1900" in: *Designwissenschaftl. Beiträge 6* (Halle: Hochschule für industrielle Formgestaltung Halle – Burg Giebichenstein), p. 262.
[8] F. Reuleaux, *Briefe aus Philadelphia* (Braunschweig, 1877).
[9] Gabriele Fahr-Becker, *Jugendstil* (Cologne: Könemann, 1996).

| PLATES |

1 | WALL HANGING, 1924

Benita Koch-Otte (1892–1976)
Bauhaus Weimar
Semi-tapestry
Warp: cotton; weft: wool
H. 175.5 cm; w. 110 cm
Inventory no. XII/7516; acquired 1924 from Bauhaus Weimar

2 | PATCHWORK RUG, 1925/27 (Detail)

Helene Schmidt-Nonné (1891–1976)
Bauhaus Dessau
Warp: cotton; weft: strips of various materials
L. 328 cm; w. 68 cm
Inventory no. XII/11517; this patchwork rug originally belonged to
Marianne Brandt and was acquired for the collection in 1991.

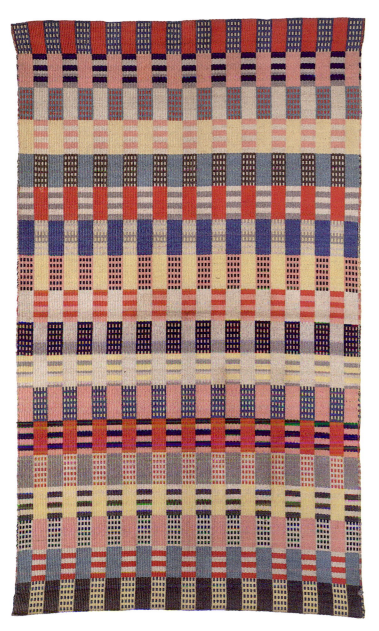

3 | GRAND PIANO COVER, 1927

Ruth Hollós-Consemüller (1904–1993)
Bauhaus Dessau
Double weave
Warp: rayon; weft: rayon
H. 200 cm; w. 119 cm
Inventory no. XIII/8279; acquired 1927

4 | NURSERY ROOM RUG, 1929

Otti Berger (1898–1944/45)
Bauhaus Dessau
Warp: cotton; weft: mercerized cotton
H. 185 cm; w. 109 cm
Marked with Bauhaus signum u. l.
Inventory no. XII/9400; acquired 1929 from Bauhaus Dessau

5 | WALL HANGING/QUILT, 1929

Bauhaus Dessau
Manufacture: Textiles studio of the Bauhaus Dessau
Two-ply cloth with filling weft
Warp: cotton; weft: wool
H. 195 cm; b. 124 cm
Marked with Bauhaus signum l. l.
Inventory no. XII/8745; acquired 1929 from Bauhaus Dessau

6 | WALL HANGING, 1928

Burg Giebichenstein – Werkstätten der Stadt Halle
Manufacture: Werkstätten der Stadt Halle/Hand Weaving, Director: Benita Otte
Warp: cotton; weft: wool, cotton
H. 300 cm; w. 175 cm
Inventory no. XII/8603; acquired 1928 from the Werkstätten der Stadt Halle

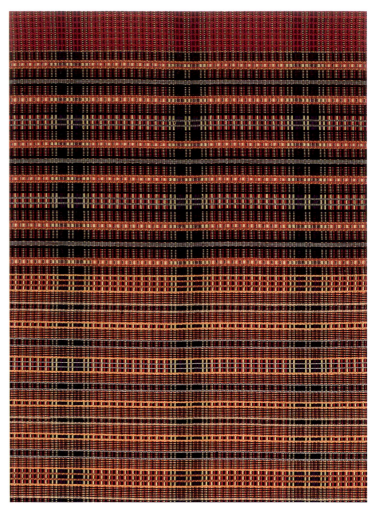

7 | DECORATIVE MATERIAL, 1930

Burg Giebichenstein – Werkstätten der Stadt Halle
Manufacture: Werkstätten der Stadt Halle/Hand Weaving, Director: Benita Otte
Warp: cotton; weft: rayon, wool
H. 140 cm; w. 115 cm
Pattern repeat: h. 9.5 cm; w. 15 cm
Inventory no. XII/9244; acquired 1930 from the Studio of the City of Halle

8 | SOFA COVERLET, 1930 (Detail)

Burg Giebichenstein – Werkstätten der Stadt Halle
Manufacture: Werkstätten der Stadt Halle/Hand Weaving, Director: Benita Otte
Warp: cotton (chenille), rayon; weft: wool, rayon
H. 250 cm; w. 158 cm
Inventory no. XII/9246; acquired 1930 from the Werkstätten der Stadt Halle

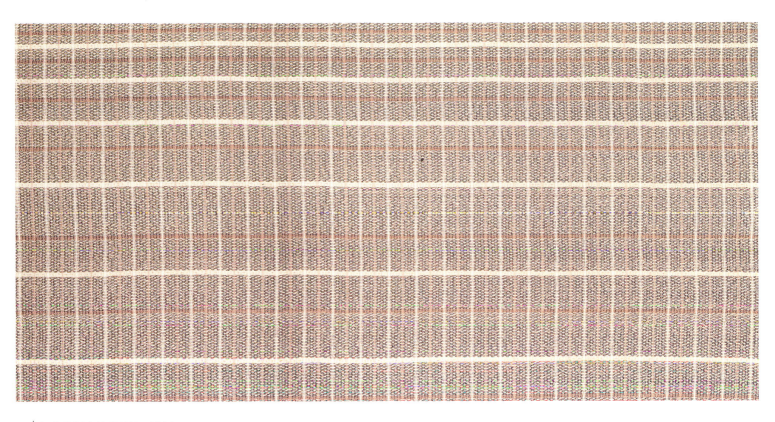

9 | CURTAIN MATERIAL, 1932

Burg Giebichenstein – Werkstätten der Stadt Halle
Manufacture: Werkstätten der Stadt Halle/Hand Weaving, Director: Benita Otte
Warp: mercerized cotton; weft: rayon
H. 100 cm; w. 124 cm
Pattern repeat: h. 60 cm; w. 4.5 cm
Inventory no. XII/9452; acquired 1932 from the Werkstätten der Stadt Halle

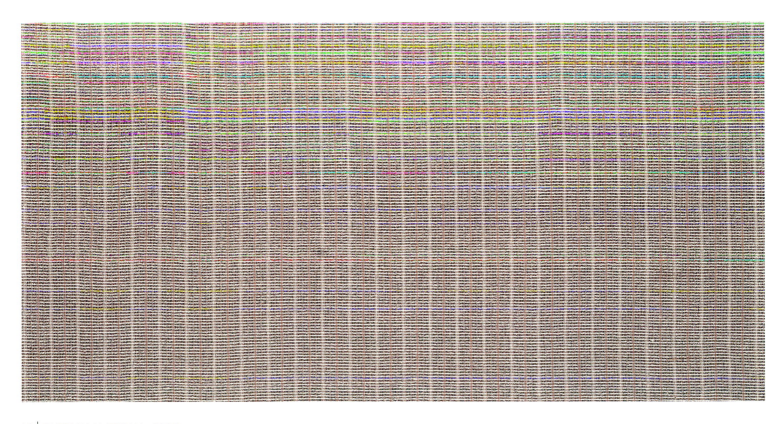

10 | CURTAIN MATERIAL, 1932

Burg Giebichenstein – Werkstätten der Stadt Halle
Manufacture: Werkstätten der Stadt Halle/Hand Weaving, Director: Benita Otte
Warp: mercerized cotton; weft: rayon
H. 97 cm; w. 3.5 cm
Pattern repeat: h. 0.3 cm; w. 3.5 cm
Inventory no. XII/9451; acquired 1932 from the Werkstätten der Stadt Halle

11 | SPRAY-PRINTED FABRIC "BIWA-LAKE", 1928

Maria May (1900–1968)
Reimann School, Berlin
Warp: rayon; weft: rayon
H. 195 cm; w. 98.5 cm
Inventory no. XVII/8418; acquired 1928 from the Reimann School, Berlin

12 | SPRAY-PRINTED FABRIC "BLACK–WHITE–GREY", 1928

Maria May (1900–1968)
Reimann School, Berlin
Warp: rayon; weft: rayon
H. 199 cm; w. 90 cm
Pattern repeat: h. 49 cm; w. 34 cm
Inventory no. XVII/8416; acquired 1928 from Reimann School, Berlin

13 | SPRAY-PRINTED FABRIC "ODETTE", 1928

Maria May (1900–1968)
Reimann School, Berlin
Warp: rayon; weft: rayon
H. 195 cm; w. 89 cm
Pattern repeat: h. 57.5 cm; w. = web width
Inventory no. XVII/8417; acquired 1928 from the Reimann School, Berlin

14 | SPRAY-PRINTED FABRIC "FRUIT BOWL", 1928

Maria May (1900–1968)
Reimann School, Berlin
Warp: rayon; weft: rayon
H. 193 cm; w. 89 cm
Pattern repeat: h. 62 cm; w. = web width
Inventory no. XVII/8580; acquired 1928 from the Reimann School, Berlin

15 | SPRAY-PRINTED FABRIC, 1928

Maria May (1900–1968)
Reimann School, Berlin
Warp: rayon; weft: rayon
H. 190 cm; w. 90 cm
Pattern repeat: h. 62 cm; w. = web width
Inventory no. XVII/8579; acquired 1928 from the Reimann School, Berlin

16 | SPRAY-PRINTED FABRIC "PARIS", 1930

Maria May (1900–1968)
Reimann School, Berlin
Warp: rayon; weft: rayon
H. 237 cm; w. 117 cm
Pattern repeat: h. 127 cm; w. = web width
Inventory no. XVII/9099; acquired 1930 from the Reimann School, Berlin

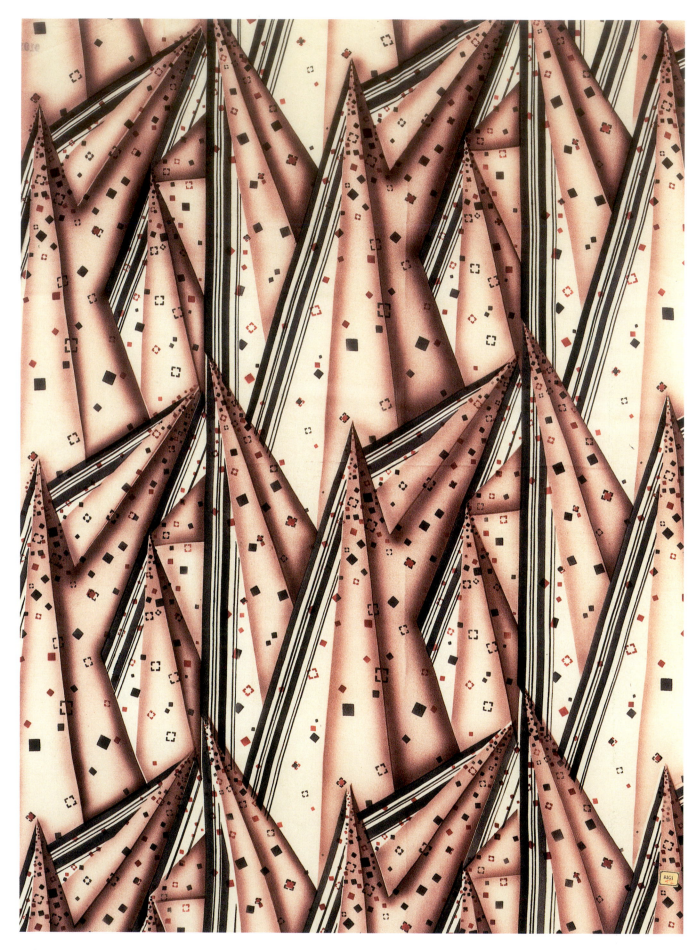

17 | SPRAY-PRINTED FABRIC "LACE", 1930

Maria May (1900–1968)
Reimann School, Berlin
Warp: rayon; weft: rayon
H. 147 cm; w. 118 cm
Pattern repeat: h. 50 cm; w. 44 cm
Inventory no. XVII/9101; acquired 1930 from the Reimann School, Berlin

18 | SPRAY-PRINTED FABRIC "HUNGARIA", 1930

Maria May (1900–1968)
Reimann School, Berlin
Warp: cotton; weft: cotton
H. 176 cm; w. 98 cm
Pattern repeat: h. 89 cm; w. 35 cm
Inventory no. XVII/9100; acquired 1930 from the Reimann School, Berlin

19| UPHOLSTERY FABRIC, 1929

Sigmund von Weech (1888–1982)
Manufacture: Hand Weaving Studio Sigmund von Weech, Schaftlach
Warp: cotton, rayon; weft: rayon, cotton (chenille)
H. 116 cm; w. 129 cm
Pattern repeat: h. 40 cm; w. 21 cm
Inventory no. XII/8687; acquired 1929 from Friedemann und Weber, Berlin

20 | UPHOLSTERY FABRIC, 1929

Sigmund von Weech (1888–1982)
Manufacture: Hand Weaving Studio Sigmund von Weech, Schaftlach
Warp: cotton, rayon; weft: cotton (chenille)
H. 126 cm; w. 129 cm
Pattern repeat: h. 65.5 cm; w. 42.5 cm
Inventory no. XII/8688; acquired 1929 from Friedemann und Weber, Berlin

21│SOFA COVERLET, 1929

Sigmund von Weech (1888–1982)
Manufacture: Hand Weaving Studio Sigmund von Weech, Schaftlach
Warp: cotton; weft: cotton
H. 300 cm; w. 150 cm
Inventory no. XII/8895; acquired 1929 from Schneider und Königs, Düsseldorf

22 | BAYCO GOLD STRETCH FABRIC, 1927

Hand Weaving Studio Hohenhagen, Bremen
Warp: cotton; weft: silk, rayon, bayco yarn (metallic yarn)
H. 323 cm; w. 178 cm
Inventory no. XII/8265; acquired 1927 from Schneider und Königs, Düsseldorf

23 | UPHOLSTERY FABRIC, 1927

Hand Weaving Studio
Hohenhagen, Bremen
Warp: cotton; weft: cotton (chenille)
H. 178 cm; w. 150 cm
Pattern repeat: h. 20 cm; w. 150 cm
Inventory no. XII/8264; acquired 1927 from Schneider und Königs, Düsseldorf

24 | WALL FABRIC, 1930

Polytex Textilgesellschaft mbH, Berlin
Warp: rayon; weft: cotton (chenille), rayon
H. 176 cm; w. 131 cm
Inventory no. XII/9249; acquired 1930 from Polytex Textilgesellschaft mbH, Berlin

25 | UPHOLSTERY FABRIC, 1930

Polytex Textilgesellschaft mbH, Berlin
Warp: rayon; weft: cotton (chenille), rayon
H. 213 cm; w. 132 cm
Pattern repeat: h. 159 cm; w. 65 cm
Inventory no. XII/951; acquired 1930 from Polytex Textilgesellschaft mbH, Berlin

Fig. English armchair

30 | UPHOLSTERY FABRIC (looped pile fabric), 1927

Vereinigte Werkstätten, Munich
Warp: wool; weft: cotton
H. 136 cm; w. 130 cm
Pattern repeat: h. 20 cm; w. 130 cm
Inventory no. VI/8229; acquired 1927 from the Vereinigte Werkstätten, Munich

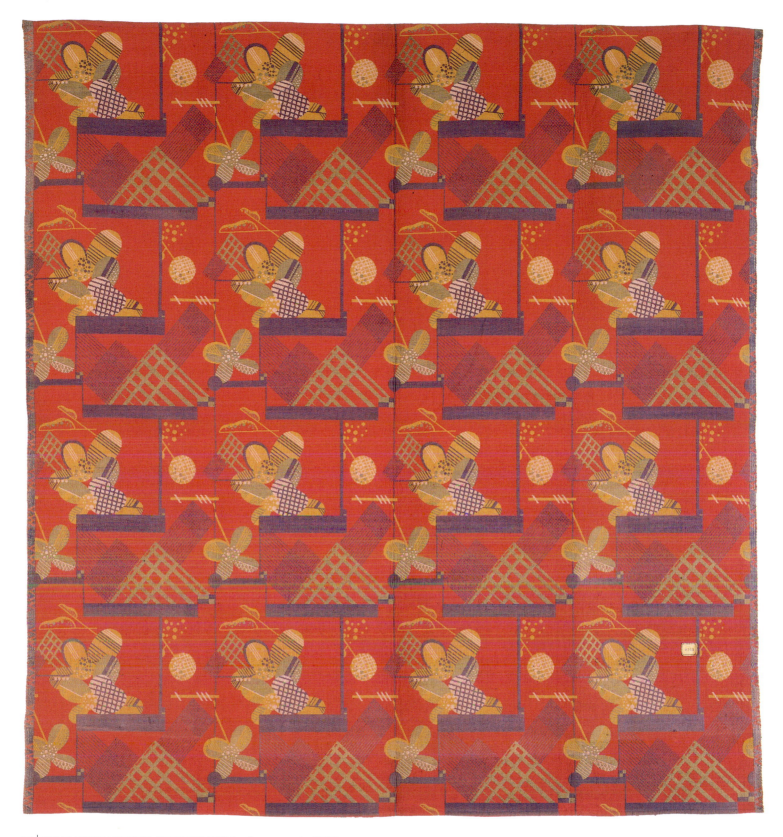

31 | UPHOLSTERY FABRIC "PAPAGENO" (weft tapestry), 1929

Paul László (born 1900)
Vereinigte Werkstätten, Munich
Warp: cotton; weft: cotton, wool
H. 135 cm; w. 128 cm
Pattern repeat: h. 34 cm; w. 31 cm
Mark in the selvage: V.W.
Inventory no. II/8743; acquired 1929 from the Vereinigte Werkstätten für Kunst im Handwerk, Düsseldorf

32 | UPHOLSTERY FABRIC (weft tapestry), 1928

E. Engelbrecht
Vereinigte Werkstätten, Munich
Warp: cotton; weft: cotton, wool
H. 148 cm; w. 128 cm
Pattern repeat: h. 52 cm; w. 31.5 cm
Mark in the selvage: V.W.
Inventory no. III/8587; acquired 1928 from the
Vereinigte Werkstätten, Munich

33 | BROCADE UPHOLSTERY FABRIC, 1928

Studio F. A. Breuhaus
Vereinigte Werkstätten, Munich
Warp: cotton; weft: cotton, rayon (chenille), false lamé
H. 96.5 cm; w. 130 cm
Pattern repeat: h. 38.5 cm; w. 63.5 cm
Inventory no. I/9671; acquired 1933 from the Vereinigte Werkstätten

Fig. F. A. Breuhaus: Library of the Steam Liner "Bremen", in: *ID*, 1929, Vol. XI, p. 448

34 | UPHOLSTERY FABRIC (brocade velour), 1929

Studio F. A. Breuhaus
Vereinigte Werkstätten, Munich
Warp: cotton; weft: cotton, wool, false lamé
H. 106 cm; w. 135 cm
Pattern repeat: h. 47 cm; w. 33 cm
Inventory no. V/8874; acquired 1929 from the
Vereinigte Werkstätten für Kunst im Handwerk,
Düsseldorf

35 | UPHOLSTERY FABRIC (terry pile), 1929

Studio F.A. Breuhaus
Vereinigte Werkstätten, Munich
Warp: cotton; weft: cotton, rayon
H. 133 cm; w. 136 cm
Pattern repeat: h. 36 cm; w. 33 cm
Inventory no. V/9329; acquired 1931 from H. G.
Schrödter, Leipzig

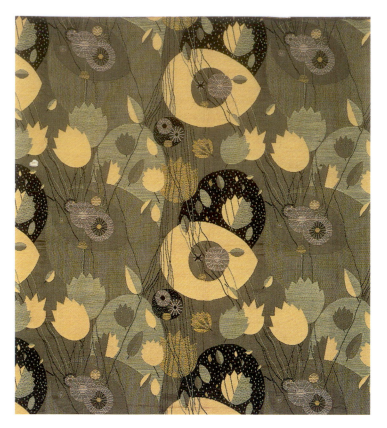

36 | BEZUGSSTOFF "VENUS", around 1932

Vereinigte Werkstätten, Munich
Warp: mercerized cotton; weft: rayon
H. 135 cm; w. 129 cm
Musterrapport: H. 49 cm; B. 63 cm
Mark in the selvage: V.W. VENUS
Inventory no. I/9667; acquired 1933 from the Vereinigte Werkstätten, Munich

37 | UPHOLSTERY FABRIC, 1935

Vereinigte Werkstätten, Munich
Warp: cotton; weft: wool, cotton
H. 100 cm; w. 37 cm
Pattern repeat: h. 41 cm; w. 36.5 cm
Inventory no. I/9975; acquired 1935 from the Vereinigte Werkstätten, Munich

38 | UPHOLSTERY FABRIC, 1935

Vereinigte Werkstätten, Munich
Warp: cotton; weft: wool, cotton
H. 97 cm; w. 145.5 cm
Pattern repeat: h. 54 cm; w. 71 cm
Inventory no. I/9976; acquired 1935 from the Vereinigte Werkstätten, Munich

39 | UPHOLSTERY FABRIC (weft tapestry), 1927

Deutsche Werkstätten, Dresden
Warp: cotton; weft: wool
H. 102 cm; w. 128 cm
Pattern repeat: h. 36 cm; w. 31 cm
Inventory no. II/7805; acquired 1926 from the Deutsche Werkstätten

40│UPHOLSTERY FABRIC (cotton velour), 1927

Deutsche Werkstätten, Dresden
Warp: cotton; weft: cotton
H. 95 cm; w. 128 cm
Pattern repeat: h. 7.5 cm; w. 8 cm
Inventory no. XXIV/8117; acquired 1927 from the Deutsche Werkstätten

Fig. Living Room, Düsseldorf; in: *ID,* July 1928, p. 289

45 | PRINTED FABRIC, around 1930

Deutsche Werkstätten, Dresden
Warp: rayon; weft: cotton
H. 47 cm; w. 54 cm
Pattern repeat: h. 30 cm; w. 32 cm
Inventory no. XIV/11380-88; part of the DE-
WE-TEX pattern-book; donated by Möbelstoff-
weberei Tannenhauer, Braunsdorf, 1982

Fig. Deutsche Werkstätten: living and dining
room; in: *ID*, 1934, p. 343

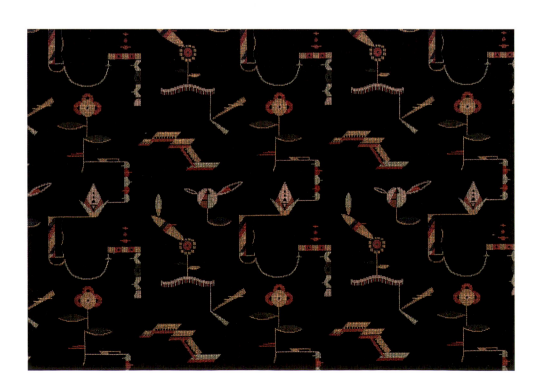

46 | UPHOLSTERY FABRIC
(looped pile fabric), 1926

Vorwerk & Co., Barmen
Warp: wool; weft: cotton
H. 140 cm; w. 128 cm
Pattern repeat: h. 31 cm; w. 32 cm
Marked and woven into the reverse side:
VORWERK
Inventory no. VI/7797; acquired 1926 from
Riedel & Rothe, Berlin

40 | UPHOLSTERY FABRIC (cotton velour), 1927

Deutsche Werkstätten, Dresden
Warp: cotton; weft: cotton
H. 95 cm; w. 128 cm
Pattern repeat: h. 7.5 cm; w. 8 cm
Inventory no. XXIV/8117; acquired 1927 from the Deutsche Werkstätten

Fig. Living Room, Düsseldorf; in: *ID,* July 1928, p. 289

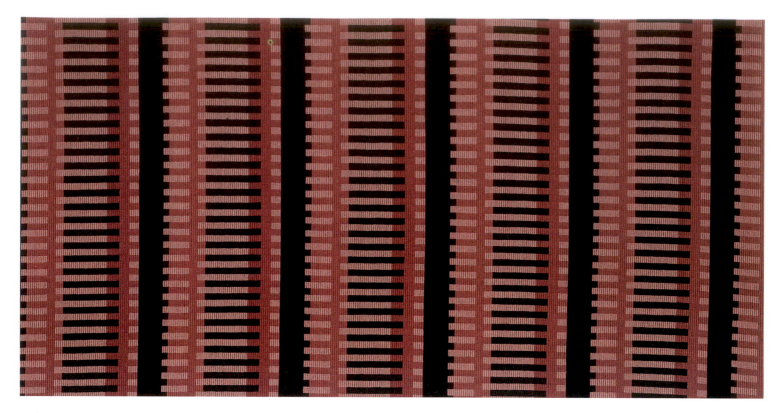

41 | UPHOLSTERY FABRIC, 1927

Deutsche Werkstätten, Dresden
Warp: wool; weft: wool
H. 100 cm; w. 135 cm
Pattern repeat: h. 2 cm; w. 21.5 cm
Inventory no. II/8114; acquired 1927 from the Deutsche Werkstätten

42 | DECORATIVE MATERIAL, 1926

Deutsche Werkstätten, Dresden
Printed fabric, block printing
Warp: cotton; weft: wool
H. 54.5 cm; w. 62 cm
Pattern repeat: indeterminate
Inventory no. XVII/7889; acquired 1926 from
A. Eick u. Söhne, Essen

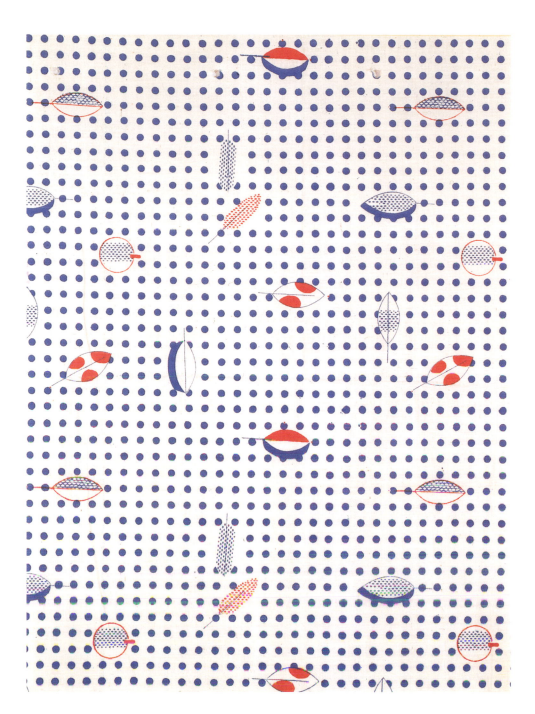

43 | PRINTED FABRIC, around 1925

Josef Hillerbrand (1892–1981)
Deutsche Werkstätten, Dresden
Warp: cotton; weft: cotton
H. 97 cm; w. 106.5 cm
Pattern repeat: h. 22 cm; w. 26.5 cm
Marked on selvage: ENTWURF HILLER-
BRAND 538 DEWETEX. DRESDEN
Inventory no. XIV/11380-150; donated by
Hofmann, 1988

44 | PRINTED FABRIC, around 1929

Deutsche Werkstätten, Dresden
Warp: rayon; weft: cotton
H. 23.5 cm; w. 59.5 cm
Pattern repeat: h. indeterminate; w. 31.5 cm
Inventory no. XIV/11380-89; part of the DE-
WE-TEX pattern-book; donated by Möbelstoff-
weberei Tannenhauer, Braunsdorf, 1982

45 | PRINTED FABRIC, around 1930

Deutsche Werkstätten, Dresden
Warp: rayon; weft: cotton
H. 47 cm; w. 54 cm
Pattern repeat: h. 30 cm; w. 32 cm
Inventory no. XIV/11380-88; part of the DE-WE-TEX pattern-book; donated by Möbelstoff-weberei Tannenhauer, Braunsdorf, 1982

Fig. Deutsche Werkstätten: living and dining room; in: *ID*, 1934, p. 343

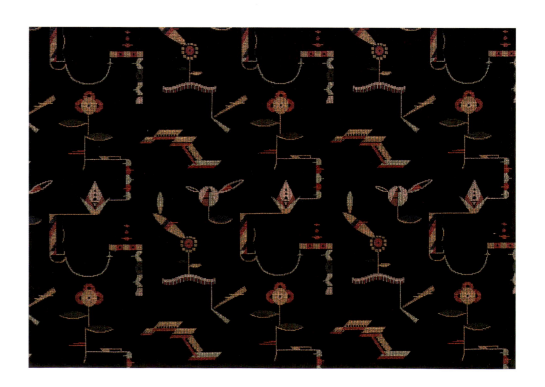

46 | UPHOLSTERY FABRIC
(looped pile fabric), 1926

Vorwerk & Co., Barmen
Warp: wool; weft: cotton
H. 140 cm; w. 128 cm
Pattern repeat: h. 31 cm; w. 32 cm
Marked and woven into the reverse side:
VORWERK
Inventory no. VI/7797; acquired 1926 from
Riedel & Rothe, Berlin

47 | UPHOLSTERY FABRIC (looped pile fabric), 1926

Vorwerk & Co., Barmen
Warp: wool; weft: cotton
H. 129 cm; w. 127 cm
Pattern repeat: h. 33 cm; w. 32 cm
Marked and woven into the reverse side: VORWERK
Inventory no. VI/7796; acquired 1926 from Riedel & Rothe, Berlin

48 | UPHOLSTERY FABRIC (looped pile fabric), 1927

Vorwerk & Co., Barmen
Warp: wool; weft: cotton
H. 138 cm; w. 128 cm
Pattern repeat: h. 29 cm; w. 32.5 cm
Marked and woven into the reverse side: VORWERK
Inventory no. VI/8091; acquired 1927 from Fischer & Wolf, Cologne

49 | UPHOLSTERY FABRIC (looped pile fabric), 1928

Vorwerk & Co., Barmen
Warp: wool, cotton; weft: cotton
H. 140 cm; w. 128 cm
Pattern repeat: h. 27 cm; w. 31.5 cm
Marked and woven into the reverse side: VORWERK
Inventory no. VI/8383; acquired 1928 from Brüggemann & Barkmann, Hamburg

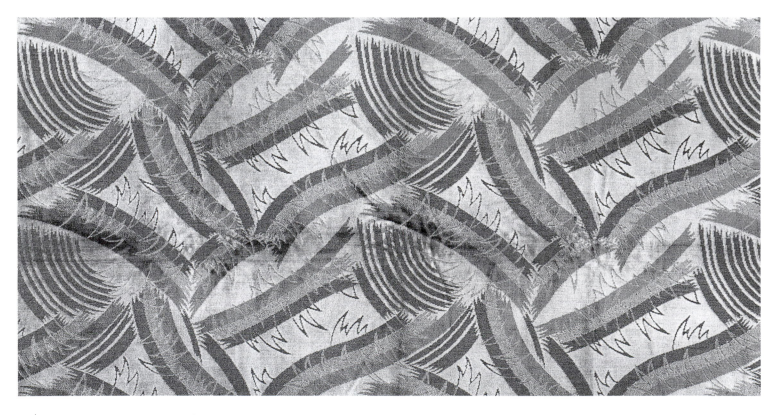

50 | UPHOLSTERY FABRIC (terry pile), 1930

Vorwerk & Co., Barmen
Warp: cotton, rayon; weft: cotton
H. 142 cm; w. 132 cm
Pattern repeat: h. 62 cm; w. 32.5 cm
Marked in the selvage: VORWERK
Inventory no. V/9081; acquired 1930 from Brüggemann & Barkmann, Hamburg

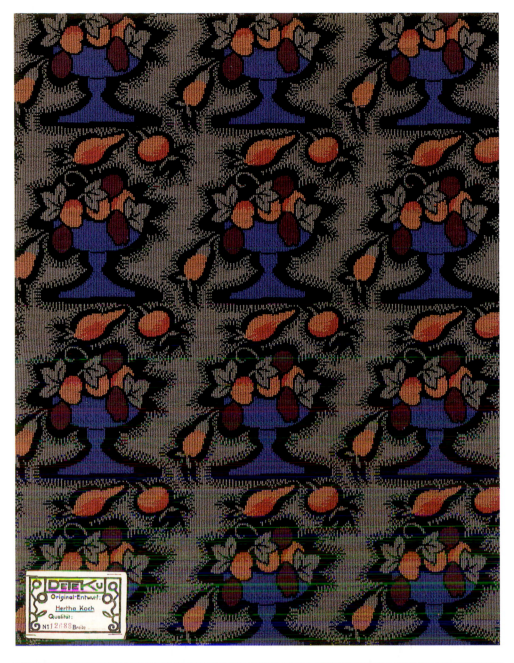

51 | UPHOLSTERY FABRIC
(looped pile fabric), 1924

Hertha Koch
DETEKU – Deutsche Textile Kunst, Leipzig
Warp: cotton; weft: wool, rayon
H. 58.5 cm; w. 60.5 cm
Pattern repeat: h. 16 cm; w. 15.5 cm
Marked on specially designed paper label:
"DETEKU, Original-Entwurf: Hertha Koch,
Qualität: No. 126788"
Inventory no. VI/7495; acquired 1924 from
DETEKU, Leipzig

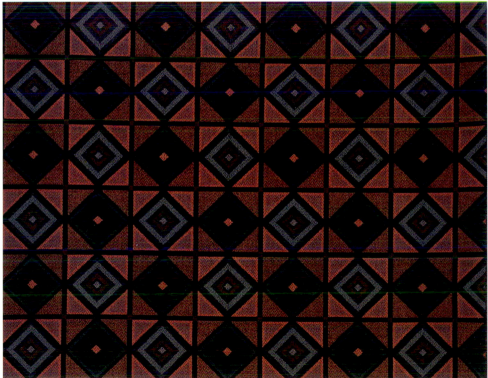

52 | UPHOLSTERY FABRIC (weft tapestry),
1924

Erich Kleinhempel (1847–1947)
DETEKU – Deutsche Textile Kunst, Leipzig
Warp: cotton; weft: wool
H. 93 cm; w. 125 cm
Pattern repeat: h. 31 cm; w. 31 cm
Inventory no. II/7496; acquired 1924 from
DETEKU, Leipzig

53 | UPHOLSTERY FABRIC (weft tapestry),
1924

Erich Kleinhempel (1847–1947)
DETEKU – Deutsche Textile Kunst, Leipzig
Warp: cotton; weft: wool
H. 132.5 cm; w. 97 cm
Pattern repeat: h. 41 cm; w. 33 cm
Inventory no. II/7499; acquired 1924 from
DETEKU, Leipzig

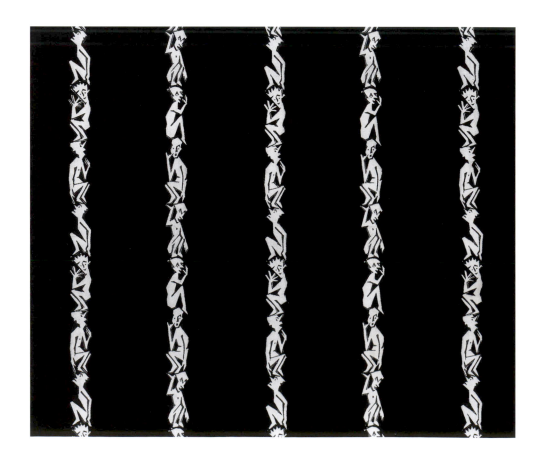

54 | PRINTED FABRIC (hand printing), 1924

Erich Kleinhempel (1847–1947)
DETEKU – Deutsche Textile Kunst, Leipzig
Warp: cotton; weft: cotton
H. 101.5 cm; w. 98 cm
Pattern repeat: h. 34 cm; w. 39 cm
Inventory no. XIV/7512; acquired 1924 from
DETEKU, Leipzig

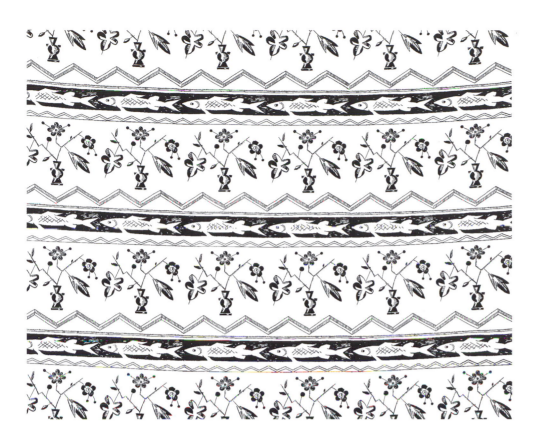

55 | PRINTED FABRIC (hand printing), 1924

Ernst Aufseeser (1880–1940)
DETEKU – Deutsche Textile Kunst, Leipzig
Warp: cotton; weft: cotton
H. 89.5 cm; w. 97 cm
Pattern repeat: h. 24 cm; w. 16.5 cm
Inventory no. XIV/7510; acquired 1924 from
DETEKU, Leipzig

56 | UPHOLSTERY FABRIC
(looped pile fabric), 1930

Adolf Toenges, Elberfeld
Warp: wool, cotton; weft: cotton
H. 148 cm; w. 130 cm
Pattern repeat: h. 45 cm; w. 64 cm
Inventory no. VI/9058; acquired 1930 from
Hans Henschel, Berlin

57 | UPHOLSTERY FABRIC (terry pile), 1930

Adolf Toenges, Elberfeld
Warp: cotton, rayon; weft: cotton
H. 134 cm; w. 129 cm
Pattern repeat: h. 60 cm; w. 64 cm
Inventory no. V/9209; acquired 1930 from Hans Henschel, Berlin

58 | PRINTED FABRIC, DESIGN 670, 1924

Ruth Hildegard Geyer-Raack (1894–1975)
Bayerische Textilwerke Tutzing
Warp: cotton; weft: cotton
H. 282 cm; w. 126 cm
Pattern repeat: h. 83.5 cm; w. 126 cm
Inventory no. XIV/7678; acquired 1925 from L. Bernheimer, Munich

59 | PRINTED FABRIC, 1928

Wilhelm Marsmann (1896–1966) and Viktor Rauch (1901–1945)
Deutsche Farbmöbel AG, Munich
Warp: rayon; weft: rayon
H. 150 cm; w. 125.5 cm
Pattern repeat: h. 68.5 cm; w. 65 cm
Inventory no. XIV/8572; acquired 1928 from Deutsche Farbmöbel AG, Munich

60 | UPHOLSTERY FABRIC (weft tapestry), 1925

Hahn und Bach, Munich
Warp: cotton; weft: wool, cotton
H. 145 cm; w. 124.5 cm
Pattern repeat: h. 70 cm; w. 62 cm
Inventory no. I/7691; acquired 1925 from Hahn und Bach, Munich

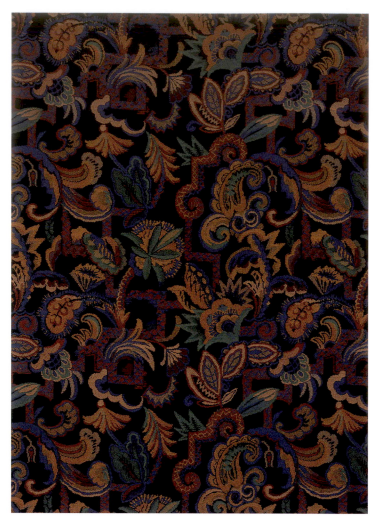

61 | UPHOLSTERY FABRIC (weft tapestry), 1924

Hahn und Bach, Munich
Warp: cotton; weft: cotton, wool
H. 90 cm; w. 130 cm
Pattern repeat: h. 68.5 cm; w. 32 cm
Inventory no. II/7768; acquired 1926 from
Hermann Gerson, Berlin

Fig. sofa in a dining room, in: *ID,* 1926, Vol. 37,
p. 115

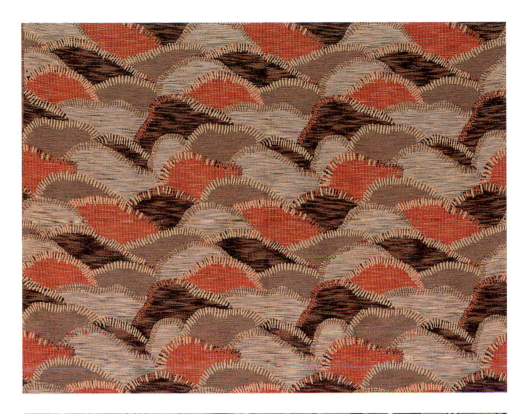

62 | UPHOLSTERY FABRIC, 1932

Hahn und Bach, Munich
Warp: cotton; weft: cotton
H. 137 cm; w. 126 cm
Pattern repeat: h. 46 cm; w. 41 cm
Inventory no. I/9660; acquired 1932 from
Richard Zieger, Chemnitz

63 | PRINTED FABRIC, 1924

Hahn und Bach, Munich
Warp: cotton; weft: flax
H. 143 cm; w. 131 cm
Pattern repeat: h. 42 cm; w. 59 cm
Inventory no. XIV/7707; acquired 1925 from
Hahn und Bach, Munich

64 | PRINTED FABRIC, 1925

Hahn und Bach, Munich
Warp: cotton; weft: flax
H. 137.5 cm; w. 129 cm
Pattern repeat: h. 38 cm; w. 60 cm
Inventory no. XIV/7716; acquired 1925 from
Hahn und Bach, Munich

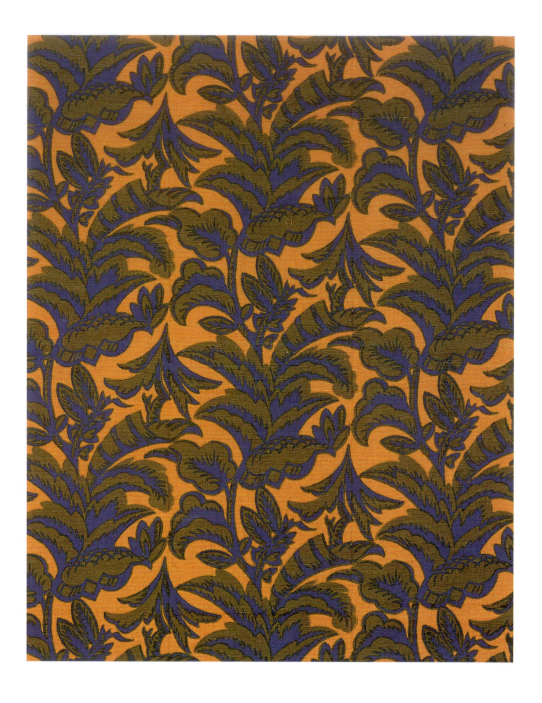

65 | PRINTED FABRIC, 1925

Hahn und Bach, Munich
Warp: flax; weft: rayon
H. 112.5 cm; w. 131 cm
Pattern repeat: h. 38 cm; w. 30 cm
Inventory no. XIV/7720; acquired 1925 from
Hahn und Bach, Munich

66 | UPHOLSTERY FABRIC (weft tapestry), 1927

Cammann & Co., Chemnitz
Warp: cotton; weft: wool, cotton
H. 131.5 cm; w. 128.5 cm
Pattern repeat: h. 20 cm; w. 32 cm
Metal signum on the reverse, u. r.: C. & Co. AG
Inventory no. II/8162; acquired 1927 from F. W. Weymar, Dresden

67 | UPHOLSTERY FABRIC (warp tapestry), 1927

Wilhelm Vogel, Chemnitz
Warp: cotton; weft: cotton
H. 65 cm; w. 126 cm
Pattern repeat: h. 33.5 cm; w. 41.5 cm
Inventory no. III/8146; acquired 1927 from Richard Zieger, Chemnitz

68 | DECORATIVE FABRIC, 1929

Germany
Warp: cotton; weft: cotton, rayon
H. 139 cm; w. 130 cm
Pattern repeat: h. 65 cm; w. 64 cm
Inventory no. IX/8660; acquired 1929 from S. A. Heßlein, Nuremberg

69 | UPHOLSTERY FABRIC, (terry pile), 1929

Germany
Warp: rayon; weft: flax
H. 140.5 cm; w. 132 cm
Pattern repeat: h. 32.5 cm; w. 32.5 cm
Inventory no. XXIV/8668; acquired 1929 from S. A. Heßlein, Nuremberg

70 | UPHOLSTERY FABRIC (pile carpet), 1925

Germany
Warp: cotton, wool; weft: cotton
H. 98.5 cm; w. 131.5 cm
Pattern repeat: h. 44 cm; w. 33 cm
Inventory no. IV/7600; acquired 1925 from
Heinrich Bremer, Bremen

71 | UPHOLSTERY FABRIC (terry pile), 1928

Germany
Warp: cotton, rayon; weft: cotton
H. 133 cm; w. 127 cm
Pattern repeat: h. 30.5 cm; w. 31.5 cm
Inventory no. V/8540; acquired 1928 from Richard Rosenberg, Cologne

Fig. F. Becker & E. Kutzner: Living room in the home of Dr. Kutzner,
Düsseldorf, in: *DK,* 1929, Vol. XXVII, p. 262

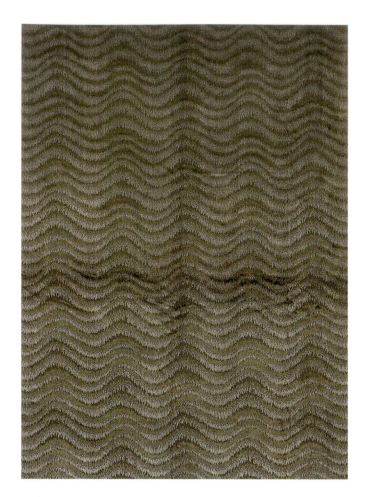

73 | UPHOLSTERY FABRIC, 1932

Germany
Warp: cotton; weft: cotton
H. 128 cm; w. 128 cm
Pattern repeat: h. 39 cm; w. 31.5 cm
Inventory no. I/9525; acquired 1932 from Pepperhoff und Rosenthal, Essen

72 | UPHOLSTERY FABRIC (terry pile), 1930

Germany
Warp: cotton, rayon; weft: cotton
H. 140 ; w. 129 cm
Pattern repeat: h. 18 cm; w. 32 cm
Inventory no. V/9165; acquired 1930 from Pepperhoff und Rosenthal, Essen

74 | UPHOLSTERY FABRIC (weft tapestry), 1930

Germany
Warp: cotton, cellophane strip; weft: cotton, wool
H. 132 cm; w. 124 cm
Pattern repeat: h. indeterminate; w. 124 cm
Inventory no. II/9064; acquired 1930 from G. A. Schrödter

75 | UPHOLSTERY FABRIC, 1930

Germany
Warp: cotton; weft: cotton
H. 123 cm; w. 62 cm
Pattern repeat: h. 34 cm; w. 31 cm
Inventory no. I/9078; acquired 1930 from Friedemann und Weber, Berlin

76 | UPHOLSTERY FABRIC (weft tapestry), 1927

Germany
Warp: cotton; weft: cotton, wool, rayon
H. 96 cm; w. 125 cm
Pattern repeat: h. 25.5 cm; w. 15.5 cm
Inventory no. II/8079; acquired 1927 from Riedel und Rother, Berlin

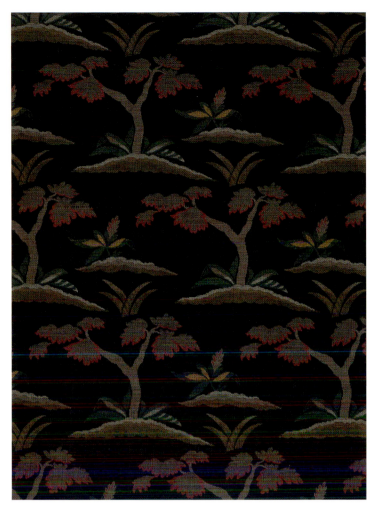

77 | UPHOLSTERY FABRIC (looped pile), 1926

Germany
Warp: wool, cotton ; weft: cotton
H. 100 cm; w. 131 cm
Pattern repeat: h. 41 cm; w. 52 cm
Inventory no. VI/7782; acquired 1926 from Friedemann und Weber, Berlin

78 | UPHOLSTERY FABRIC (weft tapestry), 1927

Germany
Warp: cotton; weft: cotton, rayon
H. 65 cm; w. 127 cm
Pattern repeat: h. 28 cm; w. 21 cm
Inventory no. II/8145; acquired 1927 from Richard Zieger, Chemnitz

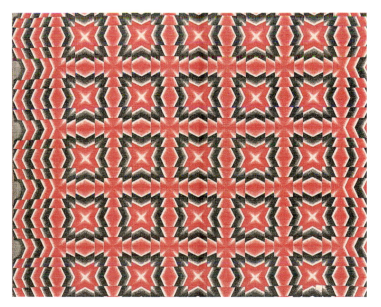

79 | UPHOLSTERY FABRIC, 1932

Germany
Warp: cotton; weft: cotton
H. 147 cm; w. 140 cm
Pattern repeat: h. 22 cm; w. 140 cm
Inventory no. I/9649; acquired 1932 from the Indanthren Haus, Frankfurt

80 | PILLOW CASE, 1931

Germany
Warp: cotton; weft: wool
H. 100 cm; w. 55 cm
Pattern repeat: h. indeterminate; w. 41 cm
Inventory no. XII/9396; acquired 1931 from Wertheim, Berlin

81 | PRINTED FABRIC, 1924

Germany
Warp: cotton; weft: cotton
H. 102 cm; w. 132 cm
Pattern repeat: h. indeterminate; w. 132 cm
Inventory no. XIV/7524; acquired 1924 from Richard Zieger, Chemnitz

Fig. Richard Straumer: View of the stairway landing, house in the Thorerstr.,
Leipzig, in: *DKuD*, Vol. 57, October 1925 – March 1926, p. 334, 335, 339

82 | PRINTED FABRIC, 1924

Germany
Warp: cotton; weft: cotton
H. 57 cm; w. 136.5 cm
Pattern repeat: h. indeterminate; w. 32 cm
Inventory no. XIV/7445; acquired 1924 from L. Bernheimer, Munich

Fig. Sanitarium am Königspark in Dresden-Loschwitz, view of the smoking and
billiards room, in: *ID*, Vol. XXII, 1922, p. 94

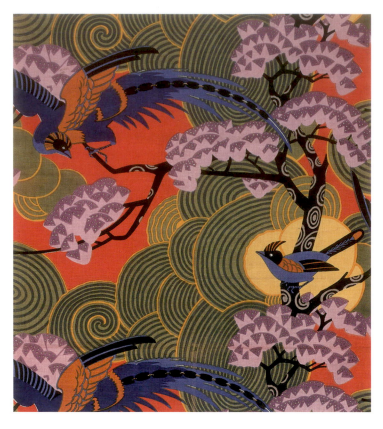

83 | PRINTED FABRIC, 1926

Germany
Warp: cotton, weft: cotton
H. 107 cm; w. 77 cm
Pattern repeat: h. 39 cm; w. 47.5 cm
Inventory no. XIV/7871; acquired 1926 from S. und R. Wahl, Barmen

84 | PRINTED FABRIC, 1926

Germany
Warp: cotton; weft: cotton
H. 138 cm; w. 78 cm
Pattern repeat: h. 58 cm; w. = web width
Inventory no. XIV/8004; acquired 1926 from Richard Zieger, Chemnitz

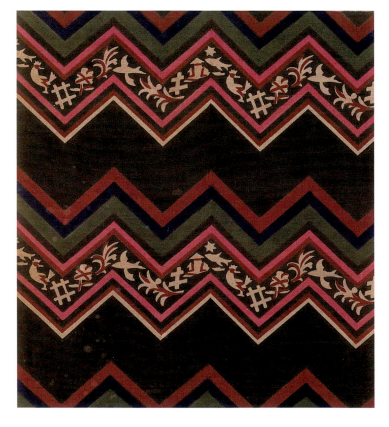

85 | PRINTED FABRIC, 1927

Germany
Warp: flax; weft: flax
H. 152 cm; w. 127 cm
Pattern repeat: h. 82 cm; w. = web width
Inventory no. XIV/8197; acquired 1927 from Bros. Schürmann, Cologne

86 | PRINTED FABRIC, ca. 1925

Germany
Warp: cotton; weft: cotton
H. 97 cm; w. 70 cm
Pattern repeat: h. 34.5 cm; w. 35 cm
Inventory no. XIV/6809, date of acquisition unknown

87 | PRINTED FABRIC (block printing), 1924

Germany
Warp: flax; weft: flax
H. 102 cm; w. 77 cm
Pattern repeat: h. 25 cm; w. 30 cm
Inventory no. XIV/7488; acquired 1924 from the Volkskunsthaus Wallach, Munich

88 | PRINTED FABRIC (block printing), 1924

Germany
Warp: flax; weft: flax
H. 102 cm; w. 77 cm
Pattern repeat: h. 36 cm; w. 28.5 cm
Inventory no. XIV/7492; acquired 1924 from the Volkskunsthaus Wallach, Munich

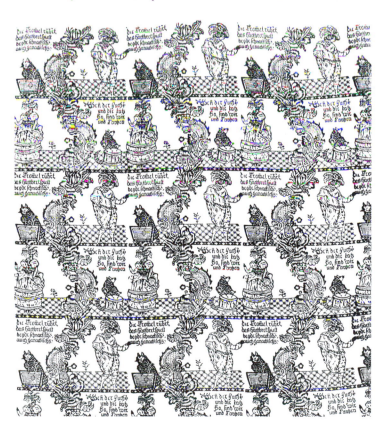

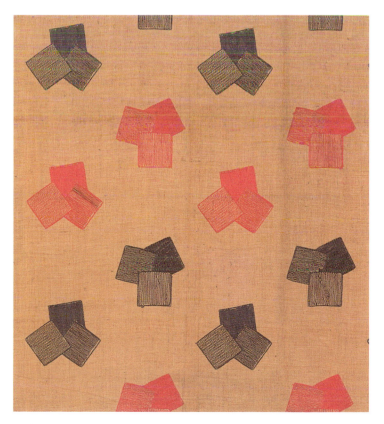

89 | PRINTED FABRIC (block printing), 1926

Germany
Warp: cotton; weft: flax
H. 129 cm; w. 78.5 cm
Pattern repeat: h. 32 cm; w. 25 cm
Inventory no. XIV/7882; acquired 1926 from Schneider und Königs, Düsseldorf

90 | CURTAIN FABRIC, 1930

Germany
Machined corded embroidery
Warp: flax; weft: flax; embroidery material: cotton
H. 193 cm; w. 137 cm
Pattern repeat: h. 64 cm; w. 40 cm
Inventory no. XII/9076; acquired 1930 from Friedemann und Weber, Berlin

91 | HORSEHAIR UPHOLSTERY FABRIC, 1925

Germany
Warp: cotton; weft: horsehair
H. 53 cm; w. 69 cm
Pattern repeat: h. 16 cm; w. 19 cm
Inventory no. I/7676; acquired 1925 from L. Bernheimer, Munich

92 | HORSEHAIR UPHOLSTERY FABRIC, 1925

Germany
Warp: cotton; weft: horsehair
H. 51 cm; w. 67 cm
Pattern repeat: h. 10 cm; w. 9 cm
Inventory no. I/7677; acquired 1925 from L. Bernheimer, Munich

93 | UPHOLSTERY FABRIC, 1930

Germany
Warp: cotton; weft: cotton
H. 125 cm; w. 131 cm
Pattern repeat: h. 16 cm; w. 41.5 cm
Inventory no. XII/9079; acquired 1930 from Friedemann und Weber, Berlin

94 | WALL HANGING "BEARS", 1928

Wenzel Hablik (1881 – 1934)
Manufacture: Hand Weaving Studio Hablik-Lindemann, Itzehoe
Warp: cotton; weft: hand-spun wool
H. 147 cm; w. 300 cm
Marked l. m. with the studio signum
Inventory no. XII/8599; acquired 1928 from Hand Weaving Studio Hablik-Lindemann, Itzehoe

95 | PILLOW "HELLHOUND"; REVERSE
   "MIRROR IMAGE", 1928

Wenzel Hablik (1881–1934)
Manufacture: Hand Weaving Studio
Hablik-Lindemann, Itzehoe
Warp: cotton; weft: wool
H. 60 cm; w. 70cm
Marked on reverse u. l. with the studio signum
Inventory no. XII/8600; acquired 1928 from
Hand Weaving Hablik-Lindemann, Itzehoe

96 | CLOTH, 1928 (Detail)

Wenzel Hablik (1881–1934)
Jacquard fabric, manufacture: Hand Weaving Studio Hablik-Lindemann, Itzehoe
Warp: tussah silk; weft: tussah silk
L. 153 cm; w. 153 cm (without fringe)
Pattern repeat: h. 19.5 cm; w. 19.5 cm
Inventory no. XII/8347; acquired 1928 from Hand Weaving Studio Hablik-Lindemann, Itzehoe

Wenzel Hablik (1881–1934)
Manufacture: Hand Weaving Studio
Hablik-Lindemann, Itzehoe
Warp: cotton; weft: chenille, various materials
H. 322 cm; w. 144 cm
Inventory no. XII/8348; acquired 1928 from
Hand Weaving Studio Hablik-Lindemann,
Itzehoe

99 | WALL HANGING, circa 1935

Valerie Jorud
Appliqué, cotton ribbons on linen; design and manufacture Valerie Jorud, Berlin
H. 190 cm; w. 148 cm
Marked u. l. V
Inventory no. XII/9901; acquired from Valerie Jorud at the Grassi Fair, Leipzig, autumn 1935

98 | WALL HANGING "ALASKA ANIMALS", 1929

Wenzel Hablik (1881–1934)
Semi-tapestry, manufacture: Hand Weaving Studio Hablik-Lindemann, Itzehoe
Warp: cotton; weft: wool
H. 280 cm; w. 135 cm
Inventory no. XII/8791; acquired 1929 from Hand Weaving Studio Hablik-Lindemann, Itzehoe

100 | WALL HANGING "RED DEER", 1927

Else Mögelin (1887–1982)
Semi-tapestry, manufactured in artist's own studio in Gildenhall/Neu-Ruppin, woven in two runs
Warp: cotton; weft: wool, rayon fibre
H. 270 cm; B: 154 cm
Inventory no. XII/8899; acquired 1929 from Else Mögelin, Gildenhall

101 | CURTAIN, 1928

Else Mögelin (1887–1982)
Manufactured in artist's own studio in Gilden-
hall/Neu-Ruppin
Warp: rayon fibre; weft: rayon fibre, wool
H. 298 cm; w. 158 cm
Inventory no. XII/8412; acquired 1928 from
Else Mögelin, Gildenhall

103 | COVERLET, 1926

Margarete Willers (1883–1977)
Germany
Hand-woven, edged border
Warp: cotton, weft: cotton, false lamé
H. 73 cm; w. 93 cm
Inventory no. XII/7891; acquired 1926 from A. Eick und Söhne, Essen

104 | WALL HANGING, 1929

Irmgard Ritter-Kauermann (born 1895)
Germany
Filet embroidery
Woven filet net: cotton; embroidery material: cotton, flax
H. 90 cm; w. 140 cm
Inventory no. XII/8993; acquired 1929 from Irmgard Ritter-Kauermann, Heidelberg

105 | SCARF, 1928

Agnes Pechuel-Lösche
Germany
Batik
Warp: silk; weft: silk
L. 190 cm; w. 93 cm
Inventory no. XXX/8606; acquired 1928 from
Agnes Pechuel-Lösche, Cologne

On the right side:

106 | SCARF, 1927

Else Fischer
Germany
Stencil spray printing
Warp: tussah silk; weft: tussah silk
L. 198 cm; w. 38 cm
Inventory no. XVII/8273; acquired 1927 from
the Schlesischer Ausstellungsverein Breslau

107 | SCARF, 1927

Edith Schwirzell
Germany
Stencil spray printing
Warp: cotton; weft: cotton
L. 200 cm; w. 60 cm
Inventory no. XVII/8274; acquired 1927 from
the Schlesischer Ausstellungsverein Breslau

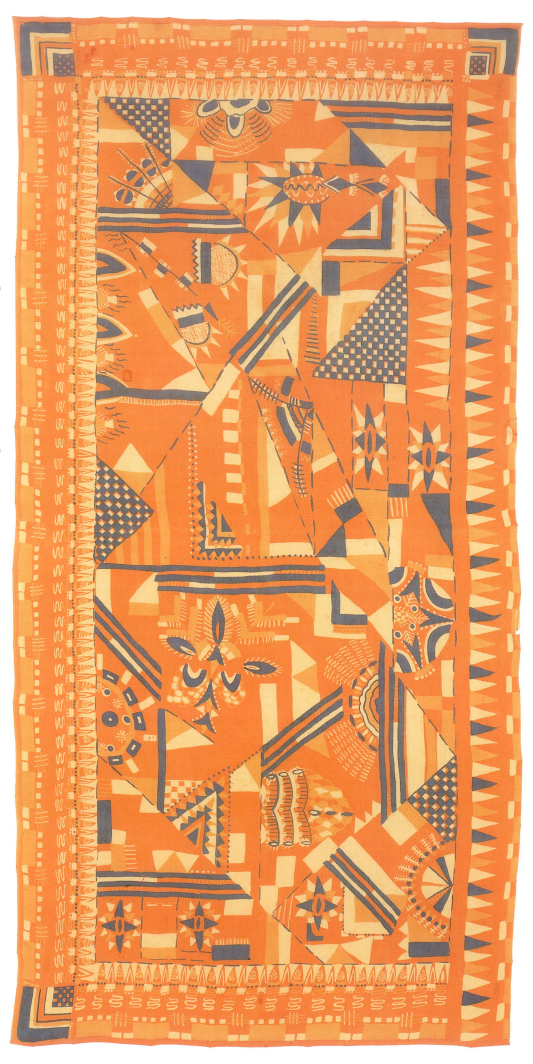

108 | DECORATIVE FABRIC, 1929

Switzerland
Stencil spray printing
Warp: cotton; weft: cotton
H. 135 cm; w. 106 cm
Pattern repeat: h. 62 cm; w. 45 cm
Inventory no. XVII/8724; acquired 1929 from G. H. Schrödter, Leipzig

109 | PRINTED FABRIC "PAN", 1919

Dagobert Peche (1887–1923)
Wiener Werkstätte, Vienna
Block print, Design no. 709
Manufacture: A. Clavel & F. Lindenmeyer,
Basle
Warp: silk; weft: silk
H. 99 cm; w. 93 cm
Pattern repeat: h. 44 cm; w. 46.5 cm
Inventory no. XVII/8028; acquired 1926 from
the Wiener Werkstätte

110 | UPHOLSTERY FABRIC "TULIPS",
(warp tapestry), 1926

Dagobert Peche (1887–1923)
Wiener Werkstätte, Vienna
Manufacture: W. Vogel, Chemnitz,
Design no. 9627
Warp: cotton; weft: cotton
H. 99 cm; w. 125 cm
Pattern repeat: h. 59.2; w. 62 cm
Inventory no. III/8031; acquired 1926 from
the Wiener Werkstätte

111 | UPHOLSTERY FABRIC (warp tapestry),
1922

Dagobert Peche (1887–1923)
Wiener Werkstätte, Vienna
Manufacture: Wilhelm Vogel, Chemnitz
Warp: cotton; weft: cotton
H. 49 cm; w. 58.5 cm
Pattern repeat: indeterminate
Inventory no. III/98/1; gift of the W. Vogel
Pattern Collection, Chemnitz, 1994

112 | PRINTED FABRIC "PARTRIDGE", 1924

Maria Likarz (1893–1971)
Wiener Werkstätte, Vienna
Block print; Design no. 872
Manufacture: G. Ziegler, Vienna; Teltscher
Warp: bourette silk; weft: bourette silk
H. 100 cm; w. 87 cm
Pattern repeat: h. 33 cm; w. 33.5 cm
Mark on the selvage: WW
Inventory no. XIV/7791; acquired 1926 from the Wiener Werkstätte

113 | PRINTED FABRIC "BRINDISI", 1925

Maria Likarz (1893–1971)
Wiener Werkstätte, Vienna
Block print; Design no. 503
Manufacture: G. Ziegler, Vienna
Warp: bourette silk; weft: bourette silk
H. 101 cm; w. 85 cm
Pattern repeat: h. 40.5 cm; w. 22.5 cm
Inventory no. XIV/7790; acquired 1926 from the Wiener Werkstätte

114 | PRINTED FABRIC "TRAMINO", 1925

Felice Rix (1893–1967)
Wiener Werkstätte, Vienna
Block print; Design no. 924
Manufacture: G. Ziegler, Vienna; Teltscher
Warp: silk; weft: silk
H. 140 cm; w. 90 cm
Pattern repeat: indeterminate
Inventory no. XVII/8259; acquired 1927 from the Wiener Werkstätte

115 | PRINTED FABRIC "POPPIES", 1929

Felice Rix (1893–1967)
Wiener Werkstätte, Vienna
Block print; Design no. 1123
Manufacture: G. Ziegler Vienna
Warp: silk; weft: silk
H. 101 cm; w. 96.5 cm
Pattern repeat: h. 43.5 cm; w. 48 cm
Mark on the selvage: WW
Inventory no. XVII/9109; acquired 1930 from the Wiener Werkstätte

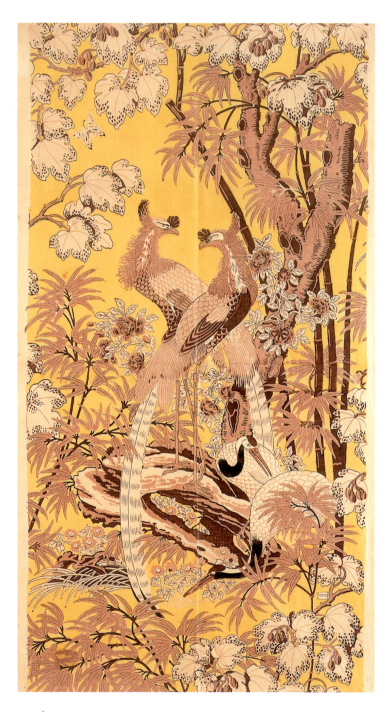

116 | PRINTED FABRIC "OLD ENGLISH SHOP SIGNS", 1927

    Minnie McLeish (1876–1957)
    Great Britain
    Manufacture: W. Foxton Ltd., London
    Warp: cotton; weft: cotton
    H. 102 cm; w. 78 cm
    Pattern repeat: h. 46 cm; w. = web width
    Inventory no. XIV/8075; acquired 1927 from Richard Zieger, Chemnitz

117 | CHINTZ "PHOENIX", 1918

    William Turner
    Great Britain
    Manufacture: G. P. & J. Baker Ltd., London
    Warp: cotton; weft: cotton
    H. 149 cm; w. 79 cm
    Inventory no. XV/10653; acquired 1939 from G. A. Skibbe, Berlin

118 | CHINTZ "FEATHERS", 1925

Great Britain
Manufacture: G. P. & J. Baker Ltd., London
Warp: cotton; weft: cotton
H. 65 cm; w. 82 cm
Pattern repeat: h. 37 cm; w. = web width
Inventory no. XIV/10133; acquired 1936 from
Arthur Benrath, Berlin

119 | PRINTED FABRIC "THE UNICORN",
1926

Great Britain
Manufacture: G. P. & J. Baker Ltd., London
Warp: flax; weft: flax
H. 139 cm; w. 133 cm
Pattern repeat: h. 54 cm; w. = web width
Inventory no. XIV/7964; acquired 1926 from
L. Bernheimer, Munich

Fig. A. Linschütz, Vienna: daybed in boudoir, in:
ID, January 1931, p. 34

120 | UPHOLSTERY FABRIC, 1929

Great Britain
Manufacture: A. H. Lee & Sons Ltd.,
Birkenhead
Warp: cotton; weft: cotton, rayon (chenille),
false lamé
H. 67 cm; w. 122 cm
Pattern repeat: h. indeterminate; w. 59 cm
Inventory no. I/8739; acquired 1929 from
Julius Katzenstein

121 | UPHOLSTERY FABRIC (looped pile), 1930

Great Britain
Manufacture: A. Lee & Sons Ltd., Birkenhead
Warp: cotton, wool; weft: cotton
H. 145 cm; w. 133 cm
Pattern repeat: 41 cm; w. 61 cm
Inventory no. VI/9002; acquired 1930 from
Richard Zieger, Chemnitz

122 | UPHOLSTERY FABRIC (pile carpet), 1930

Great Britain
Manufacture: A. Lee & Sons Ltd., Birkenhead
Warp: cotton; weft: cotton, wool
H. 99 cm; w. 131 cm
Pattern repeat: h. 35 cm; w. 25 cm
Inventory no. V/9003; acquired 1930 from
Richard Zieger, Chemnitz

123 | CHINTZ, around 1930

Great Britain
Manufacture: Ramm Son & Crocker Ltd., London
Warp: cotton; weft: cotton
H. 102 cm; w. 133 cm
Pattern repeat: h. 50 cm; w. 31 cm
Mark l. l. MADE IN ENGLAND (stamp); paper label R. S. & C. Ltd.
Inventory no. XV/10361; acquired 1937 from Hans Henschel, Berlin

124 | PRINTED FABRIC "ROSEBANK", 1934

Great Britain
Manufacture: Turnbull & Stockdale Ltd., Ramsbottom
Warp: flax; weft: flax
H. 98 cm; w. 78 cm
Pattern repeat: h. 45 cm; w. = web width
Inventory no. XIV/9728; acquired 1934 from Turnbull & Stockdale, Ramsbottom

125 | PRINTED FABRIC, 1932

Great Britain
Manufacture: Turnbull & Stockdale Ltd., Ramsbottom
Warp: flax; weft: flax
H. 154 cm; w. 75 cm
Pattern repeat: h. 45 cm; w. 32 cm
Inventory no. XIV/9627a; acquired 1932 from Turnbull & Stockdale, Ramsbottom

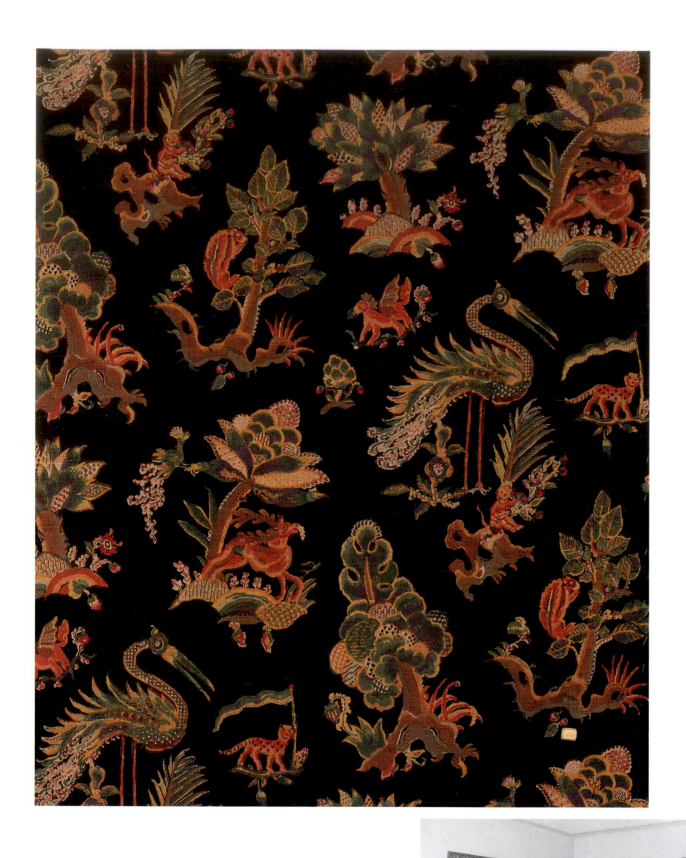

126 | PRINTED FABRIC, 1928

Great Britain
Warp: flax; weft: flax
H. 197 cm; w. 129 cm
Pattern repeat: h. 126 cm; w. = web width
Inventory no. XIV/9479, acc. to inventory of English origin; acquired 1932

Fig. B. Ludwig, Vienna: Living Room, in: *DKuD,* 1928, p. 334

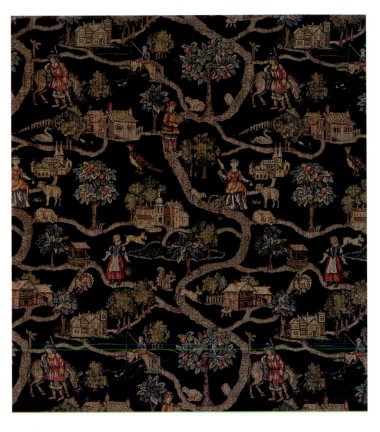

127 | UPHOLSTERY FABRIC (weft tapestry), 1925

Great Britain
Warp: cotton; weft: wool
H. 60 cm; w. 142 cm
Pattern repeat: h. 37 cm; w. 70 cm
Inventory no. II/7580, acc. to inventory of English origin; acquired 1925 from
L. Phil. Schäfer, Cologne

128 | UPHOLSTERY FABRIC (looped pile), 1927

Great Britain
Warp: cotton, wool; weft: cotton
H. 139 cm; w. 129 cm
Pattern repeat: h. 80 cm; w. 60 cm
Inventory no. VI/8168, acc. to inventory of English origin; acquired 1927
from F. W. Weymar, Dresden

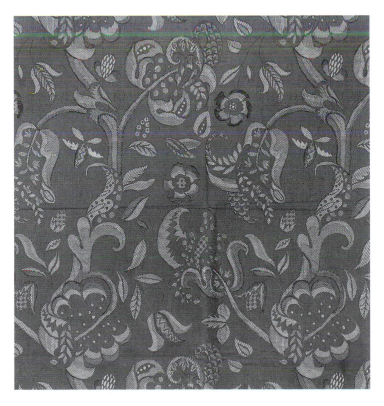

129 | UPHOLSTERY FABRIC (weft tapestry), 1925

Great Britain
Warp: cotton; weft: cotton, wool
H. 178 cm; w. 140 cm
Pattern repeat: h. 96 cm; w. 69 cm
Inventory no. II/7584, acc. to inventory of English origin; acquired 1925 from
L. Phil. Schäfer, Cologne

130 | UPHOLSTERY FABRIC (weft tapestry), 1927

Great Britain
Warp: cotton; weft: cotton, wool
H. 141 cm; w. 138 cm
Pattern repeat: h. 84 cm; w. = web width
Inventory no. II/8218, acc. to inventory of English origin; acquired 1927 from
L. Phil. Schäfer, Cologne

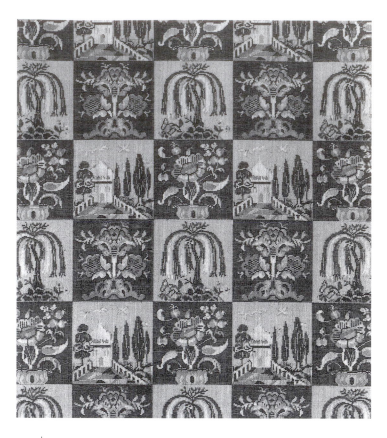

131 | UPHOLSTERY FABRIC (looped pile), 1926

Great Britain
Warp: cotton, wool; weft: cotton
H. 101 cm; w. 69 cm
Pattern repeat: h. 25 cm; w. 25 cm
Inventory no. VI/7996, acc. to inventory of English origin; acquired 1926
from Richard Zieger, Chemnitz

132 | UPHOLSTERY FABRIC (looped pile), 1926

Great Britain
Warp: cotton, wool; weft: cotton
H. 66 cm; w. 68 cm
Inventory no. VI/7995, acc. to inventory of English origin; acquired 1926
from Richard Zieger, Chemnitz

133 | UPHOLSTERY FABRIC, 1928

Great Britain
Warp: cotton; weft: wool, cotton
H. 97 cm; w. 144 cm
Pattern repeat: h. 54 cm; w. 70 cm
Inventory no. II/8515, acc. to inventory of English origin; acquired 1928 from
L. Phil. Schäfer, Cologne

134 | UPHOLSTERY FABRIC, 1926

Great Britain
Warp: cotton; weft: wool
H. 54 cm; w. 143 cm
Pattern repeat: h. 16 cm; w. 23.5 cm
Inventory no. I/7893, acc. to inventory of English origin; acquired 1926 from
L. Ernst, Düsseldorf

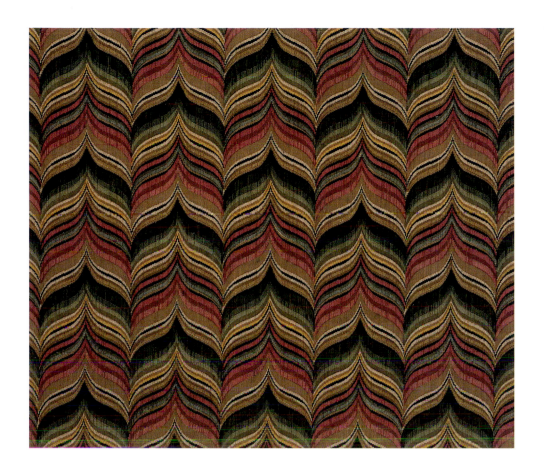

135 | UPHOLSTERY FABRIC (looped pile), 1928

Great Britain
Warp: cotton, wool; weft: cotton
H. 98.5 cm; w. 132.5 cm
Pattern repeat: h. 20 cm; w. 31 cm
Inventory no. VI/8514, acc. to inventory of
English origin; acquired 1928 from L. Phil.
Schäfer, Cologne

136 | UPHOLSTERY FABRIC, 1930

Great Britain
Manufacture: Gainsborough Silk Weaving Co.
Ltd., Sudbury
Warp: cotton; weft: cotton
H. 89 cm; w. 124 cm
Pattern repeat: h. 91.5 cm; w. 19 cm
Inventory no. IX/9026; acquired 1930 from
Richard Zieger, Chemnitz

137 | UPHOLSTERY FABRIC, 1931

Great Britain
Manufacture: Donald Brothers Ltd., Dundee
Warp: cotton; weft: rayon, mercerized cotton
H. 96 cm; w. 64.5 cm
Pattern repeat: h. 20 cm; w. 12.5 cm
Inventory no. I/9323; acquired 1931 from Lorenzo Rubelli e Figlio, Venice

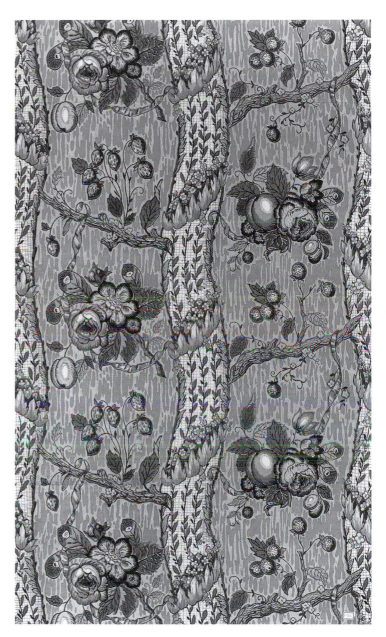

138 | PRINTED FABRIC, 1926

Great Britain
Warp: cotton; weft: cotton
H. 155 cm; w. 74 cm
Pattern repeat: h. 78 cm; w. = web width
Inventory no. XIV/7956, acc. to inventory of English origin; acquired 1926
from L. Bernheimer, Munich

139 | PRINTED FABRIC, 1926

Great Britain
Warp: cotton; weft: cotton
H. 151 cm; w. 74 cm
Pattern repeat: h. 50 cm; w. = web width
Inventory no. XIV/8022, acc. to inventory of English origin; acquired 1926
from Teppich- und Möbelstoffindustrie Langer & Co.

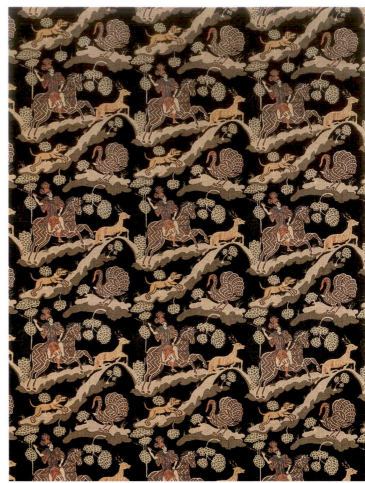

140 | PRINTED FABRIC, 1926

    Great Britain?
    Warp: flax; weft: flax
    H. 140 cm; w. 124 cm
    Pattern repeat: h. 54.5 cm; w. 78 cm
    Inventory no. XIV/7902; acquired 1926 from Paul Braess, Düsseldorf

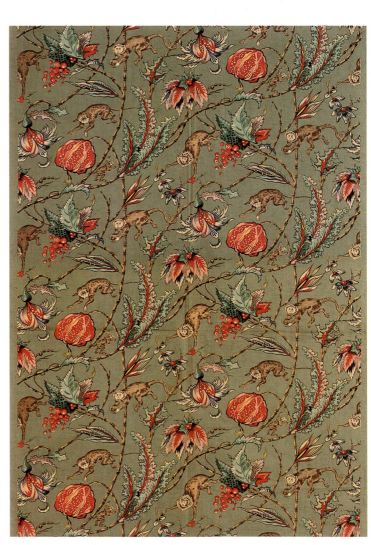

141 | PRINTED FABRIC, 1926

    Great Britain?
    Warp: flax; weft: flax
    H. 150 cm; w. 132 cm
    Pattern repeat: h. 27 cm; w. 25.5 cm
    Inventory no. XIV/8018; acquired 1926 from Teppich- und Möbelstoff-
    industrie Langer & Co.

142 | PRINTED FABRIC, 1926

    Great Britain?
    Warp: cotton; weft: cotton
    H. 141 cm; w. 81 cm
    Pattern repeat: h. 38.5 cm; w. 76.5 cm
    Mark u. r. and l. r.: S.F.A. (stamped)
    Inventory no. XIV/8020; acquired 1926 from Teppich- und Möbelstoff-
    industrie Langer & Co.

143 | PRINTED FABRIC, 1926

    Great Britain?
    Warp: cotton; weft: cotton
    H. 136 cm; w. 79 cm
    Pattern repeat: h. 60 cm; w. = web width
    Mark u. l. and l. l.: S.F.A. (stamped)
    Inventory no. XIV/8023; acquired 1926 from Teppich- und Möbelstoff-
    industrie Langer & Co.

144 | PRINTED FABRIC, 1924

    Great Britain?
    Warp: cotton; weft: cotton
    H. 153 cm; w. 131 cm
    Pattern repeat: h. 62 cm; w. = web width
    Mark l. l. and l. r.: FTL (stamped)
    Inventory no. XIV/7447; acquired 1924 from L. Bernheimer, Munich

Great Britain?
Warp: cotton; weft: flax
H. 106 cm; w. 90 cm
Pattern repeat: h. 74 cm; w. = web width
Inventory no. XIV/7443; acquired 1924 from
L. Bernheimer, Munich

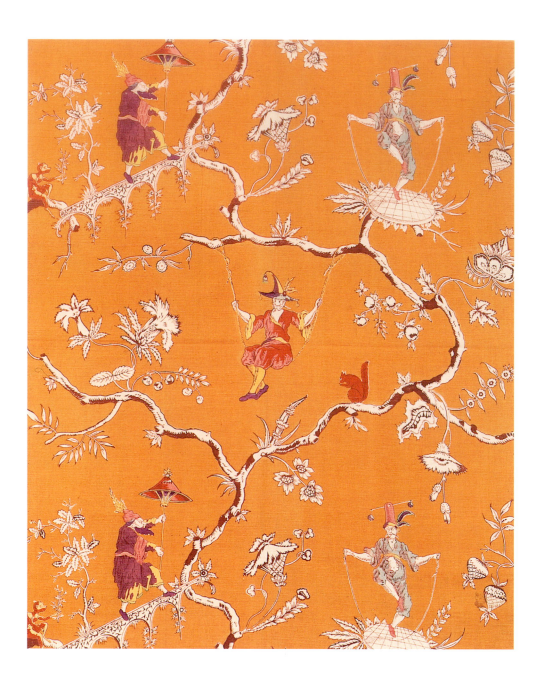

146 | PRINTED FABRIC, 1926

Great Britain?
Warp: flax; weft: flax
H. 140 cm; w. 125 cm
Pattern repeat: h. 67.5 cm; w. = web width
Inventory no. XIV/8014; acquired 1926 from
Teppich- und Möbelstoffindustrie Langer & Co.

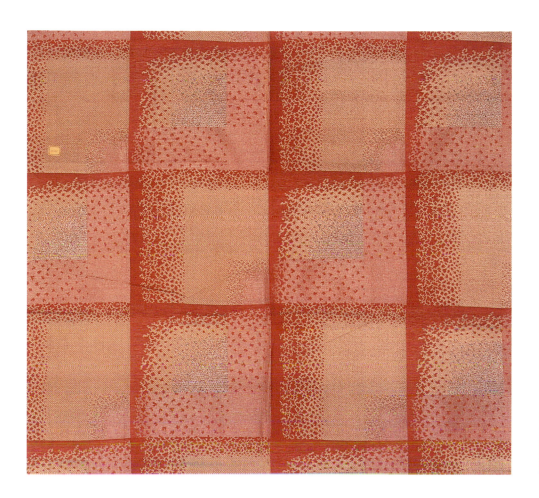

| UPHOLSTERY FABRIC, 1929

Eric Bagge (born 1890)
France
Manufacture: Lucien Bouix
Warp: rayon; weft: rayon, cotton
H. 136 cm; w. 129 cm
Pattern repeat: h. 62 cm; w. 64 cm
Inventory no. IX/9290; acquired 1931 from
Benrath und Bretsch, Berlin

Fig. Emmerich Révész, Vienna: Bedroom, in:
ID, 1931, Vol. XLII, p. 285

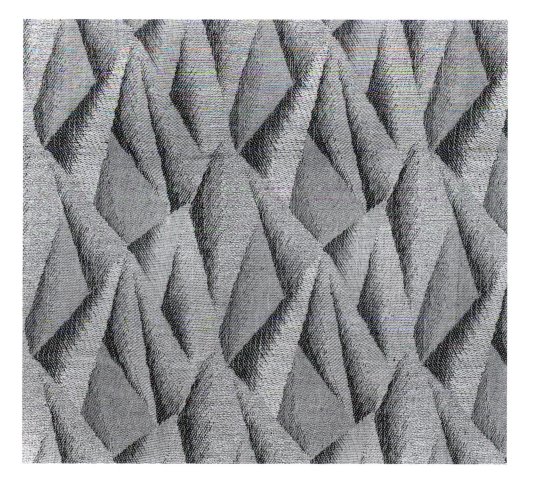

148 | UPHOLSTERY FABRIC, 1928

France
Warp: cotton; weft: cotton, jute
H. 120 cm; w. 130 cm
Pattern repeat: h. 29 cm; w. 32 cm
Inventory no. IX/8399, acc. to inventory of
French origin; acquired 1928 from Gustav
Cords, Berlin

Fig. Joubert et Petit, Paris: Fireplace in the
living room of the Comte de Mun, in:
ID, 1932, Vol. XLIII, p. 116

155 | UPHOLSTERY FABRIC, 1929

France
Warp: cotton; weft: jute
H. 134 cm; w. 133 cm
Pattern repeat: h. 23 cm; w. 32.5 cm
Inventory no. IX/8685, acc. to inventory of French origin; acquired 1929 from Friedemann und Weber, Berlin

156 | UPHOLSTERY FABRIC, 1929

France
Warp: cotton; weft: cotton, rayon
H. 125 cm; w. 126 cm
Pattern repeat: h. 32 cm; w. 31 cm
Inventory no. IX/8677, acc. to inventory of French origin; acquired 1929 from Riedel und Rother, Berlin

157 | UPHOLSTERY FABRIC, 1928

France?
Warp: cotton; weft: rayon
H. 124 cm; w. 125 cm
Pattern repeat: h. 38 cm; w. 30.5 cm
Inventory no. I/8640; acquired 1928 from Richard Zieger, Chemnitz

158 | UPHOLSTERY FABRIC, 1929

France
Warp: cotton; weft: jute
H. 146 cm; w. 130 cm
Pattern repeat: h. 64 cm; w. 64 cm
Inventory no. I/8695, acc. to inventory of French origin; acquired 1929 from Benrath und Bretsch, Berlin

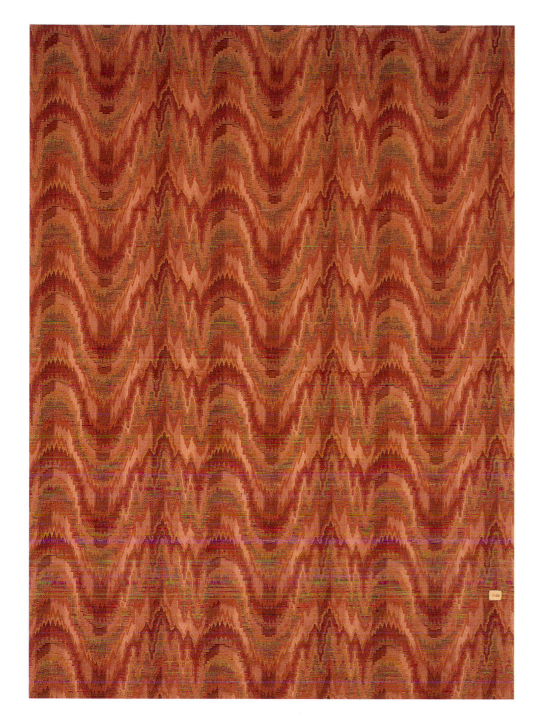

159 | UPHOLSTERY FABRIC, 1930

France
Warp: cotton; weft: mercerized cotton
H. 132 cm; w. 127.5 cm
Pattern repeat: h. 16 cm; w. 31 cm
Inventory no. I/9188, acc. to inventory of
French origin; acquired 1930 from Hans
Henschel, Berlin

**160 | UPHOLSTERY FABRIC
(brocade velour), 1932**

France
Warp: cotton, rayon, flax; weft: cotton,
false lamé
H. 136 cm; w. 134.5 cm
Pattern repeat: h. 64 cm; w. 65 cm
Inventory no. XXIV/9621, acc. to inventory of
French origin; acquired 1932 from Hugo
Schubert, Berlin

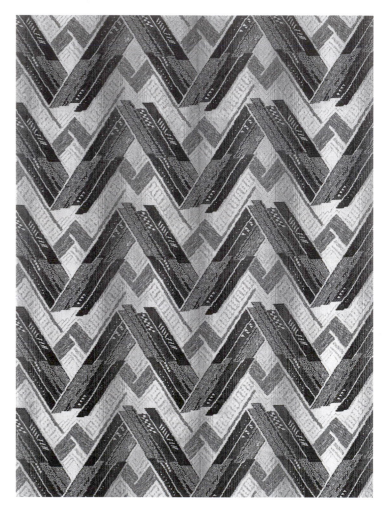

161 | UPHOLSTERY FABRIC (terry pile), 1931

France
Warp: cotton, mercerized cotton, flax; weft: cotton
H. 135 cm; w. 132 cm
Pattern repeat: h. 46 cm; w. 32.5 cm
Inventory no. V/9316, acc. to inventory of French origin; acquired 1931 from
Jules Pensu, Paris, via Hugo Schubert, Berlin

162 | UPHOLSTERY FABRIC (terry pile), 1930

France
Warp: cotton; weft: cotton
H. 137 cm; w. 130 cm
Pattern repeat: h. 25 cm; w. 64 cm
Inventory no. V/9015, acc. to inventory of French origin; acquired 1930 from
Richard Zieger, Chemnitz

163 | UPHOLSTERY FABRIC (terry pile), 1930

France
Warp: cotton, rayon; weft: cotton
H. 133 cm; w. 131 cm
Pattern repeat: h. 26.5 cm; w. 64.5 cm
Inventory no. IV/9016, acc. to inventory of French origin; acquired from Jules
Pensu, Paris, via Richard Zieger, Chemnitz

164 | UPHOLSTERY FABRIC (terry pile), 1928

France
Warp: cotton; weft: cotton, flax
H. 133 cm; w. 129 cm
Pattern repeat: h. 41 cm; w. 42 cm
Inventory no. V/8503, acc. to inventory of French origin; acquired 1928 from
Richard Zieger, Chemnitz

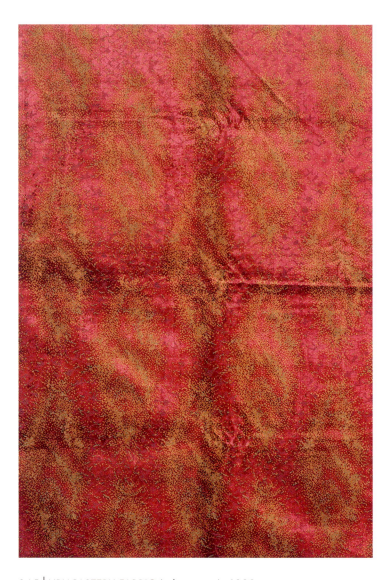

165 | UPHOLSTERY FABRIC (pile carpet), 1929

France
Warp: cotton, mercerized cotton, rayon; weft: cotton
H. 140 cm; w. 130 cm
Pattern repeat: h. 46 cm; w. 32 cm
Inventory no. XXIV/8887, acc. to inventory of French origin; acquired 1929
from Pepperhoff und Rosenthal, Essen

166 | UPHOLSTERY FABRIC (pile carpet), 1930

France
Warp: cotton; weft: cotton
H. 130 cm; w. 131 cm
Pattern repeat: h. 51.5 cm; w. 16 cm
Inventory no. IV/9014, acc. to inventory of French origin; acquired 1930 from
Jules Pensu, Paris, via Richard Zieger, Chemnitz

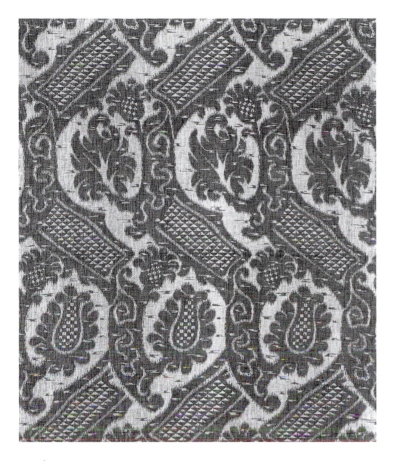

167 | UPHOLSTERY FABRIC, 1926

France
Warp: cotton; weft: cotton
H. 137 cm; w. 126 cm
Pattern repeat: h. 92.5 cm; w. 31 cm
Inventory no. IX/7974, acc. to inventory of French origin; acquired 1926 from
Richard Zieger, Chemnitz

168 | UPHOLSTERY FABRIC, 1924

France
Warp: cotton; weft: cotton
H. 104 cm; w. 128 cm
Pattern repeat: 72.5 cm; w. 63 cm
Inventory no. VII/7527, acc. to inventory of French origin; acquired 1924
from Richard Zieger, Chemnitz

169 | WALL FABRIC, 1928

France
Warp: cotton; weft: jute
H. 134 cm; w. 64 cm
Pattern repeat: h. 69.5 cm; w. 64 cm
Inventory no. I/8544, acc. to inventory of French origin; acquired 1928 from
Richard Rosenberg, Cologne

170 | DECORATIVE FABRIC, 1927

France
Warp: silk; weft: rayon, silk
H. 95 cm; w. 85 cm
Pattern repeat: h. 75 cm; w. 28 cm
Inventory no. LIII/8137; acquired 1927

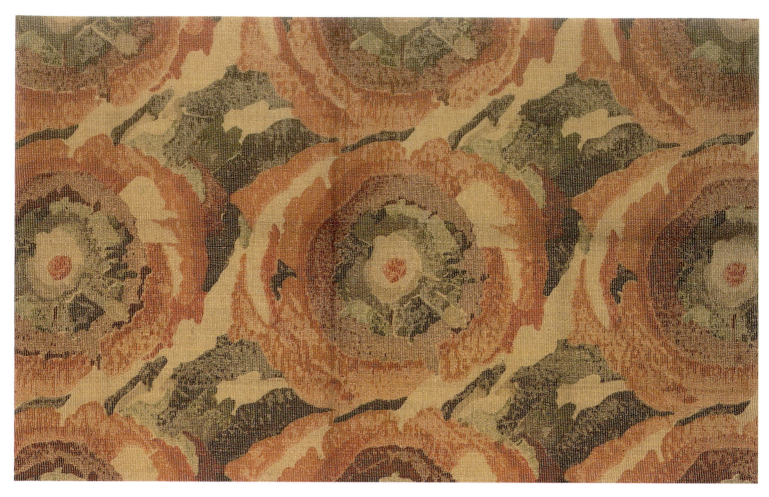

171 | DECORATIVE FABRIC, 1927

France?
Warp: silk, false lamé; weft: silk, wool
H. 99 cm; w. 92 cm
Pattern repeat: h. 39 cm; w. 30.5 cm
Inventory no. LIII/8130; acquired 1927

172 | DECORATIVE FABRIC, 1926

France?
Warp: silk; weft: silk, false lamé
H. 98.5 cm; w. 89 cm
Pattern repeat: h. 86 cm; w. 29 cm
Inventory no. LIII/7772; acquired 1926 from
Benrath und Bretsch

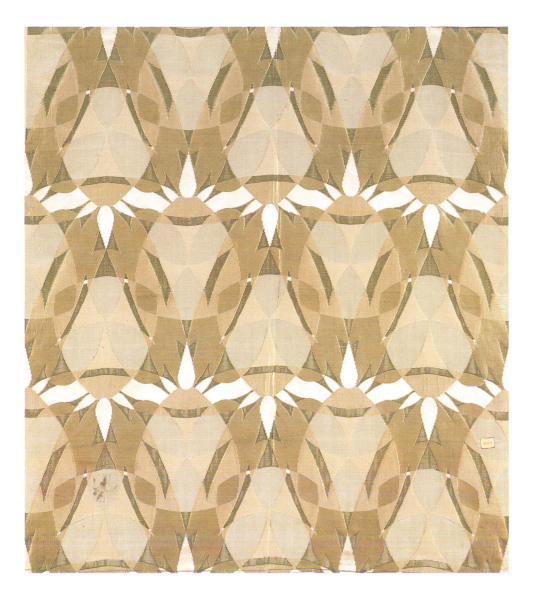

173 | BROCADE, 1929

France
Warp: silk; weft: rayon, false lamé
H. 98.5 cm; w. 88.5 cm
Pattern repeat: h. 34 cm; w. 29 cm
Inventory no. XXXIII/9239, acc. to inventory
of French origin; acquired 1929 from
G. Cords, Essen

174 | DECORATIVE FABRIC, 1925

France?
Warp: silk; weft: silk, false lamé
H. 51 cm; w. 89 cm
Pattern repeat: h. 46.5 cm; w. 29 cm
Inventory no. LIII/7666; acquired 1925 from
Eduard Schott, Frankfurt/Main

175 | PRINTED FABRIC, 1926

Mariano Fortuny (1871–1949)
Italy
Manufacture: Società Anonima Fortuny
Warp: cotton; weft: cotton
H. 136.5 cm; w. 131 cm
Pattern repeat: h. 56.5 cm; w. 63 cm
Inventory no. XIV/7966; acquired 1926 from L. Bernheimer, Munich

176 | PRINTED FABRIC, 1926

Mariano Fortuny (1871–1949)
Italy
Manufacture: Società Anonima Fortuny
Warp: cotton; weft: cotton
H. 147.5 cm; w. 110 cm
Pattern repeat: h. 124 cm; w. 53 cm
Inventory no. XIV/7967; acquired 1926 from L. Bernheimer, Munich

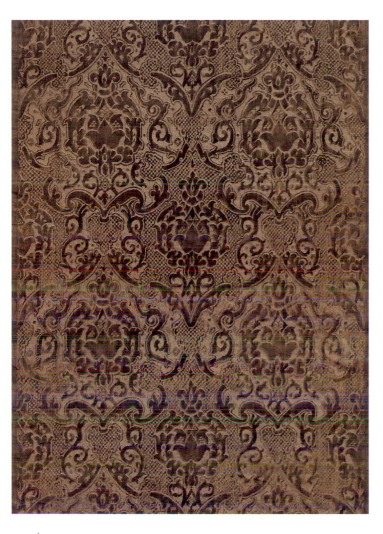

177 | PRINTED FABRIC, 1926

Mariano Fortuny (1871–1949)
Italy
Manufacture: Società Anonima Fortuny
Warp: cotton; weft: cotton
H. 121.5 cm; w. 63 cm
Pattern repeat: h. 36 cm; w. 30 cm
Inventory no. XIV/7968; acquired 1926 from L. Bernheimer, Munich

178 | PRINTED FABRIC, around 1930

Mariano Fortuny (1871–1949)
Italy
Manufacture: Società Anonima Fortuny
Warp: cotton; weft: cotton
H.161.5 cm; w. 108 cm
Pattern repeat: h. 139 cm; w. 52 cm
Inventory no. XIV/10776; acquired 1941 from the Münchner Kunsthandels-
gesellschaft

179 | PRINTED FABRIC, around 1930

Mariano Fortuny (1871–1949)
Italy
Manufacture: Società Anonima Fortuny
Warp: cotton; weft: cotton
H. 153.5 cm; w. 145.5 cm
Pattern repeat: h. 62 cm; w. 42 cm
Mark on the selvage: SOC. AN. FORTUNY
Inventory no. XIV/10781; acquired 1941 from the Münchner Kunsthandels-
gesellschaft

Fig. Mariano Fortuny: Game Room of the Hotel Excelsior at the Lido, Venice;
in: Osma, Guillermo de: *The Life and Work of Mariano Fortuny,* New York:
Rizzoli, 1980

180 | DECORATIVE FABRIC, around 1924

woven after historical Persian silk fabric of the
Safawids (1501–1722)
Italy
Manufacture: Vittorio Ferrari, Milan
Warp: cotton; weft: silk
H. 48.5 cm; w. 62 cm
Pattern repeat: h. 25 cm; w. 15 cm
Inventory no. XXXIII/7460; acquired 1924
from L. Bernheimer, Munich

181 | UPHOLSTERY FABRIC, 1931

Italy?
Warp: cotton; weft: cotton, wool
H. 98 cm; w. 130 cm
Pattern repeat: h. 56.5 cm; w. 32 cm
Inventory no. I/9322; acquired 1931 from
Lorenzo Rubelli e Figlio, Venice

182 | UPHOLSTERY FABRIC (silk velour),
1930

Italy
Warp: silk; weft: silk, cotton, false lamé
H. 61 cm; w. 61 cm
Pattern repeat: h. 30.5 cm; w. 29 cm
Inventory no. XXIV/9045, acc. to inventory of
Italian origin; acquired 1930 from Hans
Henschel, Berlin

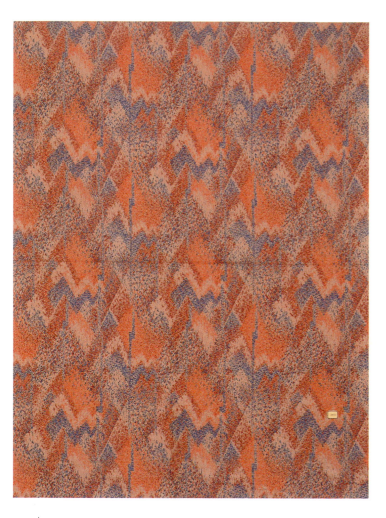

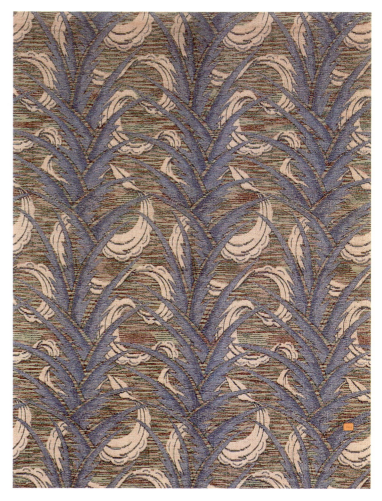

183 | UPHOLSTERY FABRIC, 1932

Italy
Manufacture: Lorenzo Rubelli e Figlio, Venice
Warp: cotton; weft: cotton
H. 120 cm; w. 124 cm
Pattern repeat: h. 32.5 cm; w. 30.5 cm
Inventory no. I/9619; acquired 1932 from H. Schubert, Berlin

184 | UPHOLSTERY FABRIC, 1932

Italy
Manufacture: Lorenzo Rubelli e Figlio, Venice
Warp: cotton; weft: cotton (chenille)
H. 132.5 cm; w. 120.5 cm
Pattern repeat: h. 51 cm; w. 30 cm
Inventory no. V/9618; acquired 1932 from H. Schubert, Berlin

185 | PRINTED FABRIC (chiné), 1931

Netherlands
Warp: cotton; weft: cotton
H. 136 cm; w. 118 cm
Pattern repeat: h. 38 cm; w. 62 cm
Inventory no. XIV/9337, acc. to inventory of Dutch origin; acquired 1931 from Richard Zieger, Chemnitz

| APPENDIX |

1 | WALL HANGING, 1924

Benita Koch-Otte (1892–1976)
Bauhaus Weimar
Semi-tapestry
Warp: cotton; weft: wool
H. 175.5 cm; w. 110 cm
Inventory no. XII/7516; acquired 1924 from
Bauhaus Weimar

At the Weimar Bauhaus, Koch-Otte was among the most talented and productive students in the weaving studio. Together with Gunta Stölzl, she took courses in Krefeld on interlacing theory and dyeing, thus laying the foundations for her studies in Weimar.
The work pictured here clearly reflects the influence of Johannes Itten and Paul Klee, both in coloration and structure. No longer is the narrative pictorial tapestry at the heart of the discourse; the focus is on a flat-constructive form in line with the new abstract art.
Of the basic forms – circle, square and triangle – the right-angled crossing of warp and weft meant that primarily rectangles and squares were chosen for use in the weaving studio. Paul Klee's series of pictures showing squares, begun in 1921, provided the weaving studio with an important impetus.
The principles of theory and form adopted by Benita Otte at the Bauhaus continued to guide her later on as director of the textiles course at Burg Giebichenstein in Halle (see nos. 6, 7, 8, 9, 10).

Lit. incl.:
Benita Koch-Otte: Vom Geheimnis der Farbe, exhibition catalogue of the Werkstatt Lydda in Bethel, 1972.
Gunta Stölzl: Weberei am Bauhaus und aus eigener Werkstatt, edited by Magdalena Droste for the Bauhaus-Archiv (Berlin: Kupfergraben, 1987).
Bauhaus 1919–1933, Meister- und Schülerarbeiten, Weimar–Dessau–Berlin, Museum für Gestaltung, Zurich, 1988, fig. p. 22.

2 | PATCHWORK RUG, 1925/27 (Detail)

Helene Schmidt-Nonné (1891–1976)
Bauhaus Dessau
Warp: cotton; weft: strips of various materials
L. 328 cm; w. 68 cm
Inventory no. XII/11517, this patchwork rug originally belonged to Marianne Brandt and was acquired for the collection in 1991.

Lit. incl.:
Bauhaus 7, issued by the Galerie am Sachsenplatz, Leipzig, Gisela and Hans-Peter Schulz, 1991, p. 87, fig. p. 47.

3 | GRAND PIANO COVER, 1927

Ruth Hollós-Consemüller (1904–1993)
Bauhaus Dessau
Double weave
Warp: rayon; weft: rayon
H. 200 cm; w. 119 cm
Inventory no. XIII/8279; aquired 1927

Lit. incl.:
Gunta Stölzl: Weberei am Bauhaus und aus eigener Werkstatt, edited by Magdalena Droste for the Bauhaus-Archiv (Berlin: Kupfergraben, 1987).
Bauhaus 1919–1933, Meister- und Schülerarbeiten, Weimar–Dessau–Berlin, Museum für Gestaltung, Zurich, 1988, fig. p. 126.
Wortmann Weltge, Sigrid, *Bauhaus-Textilien* (Schaffhausen: Edition Stemmle), 1993, fig. p. 67.

4 | NURSERY ROOM RUG, 1929

Otti Berger (1898–1944/45)
Bauhaus Dessau
Warp: cotton; weft: mercerized cotton
H. 185 cm; w. 109 cm
Marked with Bauhaus signum u. l.
Inventory no. XII/9400; acquired 1929 from
Bauhaus Dessau

In the inventory files, this object is listed under the purchase date 3 May 1929, Bauhaus Dessau, with no mention of the artist. Since Otti Berger did not take her craft exam until 1930, one may presume that until then her works were sold anonymously, marked only with the Bauhaus signum. The attribution of the nursery room rug is based on an announcement in the Bauhaus journal from April/June of the same year, reporting the purchase of a rug by Otti Berger by the Municipal Museum of Applied Arts in Chemnitz, and moreover on a contemporary illustration in the journal Kunst und Handwerk from 1930.

Lit. incl.:
bauhaus, vierteljahr-zeitschrift für gestaltung, edited by Hannes Meyer, Bauhaus Dessau, April–June 1929.
Kunst und Handwerk, vol. 80 no. III, Munich 1930, fig. p. 74.
Wortmann Weltge, Sigrid, *Bauhaus-Textilien* (Schaffhausen: Edition Stemmle), fig. p. 65.

5 | WALL HANGING/QUILT, 1929

Bauhaus Dessau
Manufacture: Textiles studio of the Bauhaus Dessau
Two-ply cloth with filling weft
warp: cotton, weft: wool
H. 195 cm; b. 124 cm
Marked with Bauhaus signum l. l.
Inventory no. XII/8745; acquired 1929 from
Bauhaus Dessau

This hanging, marked with the well-known Bauhaus seal, has not yet been attributed to any particular artist. What strikes the eye are its bright colours and weaving technique, adding to the complex two-ply or hollow weave an additional effect, a filling weft. In all of Bauhaus weaving, the stripe is one of the most important motifs, appearing in every imaginable colour and width. As this hanging demonstrates, the motif allows an intensive probing of the laws of colour and proportion. To the present-day viewer, the unusual juxtaposition of colours appears particularly bold.

Lit. incl.:
Bauhaus 1919–1933, Meister- und Schülerarbeiten, Weimar–Dessau–Berlin, Museum für Gestaltung, Zurich, 1988, fig. p. 177.

6 | WALL HANGING, 1928

Burg Giebichenstein – Werkstätten der Stadt Halle
Manufacture: Werkstätten der Stadt Halle/Hand Weaving, Director: Benita Otte
Warp: cotton; weft: wool, cotton
H. 300 cm; w. 175 cm
Inventory no. XII/8603; acquired 1928 from the
Werkstätten der Stadt Halle

On the recommendation of her predecessor, Johanna Schütz-Wolff, Benita Otte, the assistant director of the Bauhaus weaving studio, took charge of the weaving studio at Burg Giebichenstein in 1925. In friendly competition with the Bauhaus weavers (Gunta Stölzl, the directory of the weaving studio at Bauhaus Dessau, and Benita Otte were long-time friends), B. Otte developed the weaver's shop of the Burg from 1925 to 1933 into a production site for modern woven decorative materials. An outstanding example of this is the wall hanging illustrated here, which is on display at the Werkbund exhibition "Die Wohnung" in the house designed by Peter Behrens at the Weißenhof, Stuttgart.

Lit.:
Werkbund-Ausstellung Die Wohnung: Kleiner Führer durch die Werkbund-Siedlung Weißenhof, edited by the exhibition directors, Stuttgart, 1927 p. 62.
75 Jahre Burg Giebichenstein 1915–1990: Beiträge zur Geschichte, issued by Burg Giebichenstein – Hochschule für Kunst und Design Halle, 1990, fig. p. 23, fig. p. 33.
Burg Giebichenstein: Die hallesche Kunstschule von den Anfängen bis zur Gegenwart, issued by Staatliche Galerie Moritzburg Halle, Badisches Landesmuseum Karlsruhe, Burg Giebichenstein – Hochschule für Kunst und Design Halle, Halle 1993, fig. p. 227.

7 | DECORATIVE MATERIAL, 1930

Burg Giebichenstein – Werkstätten der Stadt Halle
Manufacture: Werkstätten der Stadt Halle/Hand
Weaving, Director: Benita Otte
Warp: cotton; weft: rayon, wool
H. 140 cm; w. 115 cm
Pattern repeat: h. 9.5 cm; w. 15 cm
Inventory no. XII/9244; acquired 1930 from the
Studio of the City of Halle

Lit.
*Burg Giebichenstein: Die hallesche Kunstschule von
den Anfängen bis zur Gegenwart,* issued by Staatliche
Galerie Moritzburg Halle, Badisches Landesmuseum
Karlsruhe, Burg Giebichenstein – Hochschule für
Kunst und Design Halle, Halle 1993, fig. p. 229.

8 | SOFA COVERLET, 1930

Burg Giebichenstein – Werkstätten der Stadt Halle
Manufacture: Werkstätten der Stadt Halle/Hand
Weaving, Director: Benita Otte
Warp: cotton (chenille), rayon; weft: wool, rayon
H. 250 cm; w. 158 cm
Inventory no. XII/9246; acquired 1930 from the
Werkstätten der Stadt Halle

Lit.:
*Burg Giebichenstein: Die hallesche Kunstschule von
den Anfängen bis zur Gegenwart,* issued by Staatliche
Galerie Moritzburg Halle, Badisches Landesmuseum
Karlsruhe, Burg Giebichenstein – Hochschule für
Kunst und Design Halle, Halle 1993, fig. p. 229.

9 | CURTAIN MATERIAL, 1932

Burg Giebichenstein – Werkstätten der Stadt Halle
Manufacture: Werkstätten der Stadt Halle/Hand
Weaving, Director: Benita Otte
Warp: mercerized cotton; weft: rayon
H. 100 cm; w. 124 cm
Pattern repeat: h. 60 cm; w. 4.5 cm
Inventory no. XII/9452; acquired 1932 from the
Werkstätten der Stadt Halle

10 | CURTAIN MATERIAL, 1932

Burg Giebichenstein – Werkstätten der Stadt Halle
Manufacture: Werkstätten der Stadt Halle/Hand
Weaving, Director: Benita Otte
Warp: mercerized cotton; weft: rayon
H. 97 cm; w. 3.5 cm
Pattern repeat: h. 0.3 cm; w. 3.5 cm
Inventory no. XII/9451; acquired 1932 from the
Werkstätten der Stadt Halle

11 | SPRAY-PRINTED FABRIC "BIWA-LAKE", 1928

Maria May (1900–1968)
Reimann School, Berlin
Warp: rayon; weft: rayon
H. 195 cm; w. 98.5 cm
Inventory no. XVIII/8418; acquired 1928 from the
Reimann School, Berlin

Maria May worked as a teacher at the Reimann private
art and crafts school in Berlin starting in 1922. Besides
overseeing the textiles class, she established her own
course for design and decorative painting. In collaboration with IG-Farbenindustrie, new techniques in
dyeing were tested that later found use in spray-prin-
ting and stencilling of textiles.

Lit.:
Farbe und Form, vol. 13, March 1928, no 3, fig. p. 61.

12 | SPRAY-PRINTED FABRIC
"BLACK–WHITE–GREY", 1928

Maria May (1900–1968)
Reimann School, Berlin
Warp: rayon; weft: rayon
H. 199 cm; w. 90 cm
Pattern repeat: h. 49 cm; w. 34 cm
Inventory no. XVII/8416; acquired 1928 from
Reimann School, Berlin

Maria May's pattern designs are found in both
figurative-representative and geometric-abstract
examples. Her work and materials were frequently
reported in the in-house magazine published by
the Reimann School, Farbe und Form.

Lit.:
Farbe und Form, vol. 13, March 1928, no. 3, fig.
p. 54.

13 | SPRAY-PRINTED FABRIC "ODETTE", 1928

Maria May (1900–1968)
Reimann School, Berlin
Warp: rayon; weft: rayon
H. 195 cm; w. 89 cm
Pattern repeat: h. 57.5 cm; w. = web width
Inventory no. XVII/8417; acquired 1928 from
the Reimann School, Berlin

The school presented its work in large travelling
exhibitions in Germany and the USA. In 1928 the
travelling exhibition of the Reimann School was
on display at the Textile and Applied Arts Collection in Chemnitz, including pieces by Maria May.
The purchase of her textiles proceeded in two
stages, the inventories showing five in 1928 and
three in 1930.

Lit.:
Farbe und Form, vol. 13, March 1928, no. 3, fig.
p. 60.

14 | SPRAY-PRINTED FABRIC
"FRUIT BOWL", 1928

Maria May (1900–1968)
Reimann School, Berlin
Warp: rayon; weft: rayon
H. 193 cm; w. 89 cm
Pattern repeat: h. 62 cm; w. = web width
Inventory no. XVII/8580; acquired 1928 from
the Reimann School, Berlin

Lit.:
Farbe und Form, vol. 13, March 1928, no. 3, fig.
p. 59.

15 | SPRAY-PRINTED FABRIC, 1928

Maria May (1900–1968)
Reimann School, Berlin
Warp: rayon; weft: rayon
H. 190 cm; w. 90 cm
Pattern repeat: h. 62 cm; w. = web width
Inventory no. XVII/8579; acquired 1928 from
the Reimann School, Berlin

16 | SPRAY-PRINTED FABRIC "PARIS", 1930

Maria May (1900–1968)
Reimann School, Berlin
Warp: rayon; weft: rayon
H. 237 cm; w. 117 cm
Pattern repeat: h. 127 cm; w. = web width
Inventory no. XVII/9099, acquired 1930 from
the Reimann School, Berlin

Extraordinarily popular among the students were
the annual summer studios, which took place
under the direction of a teacher in Europe and
abroad. The "Paris" and "Hungaria" fabrics are
the fruits of such summer study trips. The summer studios and the work of the Reimann School
as a whole were reported in an in-house monthly
journal. Entitled *Farbe und Form, Monatsschrift
für Kunst und Kunstgewerbe* it reported on the
activities and artistic output of the school.

Lit.:
Farbe und Form, vol. 15, Febr./March 1930, fig.
p. 32.

17 | SPRAY-PRINTED FABRIC "LACE", 1930

Maria May (1900–1968)
Reimann School, Berlin
Warp: rayon; weft: rayon
H. 147 cm; w. 118 cm
Inventory no. XVII/9101; acquired 1930 from the
Reimann School, Berlin

Lit.:
Farbe und Form, vol. 15, Febr./March 1930, fig.
p. 32.

18 | SPRAY-PRINTED FABRIC
"HUNGARIA", 1930

Maria May (1900–1968)
Reimann School, Berlin
Warp: cotton; weft: cotton
H. 176 cm; w. 98 cm
Pattern repeat: h. 89 cm; w. 35 cm
Inventory no. XVII/9100; acquired 1930 from
the Reimann School, Berlin

Lit.:
Farbe und Form, vol. 15, Febr./March 1930, fig.
p. 35.

19 | UPHOLSTERY FABRIC, 1929

Sigmund von Weech (1888–1982)
Manufacture: Hand Weaving Studio Sigmund von Weech, Schaftlach
Warp: cotton, rayon; Weft: rayon, cotton (chenille)
H. 116 cm; w. 129 cm
Pattern repeat: h. 40 cm; w. 21 cm
Inventory no. XII/8687; acquired 1929 from Friedemann und Weber, Berlin

These two clearly and functionally structured strips of material (no. 19, no. 20) probably originated in connection with designs for upholstered steel tube chairs and stools that Weech designed for JUNCKERS. The Neue Sammlung in Munich has several pages of preliminary designs. These upholstery fabrics, extraordinarily functional in appearance, clearly show the level of innovation the hand weaving studio had attained at this time, establishing a place for itself alongside the textile industry.

Lit.:
Wichmann, Hans, *Von Morris bis Memphis; Textilien der Neuen Sammlung,* (Basel, Boston, Berlin: Birkhäuser Verlag, 1990), pp. 174, 198, 199.

20 | UPHOLSTERY FABRIC, 1929

Sigmund von Weech (1888–1982)
Manufacture: Hand Weaving Studio Sigmund von Weech, Schaftlach
Warp: cotton, rayon; weft: cotton (chenille)
H. 126 cm; w. 129 cm
Pattern repeat: h. 65.5 cm; w. 42.5 cm
Inventory no. XII/8688; acquired 1929 from Friedemann und Weber, Berlin

21 | SOFA COVERLET, 1929

Sigmund von Weech (1888–1982)
Manufacture: Hand Weaving Studio Sigmund von Weech, Schaftlach
Warp: cotton; weft: cotton
H. 300 cm; w. 150 cm
Inventory no. XII/8895; acquired 1929 from Schneider und Königs, Düsseldorf

22 | BAYCO GOLD STRETCH FABRIC, 1927

Manufacture: Hand Weaving Studio Hohenhagen, Bremen
Warp: cotton; Weft: silk, rayon, bayco yarn (metallic yarn)
H. 323 cm; w. 178 cm
Inventory no. XII/8265; acquired 1927 from Schneider und Königs, Düsseldorf

The extraordinary effect of this bayco gold stretch fabric lies both in the clear artistic spatial structure and in the utilization of bayco yarns themselves. Metal yarns though similar to metal threads, are something entirely different, since they are actually metallicized textile threads. In a patented process, the yarns are covered with a thin metallic-looking coating. These yarns do not fade in the sunlight or darken from oxidation, so that even today these high-quality materials for furniture and interior decoration still possess their wonderful dull-bronze sheen.

Lit.:
Zeitschrift für die gesamte Textilindustrie, vol. 32, 1929, p. 656.

23 | UPHOLSTERY FABRIC, 1927

Manufacture: Hand Weaving Studio Hohenhagen, Bremen
Warp: cotton; weft: cotton (chenille)
H. 178 cm; w. 130 cm
Pattern repeat: h. 20 cm; w. 150 cm
Inventory no. XII/8264; acquired 1927 from Schneider und Königs, Düsseldorf

24 | WALL FABRIC, 1930

Polytex Textilgesellschaft mbH, Berlin
Warp: rayon; Weft: cotton (chenille), rayon
H. 176 cm; w. 131 cm
Inventory no. XII/9249; acquired 1930 from Polytex Textilgesellschaft mbH, Berlin

Some of the work of Polytex Textilgesellschaft was described in the inventory as "wall fabrics", although a consistent use of cotton, in this case specifically chenille, as weft and rayon fibres as warp, lend them a decidedly robust character, and they were used primarily in upholstering furniture. In the company catalogue from around 1930, both terms, i.e. wall fabric and upholstery fabric, were used interchangeably. The wall fabric pictured here is more reminiscent of contemporary forms of wall hanging, as it involves a free geometric structuring of the entire surface, with no discernible repeat.

25 | UPHOLSTERY FABRIC, 1930

Polytex Textilgesellschaft mbH, Berlin
Warp: rayon; weft: cotton (chenille), rayon
H. 213 cm; w. 132 cm
Pattern repeat: h. 159 cm; w. 65 cm
Inventory no. XII/951; acquired 1930 from Polytex Textilgesellschaft mbH, Berlin

Polytex Textilgesellschaft, Berlin, called its products POLYTEX MATERIALS. In numerous advertisements and in the company catalogue, it showcases its decorative and upholstery fabrics, created under the artistic direction of Bruno Paul. In a company catalogue from around 1930, the credits are expanded to include "Professor Bruno Paul, Bernhard Jentsch and Tillie Prill-Schloemann: artistic direction and weaving technology." The material illustrated here also appears in the same company catalogue as art. no. 248, described as "generous pattern, not dependent on repeat in upholstering." This is accompanied by an illustration showing the material used to upholstered an English armchair, plainly revealing the asymmetrical effect of the pattern.
Fig. English armchair

Lit.:
Polytex-Stoffe für Möbel und Dekorationen, issued by Polytextil GmbH Berlin, Wilhelmstr. 107, Berlin (Company catalogue), no publication date.

26 | UPHOLSTERY FABRIC, 1930

Polytex Textilgesellschaft mbH, Berlin
Warp: rayon; Weft: cotton (chenille), rayon
H. 274 cm; w. 131 cm
Pattern repeat: h. 160.5 cm; w. 65 cm
Inventory no. XII/9250; acquired 1930 from Polytex Textilgesellschaft mbH, Berlin

This material is also pictured in the company catalogue under art. no. 245 and described as follows: "Very expressive pattern. Generous but peaceful effect despite the large repeat."
Fig. day bed

Lit.:
Polytex-Stoffe für Möbel und Dekorationen, issued by Polytextil GmbH Berlin, Wilhelmstr. 107, Berlin (Company catalogue), no publication date.

27 | UPHOLSTERY FABRIC, 1928

Polytex Textilgesellschaft mbH, Berlin
Warp: rayon; weft: cotton
H. 127 cm; w. 130 cm
Pattern repeat: h. 61.5 cm; w. 130 cm
Inventory no. IX/8651; acquired 1928 from Textil- und Einrichtungshaus Richard Zieger, Chemnitz

This upholstery fabric is an example of Polytex materials with a somewhat "lighter" character than those already introduced. Instead of the fuller chenille thread, a finer cotton is used as weft material, giving the textile lighter appearance. The semi-circles in the pattern design would seem to contradict the usual right-angled crossing of warp and weft and the resulting geometrification, thus contributing to the ingenious impression of the surface design. This pattern is also in the company catalogue, under art. no. 180; moreover, it was also offered in so-called "polar quality," i.e. woven with stronger thread material, and used to cover Bruno Paul's furniture in the boardroom offices in the Kathreiner Building, Berlin.

Lit.:
Polytex-Stoffe für Möbel und Dekorationen, issued by Polytextil GmbH Berlin, Wilhelmstr. 107, Berlin (Company catalogue), no publication date.

28 | UPHOLSTERY FABRIC, 1931

Polytex Textilgesellschaft mbH, Berlin
Warp: cotton; weft: cotton
H. 135 cm; w. 125.5 cm
Pattern repeat: h. 27 cm; w. 31 cm
Inventory no. I/9346; acquired 1931 from Polytex Textilgesellschaft mbH, Berlin

29 | SCARF, 1927

Vereinigte Werkstätten, Munich
Hand-painted on small-patterned silk
Warp: silk; weft: silk
H. 148 cm; w. 46 cm
Inventory no. XVII/8235; acquired 1927 from the Vereinigte Werkstätten, Munich

30 | UPHOLSTERY FABRIC
(looped pile fabric), 1927

Vereinigte Werkstätten, Munich
Warp: wool; weft: cotton
H. 136 cm; w. 130 cm
Pattern repeat: h. 20 cm; w. 130 cm
Inventory no. VI/8229; acquired 1927 from the
Vereinigte Werkstätten, Munich

31 | UPHOLSTERY FABRIC "PAPAGENO",
(weft tapestry), 1929

Paul Lázló (born 1900)
Vereinigte Werkstätten, Munich
Warp: cotton; weft: cotton, wool
H. 135 cm; w. 128 cm
Pattern repeat: h. 34 cm; w. 31 cm
Mark in the selvage: V.W.
Inventory no. II/8743; acquired 1929 from the
Vereinigte Werkstätten für Kunst im Handwerk,
Düsseldorf

Paul László, architect and designer, is represented
with numerous works in the art magazines of the
time. Materials he designed often complement his
highly varied interiors and living spaces.

Lit.:
DKuD, October 1928/March 1929, fig. p. 429.

32 | UPHOLSTERY FABRIC (weft tapestry), 1928

E. Engelbrecht
Vereinigte Werkstätten, Munich
Warp: cotton; weft: cotton, wool
H. 148 cm; w. 128 cm
Pattern repeat: h. 52 cm; w. 31.5 cm
Mark in the selvage: V.W.
Inventory no. III/8587; acquired 1928 from the
Vereinigte Werkstätten, Munich

Another material designed by Engelbrecht, but in
this case a printed fabric is illustrated in the
DkuD, April–September 1928, p. 177. This
article is also the source of the abbreviation of the
first name.

Lit.:
DK 1927/28, vol. XXXVI, fig. p. 287.

33 | BROCADE UPHOLSTERY FABRIC, 1928

Studio F. A. Breuhaus
Vereinigte Werkstätten, Munich
Warp: cotton; weft: cotton, rayon (chenille), false
lamé
H. 96.5 cm; w. 130 cm
Pattern repeat: h. 38.5 cm; w. 63.5 cm
Inventory no. I/9671; acquired 1933 from the
Vereinigte Werkstätten

This material was used for armchairs in the library and the lounge of the "Bremen," a luxurious-
ly appointed, high-speed steamer that made its
maiden voyage on the Bremerhaven–New York
route in 1929. Fritz August Breuhaus de Groot
was responsible for designing all the first-class
salons, except for the smoking room.
Fig. F. A. Breuhaus: Library of the Steam Liner
Bremen, in: ID, 1929, vol. XI, p. 448

Lit.:
DKuD, November 1929, pp. 115, 116, fig. p.
130.
DKuD, February 1930, fig. p. 349.

34 | UPHOLSTERY FABRIC
(brocade velour), 1929

Studio F. A. Breuhaus
Vereinigte Werkstätten, Munich
Warp: cotton; weft: cotton, wool, false lamé
H. 106 cm; w. 135 cm
Pattern repeat: h. 47 cm; w. 33 cm
Inventory no. V/8874; acquired 1929 from the
Vereinigte Werkstätten für Kunst im Handwerk,
Düsseldorf

This exceedingly luxurious upholstery fabric, like
the preceding one, was also used to furnish the
luxury liner "Bremen," in this case in the ante-
room of the lounge. Of particular note is that the
pink hues were applied to the fabric using stencil
spray printing. It is interesting to compare this
with the French "brocade velour" no. 160; the almost identical selvage of the two pieces invites the
conclusion that this fabric was manufactured in
France.

Lit.:
DKuD, February 1930, fig. p. 349.
DKuD, November 1929, fig.p. 127.

35 | UPHOLSTERY FABRIC (terry pile), 1929

Studio F.A. Breuhaus
Vereinigte Werkstätten, Munich
Warp: cotton; weft: cotton, rayon
H. 133 cm; w. 136 cm
Pattern repeat: h. 36 cm; w. 33 cm
Inventory no. V/9329; acquired 1931 from H.G.
Schrödter, Leipzig

In this case the origin of the fabric can only be
guessed at. Stylistically, it represents a variation
on the pattern of the upholstery fabric "Firenze"
of the Studio F. A. Breuhaus (pictured in DKuD,
February 1930, p. 350). Here, too, we have an
exceedingly luxurious "brocade velour," whose
selvage is identical with that of the previous
upholstery fabric, so that it probably comes from
the same manufacturer.

36 | UPHOLSTERY "VENUS", around 1932

Vereinigte Werkstätten, Munich
Warp: mercerized cotton; weft: rayon
H. 135 cm; w. 129 cm
Pattern repeat: h. 49 cm; w. 63 cm
Mark in the selvage: V. W. VENUS
Inventory no. I/9667; acquired 1933 from the
Vereinigten Werkstätten, Munich

37 | UPHOLSTERY FABRIC, 1935

Vereinigte Werkstätten, Munich
Warp: cotton; weft: wool, cotton
H. 100 cm; w. 37 cm
Pattern repeat: h. 41 cm; w. 36.5 cm
Inventory no. I/9975; acquired 1935 from the
Vereinigte Werkstätten, Munich

38 | UPHOLSTERY FABRIC, 1935

Vereinigte Werkstätten, Munich
Warp: cotton; weft: wool, cotton
H. 97 cm; w. 145.5 cm
Pattern repeat: h. 54 cm; w. 71 cm
Inventory no. I/9976; acquired 1935 from the
Vereinigte Werkstätten, Munich

39 | UPHOLSTERY FABRIC (weft tapestry), 1927

Deutsche Werkstätten, Dresden
Warp: cotton; weft: cotton
H. 102 cm; w. 128 cm
Pattern repeat: h. 36 cm; w. 31 cm
Inventory no. II/7805; acquired 1926 from the
Deutsche Werkstätten

40 | UPHOLSTERY (cotton velour), 1927

Deutsche Werkstätten Dresden
Warp: cotton; weft: cotton
H. 95 cm; w. 128 cm
Pattern repeat: h. 7.5 cm; w. 8 cm
Inventory no. XXIV/8117; acquired 1927 from
the Deutsche Werkstätten

This fabric was used as upholstery fabric for an
armchair, and was on display at the "Deutsche
Kunst" exhibition in Düsseldorf in 1928.
Fig. Living Room, Düsseldorf; in: ID, July 1928,
p. 289.

41 | UPHOLSTERY FABRIC, 1927

Deutsche Werkstätten, Dresden
Warp: wool; weft: wool
H. 100 cm; w. 135 cm
Pattern repeat: h. 2 cm; w. 21.5 cm
Inventory no. II/8114; acquired 1927 from the
Deutsche Werkstätten

42 | DECORATIVE MATERIAL, 1926

Deutsche Werkstätten, Dresden
Printed fabric, block printing
Warp: cotton; weft: wool
H. 54.5 cm; w. 62 cm
Pattern repeat: indeterminate
Inventory no. XVII/7889; acquired 1926 from
A. Eick u. Söhne, Essen

Lit.:
ID, February 1926, fig. p. 83.

43 | PRINTED FABRIC, around 1925

Josef Hillerbrand (1892–1981)
Deutsche Werkstätten, Dresden
Warp: cotton; weft: cotton
H. 97 cm; w. 106.5 cm
Pattern repeat: h. 22 cm; w. 26.5 cm
Marked on selvage: ENTWURF HILLER-
BRAND 538 DEWETEX. DRESDEN
Inventory no. XIV/11380-150; donated by
Hofmann, 1988

Printed on various materials, this pattern found wide application, for instance in curtains and pillows.

Lit.:
DKuD, April–Sept. 1932, fig.p. 101.

44 | PRINTED FABRIC, around 1929

Deutsche Werkstätten, Dresden
Warp: rayon; weft: cotton
H. 23.5 cm; w. 59.5 cm
Pattern repeat: h. indeterminate; w. 31.5 cm
Inventory no. XIV/11380-89; part of the DE-WE-TEX pattern-book; donated by Möbelstoffweberei Tannenhauer, Braunsdorf, 1982

Lit.:
DKuD, April–September 1930, Vol. 66, fig. p. 332.
Wichmann, Hans, *Deutsche Werkstätten und WK-Verband 1898–1990* (Munich: Prestel, 1992), fig. p. 228.
Arnold, Klaus-Peter, *Vom Sofakissen zum Städtebau – Die Geschichte der Deutschen Werkstätten* (Dresden, Basel: Verlag der Kunst, 1993), fig. p. 270.

45 | PRINTED FABRIC, around 1930

Deutsche Werkstätten, Dresden
Warp: rayon; weft: cotton
H. 47 cm; w. 54 cm
Pattern repeat: h. 30 cm; w. 32 cm
Inventory no. XIV/11380-88; part of the DE-WE-TEX pattern-book; donated by Möbelstoffweberei Tannenhauer, Braunsdorf, 1982
Fig. Deutsche Werkstätten: Wohnraum; in: *ID*, 1934, p. 343

46 | UPHOLSTERY FABRIC
(looped pile fabric), 1926

Vorwerk & Co., Barmen
Warp: wool; weft: cotton
H. 140 cm; w. 128 cm
Pattern repeat: h. 31 cm; w. 32 cm
Marked and woven into the reverse side:
VORWERK
Inventory no. VI/7797; acquired 1926 from Riedel & Rothe, Berlin

47 | UPHOLSTERY FABRIC
(looped pile fabric), 1926

Vorwerk & Co., Barmen
Warp: wool; weft: cotton
H. 129 cm; w. 127 cm
Pattern repeat: h. 33 cm; w. 32 cm
Marked and woven into the reverse side:
VORWERK
Inventory no. VI/7796; acquired 1926 from Riedel & Rothe, Berlin

48 | UPHOLSTERY FABRIC
(looped pile fabric), 1927

Vorwerk & Co., Barmen
Warp: wool; weft: cotton
H. 138 cm; w. 128 cm

Pattern repeat: h. 29 cm; w. 32.5 cm
Marked and woven into the reverse side:
VORWERK
Inventory no. VI/8091; acquired 1927 from Fischer & Wolf, Cologne

49 | UPHOLSTERY FABRIC
(looped pile fabric), 1928

Vorwerk & Co., Barmen
Warp: wool, cotton; weft: cotton
H. 140 cm; w. 128 cm
Pattern repeat: h. 27 cm; w. 31.5 cm
Marked and woven into the reverse side:
VORWERK
Inventory no. VI/8383; acquired 1928 from Brüggemann & Barkmann, Hamburg

50 | UPHOLSTERY FABRIC (terry pile), 1930

Vorwerk & Co., Barmen
Warp: cotton, rayon; weft: cotton
H. 142 cm; w. 132 cm
Pattern repeat: h. 62 cm; w. 32.5 cm
Marked in the selvage: VORWERK
Inventory no. V/9081; acquired 1930 from Brüggemann & Barkmann, Hamburg

51 | UPHOLSTERY FABRIC
(looped pile fabric), 1924

Hertha Koch
DETEKU – Deutsche Textile Kunst, Leipzig
Warp: cotton; weft: wool, rayon
H. 58.5 cm; w. 60.5 cm
Pattern repeat: h. 16 cm; w. 15.5 cm
Marked on specially designed paper label:
"DETEKU, Original-Entwurf: Herta Koch, Qualität: No. 126788"
Inventory no. VI/7495;. acquired 1924 from DETEKU, Leipzig

Kiessling, Hiemann & Dippmann, a Leipzig company established in 1904, was a member of the Werkbund trading under the programmatic abbreviation of DETEKU (Deutsche textile Kunst) and producing a range of fabrics from designs by artists like Th. Th. Heine, H. van de Velde, J.V. Cissarz and Albin Müller. Rudolf Hiemann, the company chairman, appointed Erich Kleinhempel as artistic director. Hertha Koch designed fabrics for DETEKU both before and after the First World War. In formal terms, the example pictured here is still heavily influence by pre-World War I design concepts.

Lit.:
DK, 1917, pp. 328 ff.
DK, vol. XXV, June 1922, pp. 217 ff.

52 | UPHOLSTERY FABRIC (weft tapestry), 1924

Erich Kleinhempel (1847–1947)
DETEKU – Deutsche Textile Kunst, Leipzig
Warp: cotton; weft: wool
H. 93 cm; w. 125 cm
Pattern repeat: h. 31 cm; w. 31 cm
Inventory no. II/7496; acquired 1924 from DETEKU, Leipzig

Erich Kleinhempel's three fabric patterns make him the artist with the most exhibits in the collection from DETEKU. The material illustrated here shows a deceptively simple design that is nonetheless extraordinarily sophisticated in its subtle coloration and finely structured surface.

53 | UPHOLSTERY FABRIC (weft tapestry), 1924

Erich Kleinhempel (1847–1947)
DETEKU – Deutsche Textile Kunst, Leipzig
Warp: cotton; weft: wool
H. 132.5 cm; w. 97 cm
Pattern repeat: h. 41 cm; w. 33 cm
Inventory no. II/7499; acquired 1924 from DETEKU, Leipzig

This fabric is extraordinarily expressive in its pattern design. With its complex colour and rhythmic movements, it offers a counterpoint to the strict geometric and stripe patters of the time.

54 | PRINTED FABRIC (hand printing), 1924

Erich Kleinhempel (1847–1947)
DETEKU – Deutsche Textile Kunst, Leipzig
Warp: cotton; weft: cotton
H. 101.5 cm; w. 98 cm
Pattern repeat: h. 34 cm; w. 39 cm
Inventory no. XIV/7512; acquired 1924 from DETEKU, Leipzig

Besides the woven fabrics, there are two hand prints in the collection (cf. no. 55). It can no longer be determined whether these were produced by the company itself, or made under license.

55 | PRINTED FABRIC (hand printing), 1924

Ernst Aufseeser (1880–1940)
DETEKU – Deutsche Textile Kunst, Leipzig
Warp: cotton; weft: cotton
H. 89.5 cm; w. 97 cm
Pattern repeat: h. 24 cm; w. 16.5 cm
Inventory no. XIV/7510; acquired 1924 from DETEKU, Leipzig

56 | UPHOLSTERY FABRIC
(looped pile fabric), 1930

Adolf Toenges, Elberfeld
Warp: wool, cotton; weft: cotton
H. 148 cm; w. 130 cm
Pattern repeat: h. 45 cm; w. 64 cm
Inventory no. VI/9058; acquired 1930 from Hans Henschel, Berlin

57 | UPHOLSTERY FABRIC (terry pile), 1930

Adolf Toenges, Elberfeld
Warp: cotton, rayon; weft: cotton
H. 134 cm; w. 129 cm
Pattern repeat: h. 60 cm; w. 64 cm
Inventory no. V/9209; acquired 1930 from Hans Henschel, Berlin

58 | PRINTED FABRIC, Design 670, 1924

Ruth Hildegard Geyer-Raack (1894–1975)
Bayerische Textilwerke Tutzing
Warp: cotton; weft: cotton
H. 282 cm; w. 126 cm
Pattern repeat: h. 83.5 cm; w. 126 cm
Inventory no. XIV/7678; acquired 1925 from
L. Bernheimer, Munich

In the 1920s, R.H. Geyer-Raack was employed
by the Deutsche Werkstätten primarily as a textile
designer. This large-pattern fabric manufactured
for the Bayerische Textilwerke Tutzing was pictured with particular frequency in contemporary
literature.

Lit.:
DK, September 1925, fig. p. 284.
Wichmann, Hans, *Von Morris bis Memphis:
Textilien der Neuen Sammlung* (Basel, Boston,
Berlin: Birkhäuser, 1990), fig. p. 138.

59 | PRINTED FABRIC, 1928

Wilhelm Marsmann (1896–1966) and Viktor
Rauch (1901–1945)
Deutsche Farbmöbel AG, Munich
Warp: rayon; weft: rayon
H. 150 cm; w. 125.5 cm
Pattern repeat: h. 68.5 cm; w. 65 cm
Inventory no. XIV/8572; acquired 1928 from
Deutsche Farbmöbel AG, Munich

Lit.:
ID, 1934, vol. XLV, fig. p. 229.
Wichmann, Hans, *Von Morris bis Memphis:
Textilien der Neuen Sammlung*, (Basel, Boston,
Berlin: Birkhäuser, 1990), fig. p. 170.

60 | UPHOLSTERY FABRIC (weft tapestry), 1925

Hahn und Bach, Munich
Warp: cotton; weft: wool, cotton
H. 145 cm; w. 124.5 cm
Pattern repeat: h. 70 cm; w. 62 cm
Inventory no. I/7691; acquired 1925 from Hahn
und Bach, Munich

The Hahn und Bach company itself operated
only a textile printing works. These woven fabrics
(nos. 60, 61, 62) were manufactured by an out-
side firm and distributed under the company's
own name.

61 | UPHOLSTERY FABRIC (weft tapestry), 1924

Hahn und Bach, Munich
Warp: cotton; weft: cotton, wool
H. 90 cm; w. 130 cm
Pattern repeat: h. 68.5 cm; w. 32 cm
Inventory no. II/7768; acquired 1926 from
Hermann Gerson, Berlin
Fig. sofa in a dining room, in: *ID*, 1926, vol. 37,
p. 115

Lit.:
ID, vol. XXXV, 1924, fig p. 364.
Fachblatt für Holzarbeiter, issued by Deutscher
Holzarbeiterverband, Berlin, 1928, fig. p. 30.

62 | UPHOLSTERY FABRIC, 1932

Hahn und Bach, Munich
Warp: cotton; weft: cotton
H. 137 cm; w. 126 cm
Pattern repeat: h. I/46 cm; w. 41 cm
Inventory no. I/9660; acquired 1932 from
Richard Zieger, Chemnitz

Lit.:
DKuD, vol. 36, part 2, 1933, fig. p. 173.

63 | PRINTED FABRIC, 1924

Hahn und Bach, Munich
Warp: cotton; weft: flax
H. 143 cm; w. 131 cm
Pattern repeat: h. 42 cm; w. 59 cm
Inventory no. XIV/7707; acquired 1925 from
Hahn und Bach, Munich

Lit.:
ID, vol. XXXV, 1924, fig. p. 364.
DK, vol. 31, 1927/28, fig. p. 156.

64 | PRINTED FABRIC, 1925

Hahn und Bach, Munich
Warp: cotton; weft: flax
H. 137.5 cm; w. 129 cm
Pattern repeat: h. 38 cm; w. 60 cm
Inventory no. XIV/7716; acquired 1925 from
Hahn und Bach, Munich

65 | PRINTED FABRIC, 1925

Hahn und Bach, Munich
Warp: flax; weft: rayon
H. 112.5 cm; w. 131 cm
Pattern repeat: h. 38 cm; w. 30 cm
Inventory no. XIV/7720; acquired 1925 from
Hahn und Bach, Munich

The printed fabrics by Hahn und Bach shown
here (nos. 63, 64, 65) were called union linen, i.e.
the weft was made of particularly strong flax tow
yarn, thus producing a strong weft rib effect.

66 | UPHOLSTERY FABRIC (weft tapestry), 1927

Cammann & Co., Chemnitz
Warp: cotton; weft: wool, cotton
H. 131.5 cm; w. 128.5 cm
Pattern repeat: h. 20 cm; w. 32 cm
Metal signum on the reverse, u. r.: C.& Co. AG
Inventory no. II/8162; acquired 1927 from F. W.
Weymar, Dresden

The peculiarity of this fabric is that it is actually a
two-coloured woven textile. All other nuances of
colour are achieved by means of stencil spray
printing on the jacquard fabric.

67 | UPHOLSTERY FABRIC
(warp tapestry), 1927

Wilhelm Vogel, Chemnitz
Warp: cotton; weft: cotton
H. 65 cm; w. 126 cm
Pattern repeat: h. 33.5 cm; w. 41.5 cm
Inventory no. III/8146; acquired 1927 from
Richard Zieger, Chemnitz

The W. Vogel company was one of the most prominent weaving mills in Germany. Early on, it
was already working from designs by well-known
artists like H. van de Velde, Peter Behrens and
Adolf Niemayer. Under an agreement with Gropius, they manufactured Bauhaus fabric designs
for distribution by H. Gerson, Berlin. At the
same time, they made contact with the Wiener
Werkstätte, with the result that designs by
Dagobert Peche were woven for the Wiener
Werkstätte in Chemnitz (nos. 110, 111).

68 | DECORATIVE FABRIC, 1929

Germany
Warp: cotton; weft: cotton, rayon
H. 139 cm; w. 130 cm
Pattern repeat: h. 65 cm; w. 64 cm
Inventory no. IX/8660; acquired 1929 from S. A.
Heßlein, Nuremberg

69 | UPHOLSTERY FABRIC (terry pile), 1929

Germany
Warp: rayon; weft: flax
H. 140.5 cm; w. 132 cm
Pattern repeat: h. 32.5 cm; w. 32.5 cm
Inventory no. XXIV/8668; acquired 1929 from
S. A. Heßlein, Nuremberg

70 | UPHOLSTERY FABRIC (pile carpet), 1925

Germany
Warp: cotton, wool; weft: cotton
H. 98.5 cm; w. 131.5 cm
Pattern repeat: h. 44 cm; w. 33 cm
Inventory no. IV/7600; acquired 1925 from
Heinrich Bremer, Bremen

71 | UPHOLSTERY FABRIC (terry pile), 1928

Germany
Warp: cotton, rayon; weft: cotton
H. 133 cm; w. 127 cm
Pattern repeat: h. 30.5 cm; w. 31.5 cm
Inventory no. V/8540; acquired 1928 from Rich-
ard Rosenberg, Cologne

Fig. F. Becker & E. Kutzner: Living room in the
home of Dr. Kutzner, Düsseldorf, in: *DK*, 1929,
Vol. XXVII, p. 262

72 | UPHOLSTERY FABRIC (terry pile), 1930

Germany
Warp: cotton, rayon; weft: cotton
H. 140 ; w. 129 cm
Pattern repeat: h. 18 cm; w. 32 cm
Inventory no. V/9165; acquired 1930 from
Pepperhoff und Rosenthal, Essen

73 | UPHOLSTERY FABRIC, 1932

Germany
Warp: cotton; weft: cotton
H. 128 cm; w. 128 cm
Pattern repeat: h. 39 cm; w. 31.5 cm
Inventory no. I/9525; acquired 1932 from
Pepperhoff und Rosenthal, Essen

74 | UPHOLSTERY FABRIC (weft tapestry), 1930

Germany
Warp: cotton, cellophane strip; weft: cotton, wool
H. 132 cm; w. 124 cm
Pattern repeat: h. indeterminate; w. 124 cm
Inventory no. II/9064; acquired 1930 from G. A. Schrödter

75 | UPHOLSTERY FABRIC, 1930

Germany
Warp: cotton; weft: cotton
H. 123 cm; w. 62 cm
Pattern repeat: h. 34 cm; w. 31 cm
Inventory no. I/9078; acquired 1930 from Friedemann und Weber, Berlin

76 | UPHOLSTERY FABRIC (weft tapestry), 1927

Germany
Warp: cotton; weft: cotton, wool, rayon
H. 96 cm; w. 125 cm
Pattern repeat: h. 25.5 cm; w. 15.5 cm
Inventory no. II/8079; acquired 1927 from Riedel und Rother, Berlin

77 | UPHOLSTERY FABRIC (looped pile), 1926

Germany
Warp: wool, cotton ; weft: cotton
H. 100 cm; w. 131 cm
Pattern repeat: h. 41 cm; w. 52 cm
Inventory no. VI/7782; acquired 1926 from Friedemann und Weber, Berlin

78 | UPHOLSTERY FABRIC (weft tapestry), 1927

Germany
Warp: cotton; weft: cotton, rayon
H. 65 cm; w. 127 cm
Pattern repeat: h. 28 cm; w. 21 cm
Inventory no. II/8145; acquired 1927 from Richard Zieger, Chemnitz

79 | UPHOLSTERY FABRIC, 1932

Germany
Warp: cotton; weft: cotton
H. 147 cm; w. 140 cm
Pattern repeat: h. 22 cm; w. 140 cm
Inventory no. I/9649; acquired 1932 from Indanthren Haus, Frankfurt

80 | PILLOW CASE, 1931

Germany
Warp: cotton; weft: wool
H. 100 cm; w. 55 cm
Pattern repeat: h. indeterminate; w. 41 cm
Inventory no. XII/9396; acquired 1931 from Wertheim, Berlin

81 | PRINTED FABRIC, 1924

Germany
Warp: cotton; weft: cotton
H. 102 cm; w. 132 cm
Pattern repeat: h. indeterminate; w. 132 cm
Inventory no. XIV/7524; acquired 1924 from

Richard Zieger, Chemnitz
Fig. Richard Straumer: View of the stairway landing, house in the Thorerstr., Leipzig, in: *DKuD*, vol. 57, October 1925 – March 1926, p. 334, 335, 339

82 | PRINTED FABRIC, 1924

Germany
Warp: cotton; weft: cotton
H. 57 cm; w. 136.5 cm
Pattern repeat: h. indeterminate; w. 32 cm
Inventory no. XIV/7445; acquired 1924 from L. Bernheimer, Munich

The illustration reveals that the artistic currents of the pre-war era continued far into the 1920s, with buildings and rooms still being furnished in that tradition.
Fig. Sanitarium am Königspark in Dresden-Loschwitz, view of the smoking and billiards room, in: *ID*, vol. XXII, 1922, p. 94

83 | PRINTED FABRIC, 1926

Germany
Warp: cotton, weft: cotton
H. 107 cm; w. 77 cm
Pattern repeat: h. 39 cm; w. 47.5 cm
Inventory no. XIV/7871; acquired 1926 from S. und R. Wahl, Barmen

84 | PRINTED FABRIC, 1926

Germany
Warp: cotton; weft: cotton
H. 138 cm; w. 78 cm
Pattern repeat: h. 58 cm; w. = web width
Inventory no. XIV/8004; acquired 1926 from Richard Zieger, Chemnitz

85 | PRINTED FABRIC, 1927

Germany
Warp: flax; weft: flax
H. 152 cm; w. 127 cm
Pattern repeat: h. 82 cm; w. = web width
Inventory no. XIV/8197; acquired 1927 from Bros. Schürmann, Cologne

86 | PRINTED FABRIC, ca. 1925

Germany
Warp: cotton; weft: cotton
H. 97 cm; w. 70 cm
Pattern repeat: h. 34.5 cm; w. 35 cm
Inventory no. XIV/6809; date of acquisition unknown

Lit.:
DK, vol. 31, 1927–28, vol. XXXVI, fig. p. 157.

87 | PRINTED FABRIC (block printing), 1924

Germany
Warp: flax; weft: flax
H. 102 cm; w. 77 cm
Pattern repeat: h. 25 cm; w. 30 cm
Inventory no. XIV/7488; acquired 1924 from the Volkskunsthaus Wallach, Munich

Even before the First World War, block prints with old designs and motifs were popular, influencing the pattern designs of a number of artists. Prominent in this regard are the fabric patterns of C. O. Czeschka for the Wiener Werkstätte. These two block prints on linen (nos. 87, 88) are printed in rich, forceful colours after old popular art motifs, and, if one credits the historical inventory entries, are called "Holstein" and "Transylvanian" respectively.

88 | PRINTED FABRIC (block printing), 1924

Germany
Warp: flax; weft: flax
H. 102 cm; w. 77 cm
Pattern repeat: h. 36 cm; w. 28.5 cm
Inventory no. XIV/7492; acquired 1924 from the Volkskunsthaus Wallach, Munich

89 | PRINTED FABRIC (block printing), 1926

Germany
Warp: cotton; weft: flax
H. 129 cm; w. 78.5 cm
Pattern repeat: h. 32 cm; w. 25 cm
Inventory no. XIV/7882; acquired 1926 from Schneider und Königs, Düsseldorf

90 | CURTAIN FABRIC, 1930

Germany
Machined corded embroidery
Warp: flax; weft: flax; embroidery material: cotton
H. 193 cm; w. 137 cm
Pattern repeat: h. 64 cm; w. 40 cm
Inventory no. XII/9076; acquired 1930 from Friedemann und Weber, Berlin

91 | HORSEHAIR UPHOLSTERY FABRIC, 1925

Germany
Warp: cotton; weft: horsehair
H. 53 cm; w. 69 cm
Pattern repeat: h. 16 cm; w. 19 cm
Inventory no. I/7676; acquired 1925 from L. Bernheimer, Munich

92 | HORSEHAIR UPHOLSTERY FABRIC, 1925

Germany
Warp: cotton; weft: horsehair
H. 51 cm; w. 67 cm
Pattern repeat: h. 10 cm; w. 9 cm
Inventory no. I/7677; acquired 1925 from L. Bernheimer, Munich

93 | UPHOLSTERY FABRIC, 1930

Germany
Warp: cotton; weft: cotton
H. 125 cm; w. 131 cm
Pattern repeat: h. 16 cm; w. 41.5 cm
Inventory no. XII/9079; acquired 1930 from Friedemann und Weber, Berlin

94 | WALL HANGING "BEARS", 1928

Wenzel Hablik (1881–1934)
Manufacture: Handweberei Hablik-Lindemann,

Itzehoe
Warp: cotton; weft: hand-spun wool
H. 147 cm; w. 300 cm
Marked l.m. with the studio signum
Inventory no. XII/8599; acquired 1928 from
Handweberei Hablik-Lindemann

Hablik's particular interest in the transformation
of animal forms into abstract geometries was presumably inspired by a trip to South America. But
it was also a feature of the times, cf. the geometrification of animal images in E. Mögelin (no. 100).

Lit. incl.:
Moderne Bildwirkereien, Exhibition catalogue,
Dessau, 1930.
Fuchs-Belhamri, Elisabeth, *Wenzel Hablik –
Textilkunst und Mode* (Heide: Boyens & Co,
1993), fig. p. 52.

95 | PILLOW "HELLHOUND";
REVERSE "MIRROR IMAGE", 1928

Wenzel Hablik (1881–1934)
Manufacture: Hand Weaving Studio
Hablik-Lindemann, Itzehoe
Warp: cotton; weft: wool
H. 60 cm; w. 70cm
Marked on reverse u.l. with the studio signum
Inventory no. XII/8600; acquired 1928 from
Hand Weaving Studio Hablik-Lindemann, Itzehoe

Both the geometric pattern of horizontal and vertical interlocking stripes and surfaces of the reverse side and the motif of the front were produced
as wall hangings.

Lit.:
Studio catalogue 1928/29, no pp.
Fuchs-Belhamri, Elisabeth: *Wenzel Hablik –
Textilkunst und Mode* (Heide: Boyens & Co.,
1993), fig. p. 55.

96 | CLOTH, 1928 (Detail)

Wenzel Hablik (1881–1934)
Jacquard fabric, manufacture: Hand Weaving
Studio Hablik-Lindemann, Itzehoe
Warp: tussah silk; weft: tussah silk
L. 153 cm; w. 153 cm (without fringe)
Pattern repeat: h. 19.5 cm; w. 19.5 cm
Inventory no. XII/8347; acquired 1928 from
Hand Weaving Studio Hablik-Lindemann, Itzehoe

Lit.:
Fuchs-Belhamri, Elisabeth, *Wenzel Hablik – Textilkunst und Mode* (Heide: Boyens & Co., 1993),
fig. p. 54.

97 | WALL HANGING "CORAL TREE", 1928

Wenzel Hablik (1881–1934)
Manufacture: Hand Weaving Studio Hablik-
Lindemann, Itzehoe
Warp: cotton; weft: chenille, various materials
H. 322 cm; w. 144 cm
Inventory no. XII/8348; acquired 1928 from
Hand Weaving Studio Hablik-Lindemann, Itzehoe

The CORAL TREE was the most successful item
produced by the studio, and was shown to great
acclaim in several exhibitions.

Contemporary critics counted it among the
"most impressive" works of the late 1920s (Parsar-
ge, Walter: Deutsche Werkkunst der Gegenwart,
Berlin 1934).
Two variations are known. With its characteristic
colorfulness, the Chemnitz hanging is notable
above all for its sophisticated combination of
materials. For the first time Hablik uses chenille
in a wall hanging. This was an extremely popular
material in the late 1920s; see, for instance, the
pieces by Siegfried van Weech and Polytex.

Lit. incl.:
Moderne Bildwirkereien, exhibition catalogue,
Dessau, 1930.
Fuchs-Belhamri, Elisabeth: *Wenzel Hablik –
Textilkunst und Mode* (Heide: Boyens & Co.,
1993), fig. p. 49.

98 | WALL HANGING
"ALASKA ANIMALS", 1929

Wenzel Hablik (1881–1934)
Semi-tapestry, manufacture: Hand Weaving
Studio Hablik-Lindemann, Itzehoe
Warp: cotton; weft: wool
H. 280 cm; w. 135 cm
Inventory no. XII/8791; acquired 1929 from
Hand Weaving Studio Hablik-Lindemann, Itzehoe

Images of motifs like sailboats, islands and croco-
diles in abstract geometrical forms corresponds to
the right-angled intersection of warp and weft
and are thus strictly oriented toward the technical
weaving process.

Lit.:
Fuchs-Belhamri, Elisabeth: *Wenzel Hablik –
Textilkunst und Mode* (Heide: Boyens & Co.,
1993), fig. p. 53.

99 | WALL HANGING, circa 1935

Valerie Jorud
Appliqué, cotton ribbons on linen; design and
manufacture Valerie Jorud, Berlin
H. 190 cm; w. 148 cm
Marked u.l. V
Inventory no. XII/9901; acquired from Valerie
Jorud at the Grassi Fair, Leipzig, autumn 1935

This piece from the first half of the 1930s is one
of the few examples in Germany showing a firm
commitment to the principles of design developed in the 1920s (geometrical, abstract), and
seems today to foreshadow the op art of the
1960s. Further works by V. Jorud are in the
Grassi Museum, Leipzig.

100 | WALL HANGING "RED DEER", 1927

Else Mögelin (1887–1982)
Semi-tapestry, manufactured in artist's own
studio in Gildenhall/Neu-Ruppin, woven in two
runs
Warp: cotton; weft: wool, rayon fibre
H. 270 cm; w. 154 cm
Inventory no. XII/8899; acquired 1929 from
Else Mögelin, Gildenhall

This wall hanging represented the work of Else
Mögelin at the 1927 International Exhibition of
the Decorative Arts in Monza.

Lit. incl.:
DKuD, December 1927, Vol. 61, 1927/28, fig.
p. 207.
International Exhibition of the Decorative Arts,
(catalogue III), Monza 1927, p. 73.
Wortmann Weltge, Sigrid, *Bauhaus-Textilien,*
(Schaffhausen: Edition Stemmle), fig. p. 87.

101 | CURTAIN, 1928

Else Mögelin (1887–1982)
Manufactured in artist's own studio in Gilden-
hall/Neu-Ruppin
Warp: rayon fibre; weft: rayon fibre, wool
H. 298 cm; w. 158 cm
Inventory no. XII/8412; acquired 1928 from
Else Mögelin, Gildenhall

Lit. incl.:
*Bauhaus 1919–1933, Meister-und Schülerarbei-
ten, Weimar–Dessau–Berlin* (Zurich: Museum für
Gestaltung, 1988), fig. p. 146.

102 | COVERLET, 1926

Margarete Willers (1883–1977)
Hand-weaving with sewn-on trim ribbon
Marked l. l. with embroidered W
Warp: cotton; weft: cotton, false lamé
H. 72 cm; w. 95 cm
Inventory no. XII/7890; acquired 1926 from A.
Eick und Söhne, Essen
No fig.

103 | COVERLET, 1926

Margarete Willers (1883–1977)
Germany
Hand-woven, edged border
Warp: cotton, weft: cotton, false lamé
H. 73 cm; w. 93 cm
Inventory no. XII/7891; acquired 1926 from
A. Eick und Söhne, Essen

From 1921 to 1922, Margarete Willers studied
at the weaving studio of the Weimar Bauhaus. In
1927 W. Gropius arranged for her to work in her
own studio at the Dessau Bauhaus. The two
works in the collection (nos. 102, 103) come
from an earlier period.

Lit.:
*Gunta Stölzl: Weberei am Bauhaus und aus eigener
Werkstatt,* edited by Magdalena Droste for the
Bauhaus-Archiv (Berlin: Kupfergraben, 1987).

104 | WALL HANGING, 1929

Irmgard Ritter-Kauermann (born 1895)
Germany
Filet embroidery
Woven filet net: cotton; embroidery material:
cotton, flax
H. 90 cm; w. 140 cm
Inventory no. XII/8993; acquired 1929 from
Irmgard Ritter-Kauermann, Heidelberg

105 | SCARF, 1928

Agnes Pechuel-Lösche
Germany
Batik
Warp: silk; weft: silk
L. 190 cm; w. 93 cm
Inventory no. XXX/8606; acquired 1928 from
Agnes Pechuel-Lösche, Cologne

106 | SCARF, 1927

Else Fischer
Germany
Stencil spray printing
Warp: tussah silk; weft: tussah silk
L. 198 cm; w. 38 cm
Inventory no. XVII/8273; acquired 1927 from
the Schlesischer Ausstellungsverein Breslau

107 | SCARF, 1927

Edith Schwirzell
Germany
Stencil spray printing
Warp: cotton; weft: cotton
L. 200 cm; w. 60 cm
Inventory no. XVII/8274; acquired 1927 from
the Schlesischer Ausstellungsverein Breslau

108 | DECORATIVE FABRIC, 1929

Switzerland
Stencil spray printing
Warp: cotton; weft: cotton
H. 135 cm; w. 106 cm
Pattern repeat: h. 62 cm; w. 45 cm
Inventory no. XVII/8724; acquired 1929 from
G. H. Schrödter, Leipzig

109 | PRINTED FABRIC "PAN", 1919

Dagobert Peche (1887–1923)
Wiener Werkstätte, Vienna
Block print, Design no. 709
Manufacture: A. Clavel & F. Lindenmeyer, Basel
Warp: silk; weft: silk
H. 99 cm; w. 93 cm
Pattern repeat: h. 44 cm; w. 46.5 cm
Inventory no. XVII/8028; acquired 1926 from
the Wiener Werkstätte

Peche's penchant for the decorative is expressed
in characteristic fashion in his famous silk fabric
"Pan." Designed as early as 1919, it saw many
uses and was sold over a long period of time, as
can be seen by the year it was acquired for this
collection. The sophisticated colours of the ombré pattern are complemented by lancet-shaped
flowering tendrils to the left and right. Peche
adopted the running stripes of the so-called "iris
prints" motif made popular in the Biedermeier
period for his ombré fabrics, displaying them in
numerous variations. This system of gradually
shaded stripes became the artist's *leitmotiv*.

Lit.:
Textilien der Wiener Werkstätte, Städtische Kunst-
sammlungen Chemnitz, Bestandskatalog der
Textil- und Kunstgewerbesammlung, edited by
S. Anna (Stuttgart: DACO Verlag, 1994), fig. p.
68.

110 | UPHOLSTERY FABRIC "TULIPS", (warp tapestry), 1926

Dagobert Peche (1887–1923)
Wiener Werkstätte, Vienna
Manufacture: W. Vogel, Chemnitz,
Design no. 9627
Warp: cotton; weft: cotton
H. 99 cm; w. 125 cm
Pattern repeat: h. 59.2 cm; w. 62 cm
Inventory no. III/8031; acquired 1926 from the
Wiener Werkstätte

Next to Kolo Moser and Josef Hoffmann,
Dagobert Peche was one of the most creative
artists of the Wiener Werkstätte. He worked in
all areas of the applied arts, with special emphasis on furniture, wallpaper, lace, fashion, fabric
patterns, etc.

For the most part, Peche's fabric designs are sophisticated, highly artificial "inventions"; this is
particularly true of the so-called "ombré patterns". Characteristic of the times, "Tulips" is an
example of Peche's beloved, oft-employed om-
bré-effect stripes, which run to the edge. In this
fabric, the effect is achieved not, as usual, in the
printing, but by the stepwise colouring of the
warp. "Tulips" is among the later of the 113
fabric patterns designed by Peche during the relatively short time he belonged to the Wiener
Werkstätte. Although he died in 1923, his characteristic surface patterns and ornamental forms
not only had a lasting influence on the artists
and products of the Wiener Werkstätte, but were
in harmony with trends in international art deco, providing innovative impulses while at the
same time representing a culmination of this development. Peche's preferred motifs include scat-
tered-flower patterns, flower bouquets and leafy
sprigs portrayed in his typical stylized fashion in
which the line plays a particularly strong role.

Lit.:
Textilien der Wiener Werkstätte, Städtische Kunst-
sammlungen Chemnitz, Bestandskatalog der
Textil- und Kunstgewerbesammlung, edited by
S. Anna (Stuttgart: DACO Verlag, 1994), fig. p.
70.

111 | UPHOLSTERY FABRIC (warp tapestry), 1922

Dagobert Peche (1887–1923)
Wiener Werkstätte, Vienna
Manufacture: Wilhelm Vogel, Chemnitz
Warp: cotton; weft: cotton
H. 49 cm; w. 58.5 cm
Pattern repeat: indeterminate
Inventory no. III/98/1; gift of the W. Vogel
Pattern Collection, Chemnitz, 1994

Both "Tulips" and this fabric were made for the
Wiener Werkstätte in Chemnitz by W. Vogel, a
well-known company that had already manufactured the demanding fabrics of the Belgian designer Henry van de Velde. In this connection, it
is intriguing that the Wiener Werkstätte, which
traditionally maintained close ties with the
German market, also had textiles produced in
Germany. This particular fabric pattern by Peche
also exists as wallpaper.

Lit.:
*Das neue Kunsthandwerk in Deutschland und
Österreich: unter Berücksichtigung der Deutschen
Gewerbeschau München 1922,* edited by
Alexander Koch, Darmstadt 1923, fig. p. 182.

112 | PRINTED FABRIC "PARTRIDGE", 1924

Maria Likarz (1893–1971)
Wiener Werkstätte, Vienna
Block print; Design no. 872
Manufacture: G. Ziegler, Vienna; Teltscher
Warp: bourette silk; weft: bourette silk
H. 100 cm; w. 87 cm
Pattern repeat: h. 33 cm; w. 33.5 cm
Mark on the selvage: W W
Inventory no. XIV/7791; acquired 1926 from
the Wiener Werkstätte

Maria Likarz is of special importance as an artist
of the Wiener Werkstätte. Her fabric design "Ireland," a purely abstract pattern from 1910, was
manufactured and sold until 1929, and was
among the most prominent achievements of the
Wiener Werkstätte. "Partridge" is one of the artist's later designs. Her work contains both geometrical patterns and stylized floral elements.

Lit.:
Völker, Angela, *Die Stoffe der Wiener Werkstätte
1910–1932* (Vienna: Christian Brandstätter
Verlag, 1990), p. 278.
Textilien der Wiener Werkstätte, Städtische Kunst-
sammlungen Chemnitz, Bestandskatalog der
Textil- und Kunstgewerbesammlung, edited by
S. Anna (Stuttgart: DACO Verlag, 1994), fig.
p. 74

113 | DRUCKSTOFF «BRINDISI», 1925

Maria Likarz (1893–1971)
Wiener Werkstätte, Vienna
Block print; Design no. 503
Manufacture: G. Ziegler, Vienna
Warp: bourette silk; weft: bourette silk
H. 101 cm; w. 85 cm
Pattern repeat: h. 40.5 cm; w. 22.5 cm
Inventory no. XIV/7790; acquired 1926 from
the Wiener Werkstätte

Maria Likarz designed roughly 200 fabric patterns for the Wiener Werkstätte from 1912 bis
1927. "Brindisi" is an example of Likarz's later
pattern development, demonstrating her creative
confrontation with the abstract tendencies of the
international art scene in the first half of the 20th
century. This fabric pattern exists in nine different colour combinations; the character of the
textile is greatly influenced by the different
colour variations.

Lit.:
Völker, Angela, *Die Stoffe der Wiener Werkstätte
1910–1932* (Vienna: Christian Brandstätter
Verlag, 1990), fig. p. 176.
Textilien der Wiener Werkstätte, Städtische Kunst-
sammlungen Chemnitz, Bestandskatalog der
Textil- und Kunstgewerbesammlung, edited by
S. Anna (Stuttgart: DACO Verlag, 1994),

114 PRINTED FABRIC "TRAMINO", 1925

Felice Rix (1893–1967)
Wiener Werkstätte, Vienna
Block print; Design no. 924
Manufacture: G. Ziegler, Vienna; Teltscher
Warp: silk; weft: silk
H. 140 cm; w. 90 cm
Pattern repeat: indeterminate
Inventory no. XVII/8259; acquired 1927 from
the Wiener Werkstätte

Felice Rix, a pupil of Josef Hoffmann, worked in
the fabrics department of the Wiener Werkstätte
both before and after the First World War. Her
design repertoire runs from the decorative to
highly abstract patterns. "Tramino" and "Poppies" are examples of her fabric designs using primarily stylized plants or plant forms, and showing her predilection for large, eye-catching re-
peats.

Lit.:
Völker, Angela, *Die Stoffe der Wiener Werkstätte
1910–1932* (Vienna: Christian Brandstätter Verlag, 1990), p. 279.
Textilien der Wiener Werkstätte, Städtische Kunstsammlungen Chemnitz, Bestandskatalog der
Textil- und Kunstgewerbesammlung, edited by
S. Anna (Stuttgart: DACO Verlag, 1994), fig.
p. 78.

115 PRINTED FABRIC "POPPIES", 1929

Felice Rix (1893–1967)
Wiener Werkstätte, Vienna
Block print; Design no. 1123
Manufacture: G. Ziegler, Vienna
Warp: silk; weft: silk
H. 101 cm; w. 96.5 cm
Pattern repeat: h. 43.5 cm; w. 48 cm
Mark on the selvage: WW
Inventory no. XVII/9109; acquired 1930 from
the Wiener Werkstätte

More than 100 fabric pattern designs are attributed to Felice Rix, making her one of the most
productive of the artists of the Wiener Werkstätte. "Poppies" is a pattern that typifies both Felice
Rix and her time, using silk as the sole material.
Her designs are not timeless, they have elements
of the modish that correspond to the decorative
concepts of the period. Colour effects, in "Poppies" the interplay of differing shades of grey, are
an important element of the design.

Lit.:
Völker, Angela, *Die Stoffe der Wiener Werkstätte
1910–1932* (Vienna: Christian Brandstätter Verlag, 1990), p. 276.
Textilien der Wiener Werkstätte, Städtische Kunstsammlungen Chemnitz, Bestandskatalog der
Textil- und Kunstgewerbesammlung, edited by
S. Anna (Stuttgart: DACO Verlag, 1994), fig.
p. 80.

**116 PRINTED FABRIC
"OLD ENGLISH SHOP SIGNS", 1927**

Minnie McLeish (1876–1957)
Great Britain
Manufacture: W. Foxton Ltd., London

Warp: cotton; weft: cotton
H. 102 cm; w. 78 cm
Pattern repeat: h. 46 cm; w. = web width
Inventory no. XIV/8075; acquired 1927 from
Richard Zieger, Chemnitz

Lit.:
*The Studio Year book of Decorative Art: a review
of the latest developments in the artistic construction, decoration and furnishing of the house*
(London: The Studio, 1927), fig. p. 167.

117 CHINTZ "PHOENIX", 1918

William Turner
Great Britain
Manufacture: G. P. & J. Baker Ltd., London
Warp: cotton; weft: cotton
H. 149 cm; w. 79 cm
Inventory no. XV/10653; acquired 1939 from
G. A. Skibbe, Berlin

This design was suggested by a Chinese silk
painting from the 16th/17th century that was
acquired by the Victoria & Albert Museum,
London, in 1911 and exhibited there. In 1983
this fabric pattern was reissued by Baker.

Lit.:
From East to West; Textiles from G. P. & J. Baker,
Victoria and Albert Museum, London, 1984,
p. 127.

118 CHINTZ "FEATHERS", 1925

Great Britain
Manufacture: G. P. & J. Baker Ltd., London
Warp: cotton; weft: cotton
H. 65 cm; w. 82 cm
Pattern repeat: h. 37 cm; w. = web width
Inventory no. XIV/10133; acquired 1936 from
Arthur Benrath, Berlin

This example shows the extraordinarily high
quality of the printed fabrics that the G. P. &
J. Baker company was capable of turning out in
the 1920s. In 1976 Baker reintroduced this
fabric pattern in an adaptation by Ann Lynch.

Lit.:
*From East to West; Textiles from G. P. &
J. Baker,* Victoria and Albert Museum, London,
1984, fig. p. 149.

119 PRINTED FABRIC "THE UNICORN", 1926

Great Britain
Manufacture: G. P. & J. Baker Ltd., London
Warp: flax; weft: flax
H. 139 cm; w. 133 cm
Pattern repeat: h. 54 cm; w. = web width
Inventory no. XIV/7964; acquired 1926 from
L. Bernheimer, Munich

This printed fabric was pictured with great frequency in contemporary literature, and was used
until well into the 1940s by numerous architects,
in Germany and Austria as well, for interiors and
room designs. Modelled on old English heraldic
and early medieval motifs, the material represents a typical example of English fabric prints of
the time. Either newly reissued patterns from the

18th and 19th centuries or new creations in the
same spirit, they stand for a type of conservative
British lifestyle that was readily adopted by
European customers.
Fig. A. Linschütz, Vienna: daybed in boudoir, in:
ID, January 1931, p. 34.

Lit.:
*The Studio Year book of Decorative Art: a review
of the latest developments in the artistic construc-
tion, decoration and furnishing of the house*
(London: The Studio, 1927), fig. p. 167.
Figs (fabric pattern on light background): *ID,*
1930, p. 130; *ID,* 1931, p. 34; *ID,* 1932, p. 66;
ID, 1935, p. 280.

120 UPHOLSTERY FABRIC, 1929

Great Britain
Manufacture: A. H. Lee & Sons Ltd.,
Birkenhead
Warp: cotton; weft: cotton, rayon (chenille),
false lamé
H. 67 cm; w. 122 cm
Pattern repeat: h. indeterminate; w. 59 cm
Inventory no. I/8739; acquired 1929 from Julius
Katzenstein

This complex hollow weave is a reproduction of
a typical example of Mortlake tapestry for armchair upholstery from the 2nd half of the 17th
century.

Lit.:
Hunton, W. Gordon, *English Decorative Textiles:
Tapestry and Chintz* (London: John Tiranti &
Comp, 1930), fig. 56.

121 UPHOLSTERY FABRIC (looped pile), 1930

Great Britain
Manufacture: A. Lee & Sons Ltd., Birkenhead
Warp: cotton, wool; weft: cotton
H. 145 cm; w. 133 cm
Pattern repeat: 41 cm; w. 61 cm
Inventory no. VI/9002; acquired 1930 from
Richard Zieger, Chemnitz

The notes for no. 119 also apply to this fabric
pattern.
The upholstery fabric was woven using only
three hues. The pink, blue and yellow hues were
achieved using stencil spray printing, which had
a beneficial effect on the end price.

122 UPHOLSTERY FABRIC (pile carpet), 1930

Great Britain
Manufacture: A. Lee & Sons Ltd., Birkenhead
Warp: cotton; weft: cotton, wool
H. 99 cm; w. 131 cm
Pattern repeat: h. 35 cm; w. 25 cm
Inventory no. V/9003; acquired 1930 from
Richard Zieger, Chemnitz

In this case, too, the colour effects were achieved
with the aid of stencil spray printing.

123 | CHINTZ, around 1930

Great Britain
Manufacture: Ramm Son & Crocker Ltd.,
London
Warp: cotton; weft: cotton
H. 102 cm; w. 133 cm
Pattern repeat: h. 50 cm; w. 31 cm
Mark l. l. MADE IN ENGLAND (stamp);
paper label R.S & C. Ltd.
Inventory no. XV/10361; acquired 1937 from
Hans Henschel, Berlin

This example, something of an exception, plainly shows the international influence of art deco on English textile design as well. Still, the majority of English chintzes from this period continued to be printed using historical models from the 18th and 19th centuries.

124 | PRINTED FABRIC "ROSEBANK", 1934

Great Britain
Manufacture: Turnbull & Stockdale Ltd.,
Ramsbottom
Warp: flax; weft: flax
H. 98 cm; w. 78 cm
Pattern repeat: h. 45 cm; w. = web width
Inventory no. XIV/9728; acquired 1934 from
Turnbull & Stockdale, Ramsbottom

This fabric was acquired in 1934 and depicted under the name "Rosebank" in *Innendekoration* that same year. In an advertisement in a later issue of the same magazine we find the name Rosebank Print Works, offering hand printed linen in the English style. From this ad it is also apparent that Hans Henschel, Berlin, was the sole distributor for Germany.

Lit.:
ID, 1934, fig. p. 71.

125 | PRINTED FABRIC, 1932

Great Britain
Manufacture: Turnbull & Stockdale Ltd.,
Ramsbottom
Warp: flax; weft: flax
H. 154 cm; w. 75 cm
Pattern repeat: h. 45 cm; w. 32 cm
Inventory no. XIV/9627; acquired 1932 from
Turnbull & Stockdale, Ramsbottom

This fabric was acquired in five different colour schemes: 9627a (red background), 9627b (brown background), 9627c (blue background), 9627d (green background) and 9727 (light brown background). The different colours in pattern and background changes the fundamental character of the fabric, giving the impression that one is looking at five different designs.

126 | PRINTED FABRIC, 1928

Great Britain
Warp: flax; weft: flax
H. 197 cm; w. 129 cm
Pattern repeat: h. 126 cm; w. = web width
Inventory no. XIV/9479, acc. to inventory of
English origin; acquired 1932

Like "Unicorn" (no. 119), this fabric was extremely popular and is illustrated in a number of contemporary publications.
Fig. B. Ludwig, Vienna: Living Room, in: *DKuD*, 1928, p. 334

Lit.:
DKuD, 1928, Vol. 62, fig. p. 311 (with light background) and fig. p. 334.
DKuD, 1932, Vol. 70, p. 43 and 45, fig. (with light background).
ID, 1934 Vol. XLV, fig. p. 96, fig. p. 258, fig. p. 267.

127 | UPHOLSTERY FABRIC (weft tapestry), 1925

Great Britain
Warp: cotton; weft: wool
H. 60 cm; w. 142 cm
Pattern repeat: h. 37 cm; w. 70 cm
Inventory no. II/7580, acc. to inventory of
English origin; acquired 1925 from L. Phil.
Schäfer, Cologne

This, too, is a fabric woven on older models to which the red, green, blue and brown hues were applied by means of stencil spray printing.

128 | UPHOLSTERY FABRIC (looped pile), 1927

Great Britain
Warp: cotton, wool; weft: cotton
H. 139 cm; w. 129 cm
Pattern repeat: h. 80 cm; w. 60 cm
Inventory no. VI/8168, acc. to inventory of
English origin; acquired 1927 from F. W.
Weymar, Dresden

Red, green, grey, brown, olive, blue and yellow hues from stencil spray printing.

129 | UPHOLSTERY FABRIC (weft tapestry), 1925

Great Britain
Warp: cotton; weft: cotton, wool
H. 178 cm; w. 140 cm
Pattern repeat: h. 96 cm; w. 69 cm
Inventory no. II/7584, acc. to inventory of
English origin; acquired 1925 from L. Phil.
Schäfer, Cologne

Red, blue and brown hues from stencil spray printing.

130 | UPHOLSTERY FABRIC (weft tapestry), 1927

Great Britain
Warp: cotton; weft: cotton, wool
H. 141 cm; w. 138 cm
Pattern repeat: h. 84 cm; w. = web width
Inventory no. II/8218, acc. to inventory of
English origin; acquired 1927 from L. Phil.
Schäfer, Cologne

Blue, red, pink, green, olive, orange and brown hues from stencil spray printing.

131 | UPHOLSTERY FABRIC (looped pile), 1926

Great Britain
Warp: cotton, wool; weft: cotton
H. 101 cm; w. 69 cm
Pattern repeat: h. 25 cm; w. 25 cm
Inventory no. VI/7996, acc. to inventory of
English origin; acquired 1926 from Richard
Zieger, Chemnitz

Woven in black and light brown. Red, orange, blue, green, olive and brown hues from stencil spray printing.

132 | UPHOLSTERY FABRIC (looped pile), 1926

Great Britain
Warp: cotton, wool; weft: cotton
H. 66 cm; w. 68 cm
Inventory no. VI/7995, acc. to inventory of
English origin; acquired 1926 from Richard
Zieger, Chemnitz

Red, blue, green and yellow hues from stencil spray printing.
On a paper label we find the statement, in English, that this chair upholstery fabric is available both with and without the central motif and without colours. In *Dekorative Kunst* 1927/28 this fabric is illustrated on a chair and stool without the central motif.

Lit.:
DK, Vol. 31, 1927–28, fig. p. 213, without central motif.

133 | UPHOLSTERY FABRIC, 1928

Great Britain
Warp: cotton; weft: wool, cotton
H. 97 cm; w. 144 cm
Pattern repeat: h. 54 cm; w. 70 cm
Inventory no. II/8515, acc. to inventory of
English origin; acquired 1928 from L. Phil.
Schäfer, Cologne

Green, blue, yellow and brown hues from stencil spray printing.

134 | UPHOLSTERY FABRIC, 1926

Great Britain
Warp: cotton; weft: wool
H. 54 cm; w. 143 cm
Pattern repeat: h. 16 cm; w. 23.5 cm
Inventory no. I/7893, acc. to inventory of
English origin; acquired 1926 from L. Ernst,
Düsseldorf

Blue, red, brown, yellow, olive and green hues from stencil spray printing.

135 | UPHOLSTERY FABRIC (looped pile), 1928

Great Britain
Warp: cotton, wool; weft: cotton
H. 98.5 cm; w. 132.5 cm
Pattern repeat: h. 20 cm; w. 31 cm
Inventory no. VI/8514, acc. to inventory of
English origin; acquired 1928 from L. Phil.
Schäfer, Cologne

Red, green, blue, olive and yellow hues from stencil spray printing.

136 | UPHOLSTERY FABRIC, 1930

Great Britain
Manufacture: Gainsborough Silk Weaving Co. Ltd., Sudbury
Warp: cotton; weft: cotton
H. 89 cm; w. 124 cm
Pattern repeat: h. 91.5 cm; w. 19 cm
Inventory no. IX/9026; acquired 1930 from Richard Zieger, Chemnitz

137 | UPHOLSTERY FABRIC, 1931

Great Britain
Manufacture: Donald Brothers Ltd., Dundee
Warp: cotton; weft: rayon, mercerized cotton
H. 96 cm; w. 64.5 cm
Pattern repeat: h. 20cm; w. 12.5 cm
Inventory no. I/9323; acquired 1931 from Lorenzo Rubelli & Figlio, Venice

Lit.:
Die Form, January 1932, no. 1, fig. p. 29.

138 | PRINTED FABRIC, 1926

Great Britain
Warp: cotton; weft: cotton
H. 155 cm; w. 74 cm
Pattern repeat: h. 78 cm; w. = web width
Inventory no. XIV/7956, acc. to inventory of English origin; acquired 1926 from L. Bernheimer, Munich

139 | PRINTED FABRIC, 1926

Great Britain
Warp: cotton; weft: cotton
H. 151 cm; w. 74 cm
Pattern repeat: h. 50 cm; w. = web width
Inventory no. XIV/8022, acc. to inventory of English origin; acquired 1926 from Teppich- und Möbelstoffindustrie Langer & Co.

140 | PRINTED FABRIC, 1926

Great Britain?
Warp: flax; weft: flax
H. 140 cm; w. 124 cm
Pattern repeat: h. 54.5 cm; w. 78 cm
Inventory no. XIV/7902; acquired 1926 from Paul Braeß, Düsseldorf

141 | PRINTED FABRIC, 1926

Great Britain?
Warp: flax; weft: flax
H. 150 cm; w. 132 cm
Pattern repeat: h. 27 cm; w. 25.5 cm
Inventory no. XIV/8018; acquired 1926 from Teppich- und Möbelstoffindustrie Langer & Co.

142 | PRINTED FABRIC, 1926

Great Britain?
Warp: cotton; weft: cotton
H. 141 cm; w. 81 cm

Pattern repeat: h. 38.5 cm; w. 76.5 cm
Mark u. r. and l. r.: S.F.A. (stamped)
Inventory no. XIV/8020; acquired 1926 from Teppich- und Möbelstoffindustrie Langer & Co.

143 | PRINTED FABRIC, 1926

Great Britain?
Warp: cotton; weft: cotton
H. 136 cm; w. 79 cm
Pattern repeat: h. 60 cm; w. = web width
Mark u.l. and l. l.: S.F.A. (stamped)
Inventory no. XIV/8023; acquired 1926 from Teppich- und Möbelstoffindustrie Langer & Co.

144 | PRINTED FABRIC, 1924

Great Britain
Warp: cotton; weft: cotton
H. 153 cm; w. 131 cm
Pattern repeat: h. 62 cm; w. = web width
Mark l. l. and l. r.: FTL (stamped)
Inventory no. XIV/7447; acquired 1924 from L. Bernheimer, Munich

145 | PRINTED FABRIC, 1924

Great Britain?
Warp: cotton; weft: flax
H. 106 cm; w. 90 cm
Pattern repeat: h. 74 cm; w. = web width
Inventory no. XIV/7443; acquired 1924 from L. Bernheimer, Munich

The numerous fabrics printed with chinoiserie allow one to draw conclusions about the popularity of such imaginative motifs. The model for the fabric pattern shown here was the series of etchings called "Chinese Huts" by the French artist J. B. Pillement (1728–1809), which was also used by the artists of the Wiener Werkstätte, foremost among them D. Peche, for their work.

Lit.:
DK, 1923, fig.p. 232.

146 | PRINTED FABRIC, 1926

Great Britain?
Warp: flax; weft: flax
H. 140 cm; w. 125 cm
Pattern repeat: h. 67.5 cm; w. = web width
Inventory no. XIV/8014; acquired 1926 from Teppich- und Möbelstoffindustrie Langer & Co.

147 | UPHOLSTERY FABRIC, 1929

Eric Bagge (born 1890)
France
Manufacture: Lucien Bouix
Warp: rayon; weft: rayon, cotton
H. 136 cm; w. 129 cm
Pattern repeat: h. 62 cm; w. 64 cm
Inventory no. IX/9290; acquired 1931 from Benrath und Bretsch, Berlin

Eric Bagge's fabric patterns consist of geometrical cubistic forms that give the impression of three-dimensional effects. Characteristic of his textiles, all of which were made by Lucien Bouix,

are strong colour contrasts achieved by the weaving process, and a reduction in hue, which emphasizes the plasticity of the forms. The "grainy structure" is typical of his fabric patterns.
Eric Bagge's fabrics are well-documented in the contemporary literature. The example illustrated here was used frequently by architects of widely varying schools.
Fig. Emmerich Révész, Vienna: Bedroom, in: *ID*, 1931, Vol. XLII, p. 285

Lit.:
Art et Décoration, Juillet–Décembre 1929, fig. p. 137.
ID, Vol. XLIV, September 1931, fig. p. 332.
ID, Vol. XLIV, 1933, fig. p. 416/417.
Fanelli, Giovanni and Rosalia, *Il Tessuto Art Déco e Anni Trenta* (Florence: Cantini Edizioni d'Arte, 1986), p. 96.

148 | UPHOLSTERY FABRIC, 1928

France
Warp: cotton; weft: cotton, jute
H. 120 cm; w. 130 cm
Pattern repeat: h. 29 cm; w. 32 cm
Inventory no. IX/8399, acc. to inventory of French origin; acquired 1928 from Gustav Cords, Berlin

The notes on Eric Bagge (no. 147) also apply to this fabric. In this example, the impression of the "spatial" is even stronger. Geometrical and cubistic forms which give the impression of three-dimensional effects by means of the technical interlacing of the weave are frequently encountered in French upholstery fabrics of that time.
Fig. Joubert et Petit, Paris: Fireplace in the living room of the Comte de Mun; in: *ID*, 1932, Vol. XLIII, p. 116

Lit.:
ID, Vol. XLI, 1930, fig.p. 237.
ID, Vol. XLIII, 1932, fig. p. 116.

149 | UPHOLSTERY FABRIC (velour), 1928

France
Manufacture: Paul Rodier, Paris
Warp: cotton; weft: cotton
H. 101 cm; w. 117 cm
Pattern repeat: h. 39 cm; w. 23 cm
Mark on the selvage: RODIER (stamped)
Inventory no. XXIV/8539; acquired 1928 from Richard Rosenberg, Cologne

150 | UPHOLSTERY FABRIC, 1929

France
Manufacture: Paul Rodier, Paris
Warp: cotton; weft: cotton
H. 125 cm; w. 128.5 cm
Pattern repeat: h. 73 cm; w. 63 cm
Mark on the selvage: RODIER (stamped)
Inventory no. IX/9033; acquired 1929 from Benrath und Bretsch, Berlin

151 | UPHOLSTERY FABRIC, 1931

France
Manufacture: Paul Rodier, Paris
Warp: cotton; weft: cotton, rayon
H. 134 cm; w. 142 cm
Pattern repeat: h. 51.5 cm; w. 46.5 cm
Mark on the selvage: RODIER (stamped)
Inventory no. IX/9291; acquired 1931 from
Benrath und Bretsch, Berlin

152 | UPHOLSTERY FABRIC (velour), 1927

France?
Warp: cotton; weft: cotton
H. 99 cm; w. 131 cm
Pattern repeat: h. 32 cm; w. 32 cm
Inventory no. XXIV/8098; acquired 1927 from
Benrath und Bertsch, Berlin

153 | UPHOLSTERY FABRIC, 1929

France
Warp: rayon; weft: cotton
H. 110 cm; w. 130 cm
Pattern repeat: h. 59 cm; w. 61 cm
Inventory no. IX/8858, acc. to inventory by
RODIER; acquired 1929 from Gustav Carl
Lehmann, Cologne

154 | UPHOLSTERY FABRIC, 1928

France
Warp: cotton; weft: cotton
H. 135 cm; w. 122 cm
Pattern repeat: h. 44 cm; w. 24 cm
Inventory no. IX/8542, acc. to inventory of
French origin; acquired 1928 from Richard
Rosenberg, Cologne

155 | UPHOLSTERY FABRIC, 1929

France
Warp: cotton; weft: jute
H. 134 cm; w. 133 cm
Pattern repeat: h. 23 cm; w. 32.5 cm
Inventory no. IX/8685, acc. to inventory of
French origin; acquired 1929 from Friedemann
und Weber, Berlin

The frequent use of jute in certain upholstery
fabrics shows the French preference for exotic
materials (nos. 148, 158).

156 | UPHOLSTERY FABRIC, 1929

France
Warp: cotton; weft: cotton, rayon
H.125 cm; w.126 cm
Pattern repeat: h. 32 cm; w. 31 cm
Inventory no. IX/8677, acc. to inventory of
French origin; acquired 1929 from Riedel und
Rother, Berlin

157 | UPHOLSTERY FABRIC, 1928

France?
Warp: cotton; weft: rayon
H. 124 cm; w. 125 cm
Pattern repeat: h. 38 cm; w. 30.5 cm
Inventory no. I/8640; acquired 1928 from
Richard Zieger, Chemnitz

158 | UPHOLSTERY FABRIC, 1929

France
Warp: cotton; weft: jute
H. 146 cm; w. 130 cm
Pattern repeat: h. 64 cm; w. 64 cm
Inventory no. I/8695, acc. to inventory of
French origin; acquired 1929 from Benrath und
Bretsch, Berlin

159 | UPHOLSTERY FABRIC, 1930

France
Warp: cotton; weft: mercerized cotton
H. 132 cm; w. 127.5 cm
Pattern repeat: h. 16 cm; w. 31 cm
Inventory no. I/9188, acc. to inventory of
French origin; acquired 1930 from Hans
Henschel, Berlin

**160 | UPHOLSTERY FABRIC
(brocade velour), 1932**

France
Warp: cotton, rayon, flax; weft: cotton, false
lamé
H. 136 cm; w. 134.5 cm
Pattern repeat: h. 64 cm; w. 65 cm
Inventory no. XXIV/9621, acc. to inventory of
French origin; acquired 1932 from Hugo
Schubert, Berlin

Stencil spray printing was used to apply the
green, yellow, pink and violet hues to this very
opulent fabric pattern with its geometrical and
abstract elements and the "grainy structure" already noted in the work of Eric Bagge (no. 147).
It is interesting to note the similarities with the
"brocade velour" from the F. A. Breuhaus studio
(no. 34) of the Vereinigte Werkstätten in
Munich. These two fabrics are the only ones of
their kind in the collection, and the selvage of
both is virtually identical. This permits the conclusion that the Vereinigte Werkstätten in
Munich also sold French upholstery fabrics or
else had their fabrics made in French weaving
mills.

161 | UPHOLSTERY FABRIC (terry pile), 1931

France
Warp: cotton, mercerized cotton, flax; weft:
cotton
H. 135 cm; w. 132 cm
Pattern repeat: h. 46 cm; w. 32.5 cm
Inventory no. V/9316, acc. to inventory of
French origin; acquired 1931 from Jules Pensu,
Paris, via Hugo Schubert, Berlin

162 | UPHOLSTERY FABRIC (terry pile), 1930

France
Warp: cotton; weft: cotton
H. 137 cm; w. 130 cm
Pattern repeat: h. 25 cm; w. 64 cm
Inventory no. V/9015, acc. to inventory of
French origin; acquired 1930 from Richard
Zieger, Chemnitz

163 | UPHOLSTERY FABRIC (terry pile), 1930

France
Warp: cotton, rayon; weft: cotton
H. 133 cm; w. 131 cm
Pattern repeat: h. 26.5 cm; w. 64.5 cm
Inventory no. IV/9016, acc. to inventory of
French origin; acquired from Jules Pensu, Paris,
via Richard Zieger, Chemnitz

164 | UPHOLSTERY FABRIC (terry pile), 1928

France
Warp: cotton; weft: cotton, flax
H. 133 cm; w. 129 cm
Pattern repeat: h. 41 cm; w. 42 cm
Inventory no. V/8503, acc. to inventory of
French origin; acquired 1928 from Richard
Zieger, Chemnitz

165 | UPHOLSTERY FABRIC (pile carpet), 1929

France
Warp: cotton, mercerized cotton, rayon; weft:
cotton
H. 140 cm; w. 130 cm
Pattern repeat: h. 46 cm; w. 32 cm
Inventory no. XXIV/8887, acc. to inventory of
French origin; acquired 1929 from Pepperhoff
und Rosenthal, Essen

166 | UPHOLSTERY FABRIC (pile carpet), 1930

France
Warp: cotton; weft: cotton
H. 130 cm; w. 131 cm
Pattern repeat: h. 51.5 cm; w. 16 cm
Inventory no. IV/9014, acc. to inventory of
French origin; acquired 1930 from Jules Pensu,
Paris, via Richard Zieger, Chemnitz

167 | UPHOLSTERY FABRIC, 1926

France
Warp: cotton; weft: cotton
H. 137 cm; w. 126 cm
Pattern repeat: h. 92.5 cm; w. 31 cm
Inventory no. IX/7974, acc. to inventory of
French origin; acquired 1926 from Richard
Zieger, Chemnitz

168 | UPHOLSTERY FABRIC, 1924

France
Warp: cotton; weft: cotton
H. 104 cm; w. 128 cm
Pattern repeat: 72.5 cm; w. 63 cm
Inventory no. VII/7527, acc. to inventory of
French origin; acquired 1924 from Richard
Zieger, Chemnitz

Aside from the fabric patterns inspired by contemporary abstract art, there were always fabrics
that used historical styles as their models. This
example shows one such adaptation of a Renaissance pattern.

169 | WALL FABRIC, 1928

France
Warp: cotton; weft: jute
H. 134 cm; w. 64 cm
Pattern repeat: h. 69.5 cm; w. 64 cm
Inventory no. I/8544, acc. to inventory of
French origin; acquired 1928 from Richard
Rosenberg, Cologne

170 | DECORATIVE FABRIC, 1927

France
Warp: silk; weft: rayon, silk
H. 95 cm; w. 85 cm
Pattern repeat: h. 75 cm; w. 28 cm
Inventory no. LIII/8137; acquired 1927

171 | DECORATIVE FABRIC, 1927

France?
Warp: silk, false lamé; weft: silk, wool
H. 99 cm; w. 92 cm
Pattern repeat: h. 39 cm; w. 30.5 cm
Inventory no. LIII/8130; acquired 1927

For its character and overall impression, this
printed fabric depends on the use of false lamé as
warp material for the ribbing (printing background).

172 | DECORATIVE FABRIC, 1926

France?
Warp: silk; weft: silk, false lamé
H. 98.5 cm; w. 89 cm
Pattern repeat: h. 86 cm; w. 29 cm
Inventory no. LIII/7772; acquired 1926 from
Benrath und Bertsch

This fabric, acc. to the inventory a lamé, could
conceivably also be used as a dress material. It is
one of the few examples of an oval field being
woven in with the aid of the broché technique
(cf. no. 181).

173 | BROCADE, 1929

France
Warp: silk; weft: rayon, false lamé
H. 98.5 cm; w. 88.5 cm
Pattern repeat: h. 34 cm; w. 29 cm
Inventory no. XXXIII/9239, acc. to inventory of
French origin; acquired 1929 from G. Cords,
Essen

Unlike the majority of fabrics illustrated here,
this is not an upholstery fabric; rather this brocade is one of the few examples designated in the
inventory as a dress material.

174 | DECORATIVE FABRIC, 1925

France?
Warp: silk; weft: silk, false lamé
H. 51 cm; w. 89 cm
Pattern repeat: h. 46.5 cm; w. 29 cm
Inventory no. LIII/7666; acquired 1925 from
Eduard Schott, Frankfurt/Main.

Recalling the influence of the Wiener Werkstätte
on French fabric patterns and fashions, the peculiarity of this example is the combination of
printing and weaving in creating the pattern, i.e.
the smaller silver flowers are woven, the larger
red ones are printed, both of them forming the
pattern.

175 | PRINTED FABRIC, 1926

Mariano Fortuny (1871–1949)
Italy
Manufacture: Società Anonima Fortuny
Warp: cotton; weft: cotton
H. 136.5 cm; w. 131 cm
Pattern repeat: h. 56.5 cm; w. 63 cm
Inventory no. XIV/7966; acquired 1926 from
L. Bernheimer, Munich

Fortuny's printed fabrics are all distinguished by
great technical refinement. Using a printing
technique he developed and in part patented
himself, and which was already surrounding by
an air of mystery during his lifetime, the artist
created unique fabrics and garments. He used
metal stencils to produce his extraordinarily
sumptuous printed fabrics, usually adapted from
old Renaissance patterns. The particular brillian-
ce of his colours was achieved with pigments,
often of silver and gold, applied under pressure.
The fabrics were then retouched by hand.

Lit.:
Marangoni, Guido, *Enciclopedia delle Moderne
Arti Decorative Italiane, V. Le Stoffe D'Arte*
(Milan: Casa Editrice Ceschina, 1928), fig.
48–59.
Osma, Guillermo de, *Fortuny: The Life and Work
of Mariano Fortuny* (New York: Rizzoli
International Publications, 1980).
Fanelli, Giovanni and Rosalia, *Il Tessuto Art Déco
e Anni Trenta* (Florence: Cantini Edizioni d'Arte,
1986), pp. 107, 108.

176 | PRINTED FABRIC, 1926

Mariano Fortuny (1871–1949)
Italy
Manufacture: Società Anonima Fortuny
Warp: cotton; weft: cotton
H. 147.5 cm; w. 110 cm
Pattern repeat: h. 124 cm; w. 53 cm
Inventory no. XIV/7967; acquired 1926 from
L. Bernheimer, Munich

Lit.:
Marangoni, Guido, *Enciclopedia delle Moderne
Arti Decorative Italiane, V. Le Stoffe D'Arte*
(Milan: Casa Editrice Ceschina, 1928), fig.
48–59.
Osma, Guillermo de: *Fortuny: The Life and
Work of Mariano Fortuny* (New York: Rizzoli
International Publications, 1980).
Fanelli, Giovanni and Rosalia, *Il Tessuto Art Déco
e Anni Trenta* (Florence: Cantini Edizioni d'Arte,
1986), pp. 107, 108.

177 | PRINTED FABRIC, 1926

Mariano Fortuny (1871–1949)
Italy
Manufacture: Società Anonima Fortuny
Warp: cotton; weft: cotton
H. 121.5 cm; w. 63 cm
Pattern repeat: h. 36 cm; w. 30 cm
Inventory no. XIV/7968; acquired 1926 from
L. Bernheimer, Munich

Marangoni, Guido, *Enciclopedia delle Moderne
Arti Decorative Italiane, V. Le Stoffe D'Arte*
(Milan: Casa Editrice Ceschina, 1928), fig.
48–59.
Osma, Guillermo de: *Fortuny: The Life and Work
of Mariano Fortuny* (New York: Rizzoli International Publications, 1980).
Fanelli, Giovanni and Rosalia, *Il Tessuto Art Déco
e Anni Trenta* (Florence: Cantini Edizioni d'Arte,
1986), pp. 107, 108.

178 | PRINTED FABRIC, circa 1930

Mariano Fortuny (1871–1949)
Italy
Manufacture: Società Anonima Fortuny
Warp: cotton; weft: cotton
H.161.5 cm; w. 108 cm
Pattern repeat: h. 139 cm; w. 52 cm
Inventory no. XIV/10776; acquired 1941 from
the Münchner Kunsthandelsgesellschaft

Lit.:
Marangoni, Guido, *Enciclopedia delle Moderne
Arti Decorative Italiane, V. Le Stoffe D'Arte*
(Milan: Casa Editrice Ceschina, 1928), fig.
48–59.
Osma, Guillermo de: *Fortuny: The Life and Work
of Mariano Fortuny* (New York: Rizzoli International Publications, 1980).
Fanelli, Giovanni and Rosalia, *Il Tessuto Art Déco
e Anni Trenta* (Florence: Cantini Edizioni d'Arte,
1986), pp. 107, 108.

179 | PRINTED FABRIC, circa 1930

Mariano Fortuny (1871–1949)
Italy
Manufacture: Società Anonima Fortuny
Warp: cotton; weft: cotton
H. 153.5 cm; w. 145.5 cm
Pattern repeat: h. 62 cm; w. 42 cm
Mark on the selvage: SOC. AN. FORTUNY
Inventory no. XIV/10781; acquired 1941 from
the Münchner Kunsthandelsgesellschaft

Here the attraction of Fortuny's creation is intensified still more by the way in which the
fabric was prepared, undergoing dyeing procedu-
res even before the actual printing in order to
give it the desired irregularities in colour. The
photo gives an idea of Fortuny's opulent treat-
ment of textiles.
Fig. Mariano Fortuny: Dining Hall at the Hotel
Excelsior on the Lido, Venice, in: Osma, Guillermo de: Fortuny, Rizzoli Publ., New York, 1988,
p. 151

Lit.: Marangoni, Guido, *Enciclopedia delle
Moderne Arti Decorative Italiane, V. Le Stoffe
D'Arte* (Milan: Casa Editrice Ceschina, 1928),
fig. 48–59.

Osma, Guillermo de: *Fortuny: The Life and Work of Mariano Fortuny* (New York: Rizzoli International Publications, 1980).
Fanelli, Giovanni and Rosalia, *Il Tessuto Art Déco e Anni Trenta* (Florence: Cantini Edizioni d'Arte, 1986), pp. 107, 108.

180 | DECORATIVE FABRIC, around 1924

woven after historical Persian silk fabric
of the Safawids (1501–1722)
Italy
Manufacture: Vittorio Ferrari, Milan
Warp: cotton; weft: silk
H. 48.5 cm; w. 62 cm
Pattern repeat: h. 25 cm; w. 15 cm
Inventory no. XXXIII/7460; acquired 1924
from L. Bernheimer, Munich

This fabric is included here as an example of the numerous woven recreations of historical textiles that were the speciality of the Milanese company Vittorio Ferrari. The encyclopaedia referenced below contains no less than 24 such recreations by this company of antique fabrics and textiles from the Renaissance and the Baroque, among them the one pictured here. Such fabrics were highly prized and widely sold in the 1920s and 1930s, being used again and again in contemporary interiors. For instance, in a 1912 fireplace design by F. A. Breuhaus, the fabric is found framed as a picture over the fireplace (ID, 1912, p. 259, fig.). The depiction on the silk fabric used as its literary model a tale from the Iranian epic Shahname, known thematically as The Prisoner. The latter is led, always on foot, by a warrior holding him by a cord.

Lit.:
Marangoni, Guido, *Enciclopedia delle Moderne Arti Decorative Italiane, V. Le Stoffe D'Arte* (Milan: Casa Editrice Ceschina, 1928), fig. 18.
Ackermann, Phyllis, "Persische Textilien," in: *Ciba-Rundschau 112*, Basel, December 1953, fig. p. 4129.
Neumann, Reingard, and Murza, Gerhard: *Persische Seiden* (Leipzig: E. A. Seemann Verlag, 1988).

181 | UPHOLSTERY FABRIC, 1931

Italy?
Warp: cotton; weft: cotton, wool
H. 98 cm; w. 130 cm
Pattern repeat: h. 56.5 cm; w. 32 cm
Inventory no. I/9322; acquired 1931 from
Lorenzo Rubelli e Figlio, Venice

Showing the influence of art deco, this chinoiserie pattern was woven using the broché technique, i.e. the pattern weft follows the pattern, reaching back and forth only within the figure itself and not, as does lance filling, running across the entire width of the cloth. Fabrics produced on broché weaving machines look as if they were embroidered; so, too, in the present example, figure and background are clearly separate from one another, giving the impression of embroidery.

182 | UPHOLSTERY FABRIC (silk velour), 1930

Italy
Warp: silk; weft: silk, cotton, false lamé
H. 61 cm; w. 61 cm
Pattern repeat: h. 30.5 cm; w. 29 cm
Inventory no. XXIV/9045, acc. to inventory of Italian origin; acquired 1930 from Hans Henschel, Berlin

183 | UPHOLSTERY FABRIC, 1932

Italy
Manufacture: Lorenzo Rubelli e Figlio, Venice
Warp: cotton; weft: cotton
H. 120 cm; w. 124 cm
Pattern repeat: h. 32.5 cm; w. 30.5 cm
Inventory no. I/9619; acquired 1932 from
H. Schubert, Berlin

184 | UPHOLSTERY FABRIC, 1932

Italy
Manufacture: Lorenzo Rubelli e Figlio, Venice
Warp: cotton; weft: cotton (chenille)
H. 132.5 cm; w. 120.5 cm
Pattern repeat: h. 51 cm; w. 30 cm
Inventory no. V/9618; acquired 1932 from
H. Schubert, Berlin

185 | PRINTED FABRIC (chiné), 1931

Netherlands
Warp: cotton; weft: cotton
H. 136 cm; w. 118 cm
Pattern repeat: h. 38 cm; w. 62 cm
Inventory no. XIV/9337, acc. to inventory of Dutch origin; acquired 1931 from Richard Zieger, Chemnitz

This fabric, called "chiné," is also known as warp printing, because the pattern is printed on the warp threads before the weft threads are woven in. As a result, there is no clear contour to the pattern, which appears slightly "runny." Such mechanically produced European warp prints were suggested and influenced by the ikats from Indonesia. Starting from Holland, the former colonial power in Indonesia, they became known and gradually spread throughout Europe. That is how the collection came to include chiné fabrics from the 19th century; the example shown here is one of the few having the art deco patterning typical of the times.

Katharina Metz and Liane Sachs

ERNST AUFSEESER

29 May 1880, Nuremberg–12 December 1940, Düsseldorf

Painter, graphic artist, designer, illustrator
Aufseeser was trained and later worked at the Steglitzer Werkstätten; Professor of Applied Art in Düsseldorf from 1919–33; involved in the artistic and architectural design of the Deutsche Gewerbeschau München in 1922; designed textiles for the Rheinische Werkstätten in Bonn und Düsseldorf and for DETEKU in Leipzig (for upholstery fabrics, curtains, wall hangings, embroidered plush materials); also designed wallpaper, ceramics and commercial graphics.
Lit.:
TKI, 1921, No. 6, pp. 145–155.
Deutsche Gewerbeschau München 1922
(Munich: Knorr & Hirth, 1922), p. 20.
Saur, Vol. 5, p. 625.

ERIC BAGGE

Born in Anthony/Seine on 10 September 1890
Architect, interior designer, commercial artist
After completing his training in art in Paris, Bagge received an appointment as an instructor for Architecture at the Ecole des Arts Décoratifs in Paris. He designed several exhibition halls for the 1925 Exposition Internationale des Arts Décoratifs et Industriels Modernes in Paris. Around 1925 he created a number of designs using Cubist geometric forms for textiles produced by Lucien Bouix. Besides interior furnishings and furniture, he also designed carpets, wallpaper and glass windows. Eric Bagge worked for Mercier Frères as a decorator in the late 1920s.
Lit.:
Saur, Vol. 6, p. 273.
Fanelli, Giovanni and Rosalia, *Il Tessuto Art Déco e Anni Trenta* (Florence: Cantini, 1986), pp. 96, 97.
Schoeser, Mary, and Dejardin, Kathleen, *French Textiles from 1760 to the Present* (London: Laurence King Ltd., 1991), p. 174.

OTTI BERGER

4 October 1898, Zmajavac, Baranja–killed in a concentration camp in 1944/45
Textile artist
Studies at the Academy of Arts in Zagreb, 1921–26; studies under Gunta Stölzl at the weaving workshop, Bauhaus Dessau from 1927–30; semester abroad in Sweden, 1929; passed her journeyman's examination and received her diploma from the Bauhaus in 1930. Otti Berger served as art director at the Fischer and Hoffmann curtain factory in Zwickau until 1931. She was director of the Bauhaus weaving department in Dessau from October 1931–August 1932, after which she established her own studio and experimental workshop in Berlin; completed a curtain material collection for the Dutch de ploeg company of Bergeyk in 1935, before moving to England, where she designed fabrics for the Helios company (Barlow and Jones) in Bolton. Otti Berger returned to Yugoslavia in 1939.

Lit.:
Gunta Stölzl: Weberei am Bauhaus und aus eigener Werkstatt, edited by Magdalena Droste for the Bauhaus-Archiv (Berlin: Kupfergraben, 1987), p. 145.

FRITZ AUGUST BREUHAUS DE GROOT

9 February 1883, Solingen–2 December 1960, Cologne
Architect, interior designer, commercial arts designer, university professor
Studies at the Baugewerbeschule Wuppertal, the Kunstgewerbeschule Düsseldorf under Peter Behrens and the Technische Hochschulen Stuttgart and Darmstadt; architect's offices in Cologne, 1920–27, Düsseldorf, 1922–27 and Berlin from 1932. De Groot was appointed professor in Munich in 1928. He designed a collection of "F. A. B." fabrics for the Vereinigte Werkstätten during the 1920s, a collection of "F. A. B." wallpapers for the Rheinische Tapetenfabrik Beuel am Rhein and "F. A. B." carpets for the Gebrüder Schoeller Teppichfabrik, Düren. De Groot carried out commissions for country houses, mansions, banks, industrial and residential buildings and ocean liner decoration and furnishings. He worked as a freelance interior designer for the Deutsche Werkstätten Hellerau beginning in the early 1930s and joined the permanent staff of the Deutsche Werkstätten in 1936. During this period he also created designs for the Verband für Wohnungskunst.
Lit.:
Originalentwürfe von Fritz August Breuhaus (catalogue), n.d.
Saur, Vol. 14, p. 174.

RUTH CONSEMÜLLER (née Hollós)

3 August 1904, Lissa/Posen–25 April 1993, Cologne
Trained at the academy of applied arts; studies at the Bauhaus in Weimar and Dessau, 1924–28; journeyman's examination in Glauchau, 1927; Bauhaus certificate, 1928; Bauhaus diploma, 1930; Ruth Consemüller became director of the weaving workshop operated by the Verein für volkstümlich Heimarbeit in Ostpreussen in Königsberg; married the Bauhaus student Erich Consemüller; returned to designs in the Gobelin style after World War II.
Lit.:
Gunta Stölzl: Weberei am Bauhaus und aus eigener Werkstatt, edited by Magdalena Droste for the Bauhaus-Archiv (Berlin: Kupfergraben, 1987), p. 147.

E. ENGELBRECHT

Dates of birth and death unknown
Designer of woven and printed fabrics
Engelbrecht worked for the Vereinigte Werkstätten during the 1920s.
Lit.:
DK, 1928, Vol. XXXVI, p. 287.
DKuD, April–September 1928, Vol. LXII, p. 177.

MARIANO FORTUNY Y MADRAZO

1871, Granada–2 May 1949, Venice
Painter, textile artist, stage designer
Son of the painter Mariano Fortuny y Carbó (1838–1874); took instruction in drawing in Paris following his father's death. A self-taught artist, he copied paintings by Tiepolo, Rubens, Titian and others; assisted in significant restoration projects in Venice. Fortuny y Madrazo painted portraits, still lifes, landscapes and floral compositions. He moved to the Palazzo Martinengo, San Gregorio, in Venice in 1889; traveled to Bayreuth to the Wagner Festival in 1892 and did illustrations on Wagnerian themes during the following years; moved into the Palazzo Pesaro Orfei in 1899. He continued to do theater work: indirect lighting (patent 1901), an indirect lighting system (patent 1903), round horizon (patent 1904); experimented with textile prints beginning in 1907, producing his first model creations of printed silks and velvet fabrics. Fortuny y Madrazo was not a couturier but rather a designer of prototypes in many variations; received a patent for his plissée process and for multi-colored textile printing using metal templates in 1909 and later expanded into large-scale industrial production. Unique features included the use of powdered dyes extracted from plants and herbs, the application of gold and silver pigments using a process of his own design and retouching after printing. He expanded the small workshops in Palazzo Orfei and founded "Società Anonima Fortuny" in 1919; launched production on the island of Guidecca in 1922. He began working with Egyptian cotton and experimenting with linen, cotton-velvet and raw silk. His works were sold in Italy and in Madrid, Zurich, London and New York (also A. H. Lee & Sons Inc.). Fortuny y Madrazo began decorating rooms with massive curtains suspended from ceiling rails in 1920; designed the Spanish pavilion at the Venice Biennale in the years 1922 to 1940; commissions for stage designs, theater costumes and church vestments during those years; appointed a member of the Royal Academy of San Fernando in Madrid in 1947.
Lit.:
Osma, Guillermo de, *Fortuny: The Life and work of Mariano Fortuny* (New York: Rizzoli, 1980).

RUTH HILDEGARD GEYER-RAACK

16 June 1894, Nordhausen/Harz–19 March 1975, Berlin
Interior designer and mural painter, designer
Studies at the Vereinigte Staatsschulen für freie und angewandte Kunst in Berlin under Bruno Paul; periods of study in France; Hildegard Geyer-Raack participated in the exhibition "Bayrisches Kunsthandwerk" in Munich in 1925; created fabric designs for the Bayerische Textilwerke Bernhard Nepker of Tutzing. Co-operated with Bruno Paul in the reconstruction of the Richmodi-Haus of the Deutsche Werkstätten in Cologne in 1926. In 1931 she served as curator of the Internationale Raumausstellung in Cologne. She created textile designs for the Deutsche Werkstätten during the 1920s; did wallpaper designs for the Strauven company of Bonn; worked as an interior designer during the 1930s.

Lit.:
DKuD, September 1925, p. 284.
DKuD, October 1933, pp. 4–7.
Vollmer, Hans (ed.), *Allgemeines Lexikon der Bildenden Künstler des 20. Jahrhunderts* (Leipzig: Seemann), Vol. 2, p. 235.
Wichmann, Hans (ed.), *Deutsche Werkstätten und WK-Verband: 1898–1990; Aufbruch zum Neuen Wohnen,* issued by the WK-Institut für Wohnkultur (Munich: Prestel, 1992), p. 323.
Wichmann, Hans (ed.), *Von Morris bis Memphis: Textilien der Neuen Sammlung; Ende 19. bis Ende 20. Jahrhundert* (Basel, Boston, Berlin: Birkhäuser, 1990); *(collection catalogue* Neue Sammlung, Vol. 3), p. 442.

WENZEL HABLIK

4 August 1881, Brüx (now Most/Czechia)–23 March 1934, Itzehoe
Painter, textile artist
Studied at the Fachschule für Tonindustrie und verwandte Gewerbe in Teplitz-Schönau from 1898 to 1902; further studies at the Kunstgewerbeschule Wien under F. v. Myrbach and others in 1902–03; created first textile pattern designs in 1904. Returning to the Kunstgewerbeschule Wien to study under C. O. Czeschka in 1905, he went on to study at the Academy of Art in Prague. Hablik worked as an artist at the hand-weaving workshop of Elisabeth Lindemann in Meldorf after 1907. Aside from works of graphic art, he also created embroidery patterns and designs for fabrics and draperies. He married Elisabeth Lindemann in 1917; continued producing prints, paintings, costumes, interior designs, textile patterns for decorative fabrics, tablecloths, pillows, draperies, carpets, runners, designs for living-room and bedroom furniture with upholstery fabrics. He exhibited works in metal at the Fall Exposition at the Grassi-Museum Leipzig in 1928; was represented in Leipzig again in 1932 with jewelry and silverware. He suffered from an eye disorder in 1931. Wenzel Hablik memorial exhibitions were held at Grassi-Museum in Leipzig and in the Textil- und Kunstgewerbesammlung in Chemnitz.
Lit.:
Fuchs-Belhamri, Elisabeth, *Wenzel Hablik; Textilkunst und Mode* (Heide, Boyens & Co., 1993).

JOSEF HILLERBRAND

2 August 1892, Bad Tölz–26 November 1981, Munich
Painter, architect, designer, university professor
Following his apprenticeship as a painter, Hillerbrand enrolled at the Kunstgewerbeschule München in 1908; appointed professor and instructor of a class in applied painting at Kunstgewerbeschule München in 1922. He was a professor at the Staatsschule für angewandte Kunst and the Akademie der Bildenden Künste from 1946 until his retirement in 1960; did freelance work in art for the Deutsche Werkstätten as one of the institution's most important contributors, providing numerous designs for textiles (printed fabrics and carpets, for example), glass, wallpaper, metal, ceramics, furniture and lamps.
Lit.:
DKuD, October 1929–March 1930, pp. 63–69.
Arnold, Klaus-Peter, *Vom Sofakissen zum Städtebau; Die Geschichte der deutschen Werkstätten und der Gartenstadt Hellerau* (Dresden, Basel: Verlag der Kunst, 1993), p. 418.
Wichmann, Hans (ed.), *Deutsche Werkstätten und WK-Verband: 1898–1990; Aufbruch zum Neuen Wohnen,* issued by the WK-Institut für Wohnkultur (Munich: Prestel, 1992), p. 326.

VALERIE JORUD

Dates of birth and death unknown
Textile artist
Valerie Jorud exhibited cloths and draperies at the spring and fall Grassi expositions in 1935. She worked at her studio in Berlin-Friedenau, Wilhelmstr. 16.
Lit.:
Ausstellerverzeichnis der Messeausstellungen 1935 (Leipzig: Grassi-Museum).

ERICH KLEINHEMPEL

9 January 1874, Leipzig–2 September 1947, Erbach/Westerwald
Architect, painter, commercial arts designer
Studied at the Kunstgewerbeschule Dresden, 1890–93; joined the staff of the Dresdner Werkstätten für Handwerkskunst in about 1899. Kleinhempel and his siblings Fritz and Gertrud founded a private school in 1900 or shortly after. He taught in the girls' section at Kunstgewerbeschule Dresden from 1906 to 1912; appointed director of the Bremen Kunstgewerbemuseum and its school in 1912. Kleinhempel was a designer of furniture, wallpaper, fabrics, carpets, book endpapers, porcelain, metal goods and toys. He served as art director and designer for DETEKU of Leipzig and other firms in the state of Sachsen.
Lit.:
Arnold, Klaus-Peter, *Vom Sofakissen zum Städtebau; Die Geschichte der deutschen Werkstätten und der Gartenstadt Hellerau* (Dresden, Basel: Verlag der Kunst, 1993), p. 420.
Wichmann, Hans (ed.), *Deutsche Werkstätten und WK-Verband: 1898–1990; Aufbruch zum Neuen Wohnen,* issued by WK-Institut für Wohnkultur (Munich: Prestel, 1992), p. 329.

HERTHA KOCH

Dates of birth and death unknown
Textile designer
Hertha Koch created textile designs for the Deutsche Textile Kunst, Kießling, Hiemann & Dippmann, Leipzig. In the article "Neue Stoffe für Raumkunst," printed in the journal Dekorative Kunst in 1917, we read [in translation]: "… its designer, Hertha Koch, is a talented artist who brings great freshness to the field of surface decoration."
Lit.:
E. H., "Neue Stoffe für Raumkunst" in: *DK,* 1917, Vol. XXV, p. 329.

BENITA KOCH-OTTE

23 May 1892, Stuttgart–26 April 1976, Bethel
Textile artist
Benita Koch-Otte attended a seminar for teachers of drawing in Düsseldorf from 1911 to 1913 and passed the state examination; state examination for handicrafts teachers at the Lettehaus in Berlin in 1915; studied at the Bauhaus in Weimar from 1920–25 and later joined the staff there; taught in Uerdingen from 1915 to 1920. She attended a course at the Färbereifachschule in Krefeld in 1922; course in bindings and materials at the Seidenwebschule in Krefeld in 1924; worked as a teacher and art director at the Werkstatt für Handweberei at the Werkstätten der Stadt Halle – Staatlich städtische Kunstgewerbeschule Burg Giebichenstein from 1925 to 1933. Benite Koch-Otte was relieved of teaching duties in 1933 and moved to Prague soon afterwards. She was director of the Bodel-schwingsche Anstalten in Bethel from 1934 until her retirement in 1957.
Lit.:
Gunta Stölzl: Weberei am Bauhaus und aus eigener Werkstatt, edited by Magdalena Droste for the Bauhaus-Archiv (Berlin: Kupfergraben, 1987), pp. 155–156.
Burg Giebichenstein; Die hallesche Kunstschule von den Anfängen bis zur Gegenwart, issued by Staatliche Galerie Moritzburg Halle, Badisches Landesmuseum Karlsruhe and Burg Giebichenstein – Hochschule für Kunst und Design Halle (Halle, 1993), p. 523.

PAL (PAUL) LÁSZLÓ

Born in Debrecen on 6 February 1900
Architect and designer
Trained in Stuttgart and in Berlin architects' offices until 1923, László won prizes in several German architectural competitions; designed mansions in Prague, Bucharest, Steinamanger (Szombathely), Stuttgart and at the Vierwaldstätter See. He worked as a designer of furniture and decorative fabrics for the Vereinigte Werkstätte beginning in the late 1920s; art director for the Stuttgart furniture producer Alfred Bühler AG during the early 1930s. Pal László emigrated to the U.S., where he was active as an architect and designer, primarily in California, till the 1960s.
Lit.:
Thieme, Ulrich, and Becker, Felix (eds.), *Allgemeines Lexikon der Bildenden Künstler* (Leipzig: Seemann, 1908–1950), Vol. 22, p. 416.
Hans Vollmer (ed.), *Allgemeines Lexikon der Bildenden Künstler des 20. Jahrhunderts* (Leipzig: Seemann, 1953–1962), Vol. 3, p. 180.

MARIA MAY

24 September 1900, Berlin–28 October 1968, Berlin
Designer of textiles, mural painter, instructor
Studied at the Staatliche Kunstschule Berlin under Bruno Paul; worked as an instructor at the Schule Reimanm in Berlin from 1922; there she worked as director for the textile class and was responsible for the development of courses in design and decorative painting; gave instruction in fabric dying, printing, spray printing, batik, painting and template printing on cloth and leather within the context of her association with the IG-Farben-Industrie. Maria May was appointed "Studienrätin" (senior instructor). She designed the "May-Stoffe" collection for the Vereinigte Werkstätten; exhibited at the Grassi-Museum in Leipzig in 1928; from 1930 she also worked for other firms, including Christian Dierig A.G. of Langenbielau, for whom she designed the collection "Deutsche Kretonne."
Lit.:
DKuD, October 1933, pp. 16–20.
Farbe und Form: Monatsschrift für Kunst und Kunstgewerbe (Berlin: Verlag Schule Reimann, 1916–34).
Wichmann, Hans (ed.), *Von Morris bis Memphis: Textilien der Neuen Sammlung; Ende 19. bis Ende 20. Jahrhundert* (Basel, Boston, Berlin: Birkhäuser, 1990); *(collection catalogue* Neue Sammlung, Vol. 3), p. 446.

MINNIE MCLEISH

1876–1957
Textile designer
Minnie McLeish worked as a freelance artist for a number of companies during the 1920s, creating numerous textile designs for W. Foxton Ltd., London, in particular. Typical of her designs are multi-colored print patterns.
Lit.:
Mendes, Valerie, *The Victoria & Albert Museum's Textile Collection; British Textiles from 1900 to 1937* (London: Victoria & Albert Museum, 1992), p. 91.

WILHELM MARSMANN

19 June 1896, Prusdorf/Pommerania–16 September 1966, Munich
Designer of wood inlays, textiles
Studied architecture in Munich as a student of Richard Riemerschmid; freelance work included wood inlay pieces for the Deutsche Werkstätten. Marsmann taught at the Kerschensteiner Meisterschule für Schreiner in Munich. In 1925 he founded the Deutsche Farbmöbel AG München together with Victor von Rauch and others.
Lit.:
Wichmann, Hans (ed.), *Deutsche Werkstätten und WK-Verband: 1898–1990; Aufbruch zum Neuen Wohnen,* issued by the WK-Institut für Wohnkultur (Munich: Prestel, 1992) p. 334.

ELSE MÖGELIN

Textile artist, instructor
20 April 1887, Berlin–31 December 1982, Kiel
Else Mögelin completed the examination in art education in Berlin in 1906; studied at the Kunstgewerbeschule Berlin/Charlottenburg under Professor Mohrbutter until 1919; studies at the Bauhaus Weimar from 1919 to 1923, where she received training in pottery and weaving under Helene Börner. She established and expanded her own weaving workshop in Gildenhall/Neuruppin from 1923 to 1927; produced numerous "woven pictures" using the Gobelin technique; exhibited at the "Ausstellung moderner Bildwirkereien 1930," which was also presented in the Textil- und Kunstgewerbesammlung Chemnitz. Mögelin served as department director for the textiles class at the Meisterschule für gestaltendes Handwerk (school for arts and crafts) in Stettin from 1927 to 1945. She completed her journeyman's examination in 1930, her master craftsman's exam in 1931. Declared a "degenerate" artist, she found only limited opportunities for work after 1933. Mögelin was appointed to the staff of the Hochschule für bildende Künste Hamburg in 1945 and directed the activities of the weaving department until her retirement in 1952. She carried out numerous commissions for public buildings, churches and museums and was a member of the Deutscher Werkbund.
Lit.:
Gunta Stölzl: Weberei am Bauhaus und aus eigener Werkstatt, edited by Magdalena Droste for the Bauhaus-Archiv (Berlin: Kupfergraben, 1987), p. 159.
Kircher, Ursula, *Von Hand gewebt; Eine Entwicklungsgeschichte der Handweberei im 20. Jahrhundert* (Marburg: Hitzeroth, 1986), pp. 129, 132.

BRUNO PAUL

19 January 1874, Seifhennersdorf–17 August 1968, Berlin
Painter, graphic artist, architect, interior and furniture designer, university professor
Studied at the Akademie der Künste Dresden, 1892–94; practical training in an architect's office; took up studies at the Akademie der Schönen Künste München in 1894; attended lectures in architecture; did drawings for the journal Jugend; contributed to Simplicissimus.
In 1898 Paul established contacts with the group associated with R. Riemerschmid, B. Pankok, K. Bertsch and F. A. O. Krüger and thus with the Vereinigte Werkstätten für Kunst im Handwerk. In 1904 he was awarded the Grand Prix at the World Fair in St. Louis for his "workroom." He played a dominant role at the Vereinigte Werkstätten from 1904 to 1910, was appointed director of the Kunstgewerbeschule Berlin and became a founding member of the Deutscher Werkbund in 1907. His association with the Deutsche Werkstätten began in 1909, where he worked as a permanent staff member from 1919 to 1928, receiving a new contract providing a guaranteed salary in 1931. Bruno Paul was a member of the Board of Supervisors of the Deutsche Werkstätten. He carried out architectural commissions in both the private and the public sectors. He was admitted to the Preußische Akademie der Künste in 1919. His program for art-school reform led to the merger of several schools to form Vereinigte Staatsschulen für freie und angewandte Kunst in 1924, where he held the post of director from 1924 to 1932. Served as art director for the Polytex-Textilgesellschaft mbH Berlin. He was expelled from the Akademie der Künste in 1937. Worked as an industrial architect in Höxter (from 1949) and Düsseldorf (from 1951) before returning to Berlin in 1957.
Lit.:
Ziffer, Alfred (ed.), *Bruno Paul: Deutsche Raumkunst und Architektur zwischen Jugendstil und Moderne* (Munich: Klinkhardt & Biermann, 1992), pp. 9–15.

DAGOBERT PECHE

3 April 1887, St. Michael im Lungau/Salzburg–16 April 1923, Mödling near Vienna
Architect, painter, designer
Studied architecture at the Technische Hochschule Wien under Karl König, Max von Ferstel and Leopold Simony from 1906 to 1910 and under Friedrich Ohmann at the Akademie für Bildende Künste Wien from 1908 to 1911. In 1911 he received the "Rompreis" and began working with the fabrics department at the Wiener Werkstätte. He joined the Wiener Werkstätte in 1915 and came to influence the "WW Style" through his work. In 1917 he established the WW branch in Zurich and served as its director; returned to Vienna in 1919; participated in the art show at the Museum für Kunst und Industrie in 1920; executed a commission from the carpet producer Flammersheim und Steinmann of Cologne in 1921; served on the artists' committee for German-Austria at the Deutsche Gewerbeschau München in 1922.
Lit.:
Mitteilungen der Deutschen Gewerbeschau München 1922 (Beiblatt der Form, Nr. 5) (Munich: Werbedienst, 1922), p. 11.
Eisler, Max, *Dagobert Peche* (Vienna: Gerlach und Weidling, 1925).
Fahr-Becker, Gabriele, *Wiener Werkstätte 1903–1932* (Cologne: Benedikt Taschen, 1994), p. 232.
Noever, Peter (ed.), *Die Überwindung der Utilität: Dagobert Peche und die Wiener Werkstätte* (Ostfildern: Hatje, 1998).

AGNES PECHUEL-LOESCHE

Painter, batik designer
Dates of birth and death unknown
Represented with works of batik art at the Grassi-Museum expositions until 1938 and in 1942; lived and worked in Cologne-Theilenbruch. Her batiks were shown at exhibitions well into the 1950s.
Lit.:
Ausstellerverzeichnisse der Messeausstellungen, Leipzig, Grassi-Museum.
Kunstchronik, 1956, No. 9, p. 212.

VICTOR VON RAUCH

21 May 1901, St. Petersburg–1 March 1945, Ulm
Painter, textile designer
Victor von Rauch moved to Munich in 1921. Founded the Deutsche Farbmöbel AG with Wilhelm Marsmann in 1925 and served the firm as a textile designer. After a stay in Vienna in 1927/28 he returned to Berlin.
Lit.:
Wichmann, Hans (ed.), *Von Morris bis Memphis: Textilien der Neuen Sammlung; Ende 19. bis Ende 20. Jahrhundert* (Basel, Boston, Berlin: Birkhäuser, 1990); (collection catalogue Neue Sammlung, Vol. 3), p. 448.

IRMGARD RITTER-KAUERMANN

Born on 17 November 1895 in Duisburg
Textile artist
Studied at the Kunstgewerbeschule Nürnberg, 1916–20, and at the Kunstgewerbeschule München from 1920 to 1924, where she received a position as assistant for the textiles class under Else Jaskolla. She taught from 1926 to 1933 at the Städtische Frauen-Arbeitsschule and later at the Städtische Webeschule in Heidelberg until 1937; instructor for hand weaving at the Akademie Karlsruhe from 1937; member of the Deutscher Werkbund.
Lit.:
Vollmer, Hans (ed.), *Allgemeines Lexikon der Bildenden Künstler des 20. Jahrhunderts* (Leipzig: Seemann, 1953–1962), Vol. 4, p. 75.

FELICE RIX (RIX-UENO)

1 June 1893–15 October 1967
Designer, professor
Studies at the Graphische Lehr- und Versuchsanstalt and at the Kunstgewerbeschule Wien from 1913 to 1917 under Oskar Strnad, Adele von Stark and Josef Hoffmann; member of the Wiener Werkstätte from 1917 to 1930. Felice Rix moved to Japan in 1935 and held a professorship at the Municipal Academy of Art in Kyoto from 1949 to 1963.
Lit.:
Fahr-Becker, Gabriele, *Wiener Werkstätte 1903–1932* (Cologne: Benedikt Taschen, 1994), p. 233.

HELENE SCHMIDT-NONNÉ

8 November 1891, Magdeburg–7 April 1976, Darmstadt
Textile artist, instructor
Studied at the Kunstgewerbeschule in Berlin from 1913; trained as a drawing teacher; continued her studies at the Bauhaus Weimar in 1924; married Joost Schmidt in 1925; moved with the Bauhaus to Dessau, where she studied under Gunta Stölzl at the weaving workshop in 1927/28; received the Bauhaus diploma in 1930. Schmidt-Nonné worked as an art teacher

from 1930 to 1933; moved to Berlin. Regarded as an "degenerate artist," she was forced to pursue her work in art without official sanction. She was appointed to the staff of the Hochschule für Gestaltung in Ulm by Max Bill in 1953/54.
Lit.:
Gunta Stölzl: Weberei am Bauhaus und aus eigener Werkstatt, edited by Magdalena Droste for the Bauhaus-Archiv (Berlin: Kupfergraben, 1987), p. 165.

MARIA STRAUSS-LIKARZ

28 March 1893, Przemysl–March 1971, Rome
Painter, graphic artist, designer, instructor
Studied at the Kunstschule für Frauen und Mädchen under Otto Friedrich from 1908 to 1910; further studies at the Kunstgewerbeschule Wien under Josef Hoffmann and Anton von Kenner, 1911–1915; served on the staff of the Wiener Werkstätte from 1912 to 1914. She directed the "Fachklasse für kunstgewerbliche Frauenarbeiten" at the Handwerker- und Kunstgewerbeschule Halle from 1916 to 1920 and supervised the enamel workshop; continued to work for the WW while teaching in Halle in 1917; worked on the staff of the WW from 1920 to 1931 as one of its most creative members. Maria Strauss-Likarz designed some 200 textile patterns with different color combinations. She emigrated to Italy in 1938.
Lit.:
Anna, S. (ed.), *Textilien der Wiener Werkstätte,* Städtische Kunstsammlungen Chemnitz (Stuttgart: Daco-Verlag Bläse, 1994).
Burg Giebichenstein; Die hallesche Kunstschule von den Anfängen bis zur Gegenwart, issued by Staatliche Galerie Moritzburg Halle, Badisches Landesmuseum Karlsruhe and Burg Giebichenstein – Hochschule für Kunst und Design Halle (Halle, 1993), p. 525.
Fahr-Becker, Gabriele, *Wiener Werkstätte 1903–1932* (Cologne: Benedikt Taschen, 1994), p. 235.
Völker, Angela, *Die Stoffe der Wiener Werkstätte 1910–1932,* issued by the Österreichisches Museum für angewandte Kunst Wien (Vienna: Brandstätter, 1990), p. 107.

WILLIAM TURNER

Dates of birth and death unknown
Designed textiles for G. P. & J. Baker Ltd. of London from 1909 to 1925. His more than 60 designs were all adapted from historical originals.
Lit.:
Mendes, Valerie, *The Victoria & Albert Museum's Textile Collection; British Textiles from 1900 to 1937* (London: Victoria & Albert Museum, 1992), p. 127.

SIGMUND VON WEECH

16 May 1888, Landsberg/Lech–27 October 1982, Munich
Graphic artist, designer, instructor
Studied architecture at the Technische Hochschule München and attended the Münchner Kunstgewerbeschule. Von Weech joined the Architecture department of the TH München as an academic assistant in 1912 and later became and instructor there. He established his own hand-weaving operation in Schaftlach (see Handweberei Sigmund von Weech) and a workshop for marble mosaic and scagliola in 1920. He exhibited at the Deutsche Gewerbeschau München in 1922 and was mentioned with praise in reviews. Von Weech served as director of the Höhere Fachschule für Textil- und Bekleidungsindustrie in Berlin from 1931 to 1943

and opened his own studio in Munich in 1948. He designed decorative fabrics (including patterns for the Möbelstoffweberei Gustav Kottmann, Krefeld), net curtains (for the Gardinenfabrik Plauen), carpets, postage stamps and coins. He was a member of the Deutscher Werkbund.
Lit.:
Deutsche Gewerbeschau München 1922, München: Knorr & Hirth, 1922, p. 8.
Wichmann, Hans (ed.), *Von Morris bis Memphis: Textilien der Neuen Sammlung; Ende 19. bis Ende 20. Jahrhundert* (Basel, Boston, Berlin: Birkhäuser, 1990); *(collection catalogue* Neue Sammlung, Vol. 3), p. 451.

MARGARETE WILLERS

30 July 1883, Oldenburg–12 June 1977, Essen
Textile designer, teaching master
Trained in painting and drawing in Düsseldorf, Munich and Paris from 1905; studied at the weaving workshop of the Bauhaus Weimar in 1921–22. Margarete Willers operated her own studio at the Bauhaus Dessau for a period of several months in 1927 and worked at the experimental hand-weaving workshop in Dessau. She received a letter of recommendation from Walter Gropius for the Folkwangschule in Essen, was director of the Department of Hand-Weaving and Embroidery at the Folkwangschule in Essen from 1928 to 1943, while continuing to work at her own workshop. She participated in the exhibition "Moderne Bildwirkereien" in 1930, which was also shown at Textil- und Kunstgewerbesammlung Chemnitz. She was teaching master at a hand-weaving plant in Bückeberg from 1943 to 1955. She produced works on an upright loom after 1955. Willers was a member of the Deutscher Werkbund.
Lit.:
Gunta Stölzl: Weberei am Bauhaus und aus eigener Werkstatt, edited by Magdalena Droste for the Bauhaus-Archiv (Berlin: Kupfergraben, 1987), p. 167.

Liane Sachs

| INDEX OF COMPANIES, WORKSHOPS AND SCHOOLS |

COMPANIES

G. P. & J. BAKER LTD., LONDON

Textile printing plant
Founded by the brothers George Percival and James Baker in 1884. George designed a significant collection of historical fabrics clearly influenced by Persian and Indian models. Many of these designs were produced for Baker Ltd. as model prints by Swaisland & Co. in Crayford, a company that was taken over by G. P. & J. Baker in 1893. Baker prints in the Art Nouveau style and their adaptations of historical patterns gained considerable fame. The company is now owned by Parker Knoll.
Lit.:
Mendes, Valerie, *The Victoria & Albert Museum's Textile Collection; British Textiles from 1900 to 1937* (London: Victoria & Albert Museum, 1992), p. 89.
From East to West; Textiles from G. P. & J. Baker, issued by G. P. & J. Baker Ltd. (London: Victoria & Albert Museum, 1984).

BAYERISCHE TEXTILWERKE BERNHARD NEPKER, TUTZING

Textile producers
Represented at the exhibition "Bayrisches Kunsthandwerk" in Munich in 1925 with a design by Ruth Hildegard Geyer-Raack. The company also exhibited print fabrics at the International Exhibition of Commercial Art in Monza in 1927. The enterprise was reincorporated as the "Tützinger Textilwerke" in May 1931.
Lit.:
Wichmann, Hans (ed.), *Von Morris bis Memphis: Textilien der Neuen Sammlung; Ende 19. bis Ende 20. Jahrhundert* (Basel, Boston, Berlin: Birkhäuser, 1990); *(collection catalogue* Neue Sammlung, Vol. 3), p. 455.

LUCIEN BIOUX

Producers of woven upholstery fabrics
Production of all designs by Eric Bagge.
Lit.:
Fanelli, Giovanni and Rosalia, *Il Tessuto Art Déco e Anni Trenta* (Florence: Cantini, 1986), pp. 96–97.

CAMMANN & CO. A.G., CHEMNITZ

Producers of woven upholstery fabrics
Established in 1886; converted to a joint-stock company in 1919. Chairman of the board of supervisors was Paul Schönherr, Director of the Sächsische Webstuhlfabrik vorm. Louis Schönherr. Paul Cammann was on the steering committee of the Deutsche Gewerbeschau München in 1922. The firm employed about 300 people in 1929. Cammann & Co. was a corporate member of Deutscher Werkbund. The company specialized in the template spray printing of woven fabrics. The enterprise was reincorporated as a private limited company under the name Cammann Gobelinmanufaktur GbR in 1992.

Lit.:
Mitteilungen der Deutschen Gewerbeschau München 1922 (Beiblatt der Form, Nr. 5), (Munich: Werbedienst, 1922), p. 5.
Die Aktiengesellschaften von Chemnitz und Umgebung (Chemnitz/Leipzig: Bayer & Heinze, 1929), p. 28.

DETEKU – DEUTSCHE TEXTILE KUNST, LEIPZIG

Textiles producers
Established in 1904 and operated as Deutsche Textile Kunst, Kießling, Hiemann & Dippmann, Leipzig, until about 1920. The firm produced decorative woven and hand-printed fabrics, expanding into wallpaper printing and weaving in 1917. Rudolf Hiemann was director of the wallpaper printing and weaving workshop. DETEKTU was represented at the Deutsche Gewerbeschau München with carpets by Otto Fischer-Essen in 1922; began producing net and lace fabrics in 1922. The company was renamed "Deutsche Textile Kunst, Rudolf Hiemann, Möbel und Dekorationsstoffe, Teppiche" in the mid-1920s. First hand-printed dress fabrics were produced in 1932. Represented at the Grassi expositions from 1920 to 1925. DETEKTU produced designs by artists including Th. Th. Heine, Albin Müller, M. Flath, J. V. Cissarz, Hertha Koch, Helene Geiringer, Valerie Petter, Herta Michel-Koch, Erich Gruner, Ferdinand Onnaschs, Ernst Aufseeser, Wilhelm Poetter and Erich Kleinhempel, who also served as art director.
Lit.:
DK, 1917, Vol. XX, p. 328.
DK, 1922, Vol. XXV, p. 217.
Deutsche Gewerbeschau München 1922 (Munich: Werbedienst, 1922), p. 8.
Die Kunst, March 1928, Vol. 26, No. 6, classified section.
ID, June 1929, classified section.
Ausstellerverzeichnisse der Messeausstellungen, Leipzig, Grassi-Museum.

DEUTSCHE FARBMÖBEL A.G., MUNICH

Textiles producers
Founded in 1925 by a group including the artists Victor von Rauch und Wilhelm Marsmann. The company specialized in the production, processing and sale of artistic utility objects and remained in operation until 1930. Production was limited primarily to the execution of designs created by the two artists.
Lit.:
Wichmann, Hans (ed.), *Von Morris bis Memphis: Textilien der Neuen Sammlung; Ende 19. bis Ende 20. Jahrhundert* (Basel, Boston, Berlin: Birkhäuser, 1990); *(collection catalogue* Neue Sammlung, Vol. 3), p. 454.

VITTORIO FERRARI, MILAN

Textiles producers
Worthy of particular note is this firm's specialization in woven reproductions of historical textile patterns of Persian, Indian and Venetian origin in velvets, damasks and brocades.
Lit.:

Marangoni, Guido, *Enciclopedia delle Moderne Arti decorative Italiane: V. Le Stoffe d'Arte e l'arredamento della casa* (Milan: Casa Editrice Ceschina, 1928), Plates 17–29.

WILLIAM FOXTON LTD., LONDON

Founded by William Foxton in 1903. After 1923, the firm made its reputation as W. Foxton Ltd., primarily producers of woven and printed fabrics based upon designs by the following artists: Constance Irving, Charles Francis Annesley Voysey, Gregory Brown, Minnie McLeish, Take Sato, D. Hutton, C. L. Fraser, Gladys Barraclough, Rex Silver and others.
Lit.:
Paulson Townsend, W. G., *Modern Decorative Art in England: Its Development & Characteristics* (London: B. T. Batsford, 1922).
Europäisches Kunstgewerbe: Berichte über die Ausstellung Europäisches Kunstgewerbe 1927, issued by Städtisches Kunstgewerbe-Museum zu Leipzig (Leipzig: Seemann, 1928).
Mendes, Valerie, *The Victoria & Albert Museum's Textile Collection; British Textiles from 1900 to 1937* (London: Victoria & Albert Museum, 1992).

GAINSBOROUGH SILK WEAVERS, SUFFOLK

Hand-weaving firm
Founded by Reginald Warner in 1903; producers until 1989.
Lit.:
Schoeser, Mary, and Rufey, Celia, *English and American Textiles: from 1790 to the present* (New York: Thames and Hudson, 1989), pp. 142, 242, 243.

HAHN & BACH, MUNICH

Traders in carpets, wallpaper, decorative and upholstery fabrics with their own textile printing operation. "Contemporary fabrics for interior decoration" were specially hand-printed using Indanthren dyes on very coarse woven cloths such as linen. The Hahn & Bach collection also included silk, cotton and woolen damasks and gobelin fabrics as well as silk and semi-silk decorative textiles. The company was owned during the 1930s by the Railing brothers.
Lit.:
ID, 1922, Vol. XXXIII, p.163.
ID, 1924, XI., pp. 363 to 365.
Wichmann, Hans (ed.), *Von Morris bis Memphis: Textilien der Neuen Sammlung; Ende 19. bis Ende 20. Jahrhundert* (Basel, Boston, Berlin: Birkhäuser, 1990); *(collection catalogue* Neue Sammlung, Vol. 3), p. 455.

HANDWEBEREI HABLIK-LINDEMANN, ITZEHOE

Elisabeth Lindemann (1879–1960) assumed control of the Meldorfer Museumswerkstätten in 1902 and selected the coat of arms of the Vogtemann family as the workshop trademark in 1909.
The workshop was moved from Meldorf to Itzehoe, where Lindemann and her husband Werner Hablik operated the business from their home, in 1917.

Johanna Schütz-Wolff completed her practical training there in 1920. The firm was regularly represented at the Grassi expositions in Leipzig from 1921–42. The workshop was moved again and expanded in 1923. Received an award at the Jahresschau Deutscher Arbeit in Dresden in 1924. Areas of specialization included the production of dress fabrics, upholstery and decorative textiles, pillows, tablecloths and models for ladies' outer garments (letter of W. Hablik to Herwarth Walden, 25 September 1924, in: Lit. p.102). The workshop employed 60 people by 1926. First motif carpets were woven on a horizontal loom in 1927. The firm was represented at the Werkbund exhibition in Stuttgart, the exhibition of commercial art in Monza and the exhibition "Europäisches Kunstgewerbe" in Leipzig the same year; participated at the exhibition "Handwerkskunst im Zeitalter der Maschine" in Mannheim in 1928 and the German exhibition tour of "Moderne Bildwirkereien" from 1928/29, which was also shown at the Textil- und Kunstgewerbesammlung Chemnitz in 1930. The company also produced woven and hooked rugs; received the "Ehrenpreis der Stadt Berlin" at the German building exhibition. Elisabeth Hablik continued to operate the workshop following Wenzel Hablik's death in 1934. The firm was represented at a number of exhibitions and won several awards during the years before its closing in 1964. Daughter Sybille Hablik moved to Pondicherry, India, where she operated the hand-weaving workshop under its old name.
Lit.:
Fuchs-Belhamri, Elisabeth, *Wenzel Hablik: Textilkunst und Mode* (Heide: Boyens & Co., 1993).

HANDWEBEREI HOHENHAGEN, HAGEN UND BREMEN

A weaving workshop was established in the craftsmen's settlement Hohenhagen, formerly the manor of Karl Ernst Osthaus, in the mid-1920s. The operation was owned by the Helbigs, a married couple who hired Ida Betge (of the Kunstgewerbeschule Hamburg) for their art staff. "Handweberei Hohenhagen G.m.b.H., modern hand-woven fabrics, shawls, traveling blankets, bast weaves; one-of-a-kind pieces only, Hagen i. Westf., Hohenhof …" (from *Handbuch des Kunstmarktes*, Berlin: Herrmann Kalkoff, 1926, p. 452, classified ad).
The merchant Ludwig Roselius moved the hand-weaving workshop to Bremen, where it reopened in 1930. Textiles for interior decoration were sold through distributors; no representation at trade fairs known.
Lit.:
Kircher, Ursula, *Von Hand gewebt: Eine Entwicklungsgeschichte der Handweberei im 20. Jahrhundert* (Marburg: Hitzeroth, 1986), pp. 128/129.

HANDWEBEREI SIGMUND VON WEECH, SCHAFTLACH

The hand-weaving operation was founded by Prof. Sigmund von Weech and his wife Angelina (1882–1962, daughter of the Berlin art dealer Gurlitt) at the manor "Bäck am Hof" in 1921. It was eventually expanded to accommodate about 60 looms; commercial offices were established in Munich. Initially, the company wove semi-woolen fabrics (cotton warp, wool filling); later moved into woolens in the "homespun" style as well as upholstery and decorative fabrics designed exclusively by Sigmund von Weech. Weavers worked with cotton dyed with Indranthen and began producing upholstery fabrics, cloths, draperies and clothing materials using chenille and cellophane threads

in about 1930. A number of young hand-weavers took practical training or worked until completion of their journeyman's examinations. Gunta Stölzl also worked with Mrs. Weech for a period of time. Following the Weeches' separation in 1931, Mrs. Weech assumed sole control of the weaving operation, which she directed until her death.
Lit.:
Die Kunst, 1931, Vol. 32, No. 6, p. 152.
Kircher, Ursula, *Von Hand gewebt: Eine Entwicklungsgeschichte der Handweberei im 20. Jahrhundert* (Marburg: Hitzeroth, 1986), pp. 126–127.

ARTHUR H. LEE & SONS LTD., BIRKENHEAD, LANCASHIRE

Weaving, Printing, Embroidery
Founded by Arthur H. Lee in Warrington 1888; moved to Birkenhead in 1908. The company produced several noteworthy examples of Art Nouveau textiles based upon designs by well-known designers between 1890 and the early years of the 20th century. Production was later concentrated primarily upon woven and embroidered upholstery and decorative fabrics. Arthur Humphrey Lee distributed textiles by Mariano Fortuny in New York and other U. S. cities. The firm went out of business in 1972.
Lit.:
Führer durch englische Stilarten (company catalogue), 1929.
Mendes, Valerie, *The Victoria & Albert Museum's Textile Collection; British Textiles from 1900 to 1937* (London, Victoria & Albert Museum, 1992), p. 91.
Osma, Guillermo de, *Fortuny: The Life and work of Mariano Fortuny* (New York: Rizzoli, 1980), pp. 170, 173.

POLYTEX TEXTILGESELLSCHAFT MBH, BERLIN

Textiles producers
Founded and operated under the artistic and technical direction of Prof. Bruno Paul, Bernhard Jentsch and Tillie Prill-Schloemann (a student of Bruno Paul's and his assistant for many years; interior designer in the Richmodishaus of Cologne in 1925; member of the delegation of the "Deutsche Werkstätten"; involved in the opening of the "Werkgemeinschaft Kunst und Handwerk" in Berlin in 1932). Textile designs were provided by the painter Erika Peters. Direct collaboration between artists and technicians led to the harmonization of weaving processes and patterns. Furniture coverings and decorative fabrics were referred to as "Polytex Fabrics." A collection of Bauhaus fabrics was established under the designation "bauhaus dessau" beginning in 1930. Polytex was granted first rights of utilization for upholstery and curtain materials. "The first collection comprised 20 original fabric patterns from the Bauhaus textiles department, for which Polytex was granted exclusive mechanical production rights" (contract between the Bauhaus Dessau and Polytextil GmbH of Berlin, in *Gunta Stölzl: Weberei am Bauhaus und aus eigener Werkstatt*, edited by Magdalena Droste for the Bauhaus-Archiv (Berlin: Kupfergraben, 1987, p. 132).
Production was carried out on the power looms of the Weberei P. Rentsch GmbH, Abt. Polytex, in Seifhennersdorf, Sachsen in 1932/33.

Lit.:
Polytex-Stoffe für Möbel und Dekorationen (company catalogue, n. d.), p. 1.
ID, Vol. XLII, April 1931, p. 150.
ID, February 1933, Vol. XLIV, p. IV (advertising supplement).
Ziffer, Alfred (ed.), *Bruno Paul: Deutsche Raumkunst und Architektur zwischen Jugendstil und Moderne* (Munich: Klinkhardt & Biermann, 1992), pp. 398–399.

RAMM, SON & CROCKER LTD., LONDON

Printed textiles
Lit.:
Lewis, F., *British Textiles* (London, Leigh-on-Sea: F. Lewis Publishers Ltd., 1951).

PAUL RODIER, PARIS

Mechanical Weaving
The Rodier company was represented by the largest number of textiles at the 1925 Exposition Internationale des Arts Décoratifs et Industriels Modernes in Paris.
Lit.:
Battersby, Martin, *The decorative twenties* (London: Philippe Garner, 1969; John Calmann and King Ltd, 1988), pp. 120–122, 142, 166, 218.
Schoeser, Mary, and Dejardin, Kathleen, *French Textiles from 1760 to the Present* (London: Laurence King Ltd., 1991), pp. 174/175, 177, 181/182.

LORENZO RUBELLI, VENICE

Textiles producers
Founded in 1858 as a hand-weaving operation; later expanded into a commercial textiles company with its own looms. Attracted significant attention during the 1920s with woven damasks, velvets and Jacquard fabrics bearing traditional Venetian patterns. Other commercial companies were associated with Rubelli, among them Lisio of Florence. The firm has outlets in New York and Dubai today.
Lit.:
Marangoni, Guido, *Enciclopedia delle Moderne Arti decorative Italiane: V. Le Stoffe d'Arte e l'arredamento della casa* (Milan: Casa Editrice Ceschina, 1928).
Wichmann, Hans (ed.), *Von Morris bis Memphis: Textilien der Neuen Sammlung; Ende 19. bis Ende 20. Jahrhundert* (Basel, Boston, Berlin: Birkhäuser, 1990); (*collection catalogue* Neue Sammlung, Vol. 3), p. 459.

ADOLF TOENGES GMBH, ELBERFELD

Upholstery fabrics producers
Founded in Barmen. The company used textile designs by artists such as Max Heidrich of Paderborn during the 1920s.
Lit.:
DK, 1917, 9 June, p. 304.
HdK, 1926, p. 541.

TURNBULL & STOCKDALE LTD., ROSEBANK PRINT WORKS, RAMSBOTTOM, LANCASHIRE

Textiles producers with printing, dying and finishing works Production of hand-printed linens, cretonnes, chintzes and chiné upholstery fabrics. Founded in 1881; Lewis F. Day was hired as art director in the same year. Most interesting during the 19th and early 20th centuries were the fabrics produced as model prints. Contributing designers included Disney Mawson and Samuel Rowe. Turnbull & Stockdale is one of the few plants in Great Britain that still produce on the basis of this traditional technique.

Lit.:
Mendes, Valerie, *The Victoria & Albert Museum's Textile Collection; British Textiles from 1900 to 1937* (London: Victoria & Albert Museum, 1992), p. 93.
Schoeser, Mary, and Rufey, Celia., *English and American Textiles: from 1790 to the present* (New York: Thames and Hudson, 1989), pp. 150, 155.

WILHELM VOGEL, CHEMNITZ

Mechanical weaving works
A commission-based business specialized in the sale of export goods from Sachsen was founded under the name Vogel, Stelling & Co. in 1830. Woven goods production was initiated in 1839. The company produced upholstery fabrics under the name "Wilhelm Vogel" beginning in 1844; power looms were introduced in about 1850. The firm continued to expand under Hermann Wilhelm Vogel (1895: 650 power looms, 50 embroidering machines). All types of upholstery fabrics were produced, alongside portieres, curtains, tablecloths, carriage fabrics, woolen damasks, etc. Production of textiles based upon patterns created by such artists as Peter Behrens, Th. Th. Heine, Walter Leistikow, Henry van de Velde and Rudolf und Fia Wille began in 1902. Woven goods were produced for the Wiener Werkstätte, including designs by Dagobert Peche. Patterns from the weaving department of the Bauhaus Weimar were produced industrially in 1924. All types of woven fabrics were produced during the 1920s. The plant was destroyed in 1945.

Lit.:
ID, 1902, Vol. XIII, p. 300.
Das Deutsche Kunstgewerbe 1906: III. Deutsche Kunstgewerbe-Ausstellung Dresden 1906, issued by the exhibition curatorial staff (Munich: F. Bruckmann AG), 1906, pp. 113, 203, 209, 263.
Wollenburg, Anneliese, née Vogel (ed.), *Chronik der Familie Wilhelm Vogel zu Chemnitz* (Leipzig, 1931; 1941 edition).
Gunta Stölzl: Weberei am Bauhaus und aus eigener Werkstatt, edited by Magdalena Droste for the Bauhaus-Archiv (Berlin: Kupfergraben, 1987), p. 28.

VORWERK & CO., BARMEN

Upholstery fabrics producers
Established in 1883 as Vorwerk & Co. Möbelstoffwerke, Barmen (with carpet works); acquisition of Jul. Schmitz & Co. of Eberfeld around 1900; acquisition of J. W. Eck Möbelstoffweberei of Kulmbach/Bad Berneck in 1918 and concentration of production facilities in Oberfranken during the same year. Upholstery fabrics were marked on the reverse with the woven "Vorwerk" name during the 1920s and 1930s. Vorwerk & Co. Möbelstoffwerke GmbH & Co. KG have been a part of the Achter & Ebels Group of Mönchengladbach since 1995.

Lit.:
Corporate profile of Vorwerk & Co Möbelstoffwerke, Kulmbach.

WORKSHOPS

DEUTSCHE WERKSTÄTTEN

"Bau-Möbelfabrik und Fabrik kunstgewerblicher Gegenstände" founded by Karl Schmidt (1873–1948) in Laubegast/Dresden in 1898. A period of intensive cooperation involving artists and the producer began with an open letter to the artists of Dresden requesting submission of designs for utility objects. A merger with a zither factory in 1899 resulted in the establishment of the "Dresdner Werkstätten für Handwerkskunst Schmidt und Müller." Karl Schmidt called for reform with respect to forms of living and commercial crafts as well as renewal in all fields of intellectual life. Designs came from artists such as R. Riemerschmid (machine furniture), J. M. Olbrich, P. Behrens, C. R. Mackintosh, M. H. Baillie Scott and A. von Salzmann. The organization merged in 1907 with the "Münchner Werkstätten für Wohnungseinrichtung" under the direction of Karl Bertsch to form the "Deutsche Werkstätten für Handwerkskunst," with a staff of 300 people. The Dresden facility was moved to Hellerau in 1910. Reincorporation as a joint-stock company followed in 1913. The development of prefabricated wood houses built from pre-cut plywood and siding elements began in 1920. Contributing artists included Prof. J. Hillerbrand, W. von Wersin, E. Wenz-Vietor, Prof. H. Tessenow, A. Niemeyer, who also submitted designs for fabrics, carpets, wallpaper, glass, ceramics, metal objects, lamps, baskets, etc. Their five sales and distribution outlets were joined in 1924 by the "Richmodishaus für Kunst und Handwerk GmbH" of Cologne under the direction of Bruno Paul. Most designs produced during the 1920s were created by Karl Bertsch. The organization was represented at the exhibition "Die Wohnung" in Stuttgart in 1927 (assembly-line furniture). Firms with membership in the Deutscher Werkbund included the Deutsche Werkstätten AG Hellerau and the Deutsche Werkstätten AG, Werkstätten für gesamte Innenausstattung of Munich. The Munich plant was liquidated in 1929. An economic upswing fueled by major furnishings commissions followed capital restructuring in 1930. Moveable assets were gradually liquidated in Hellerau beginning in 1945. The works were nationalized as the "Volkseigener Betrieb Deutsche Werkstätten Hellerau" in 1951 and reprivatized in 1990; re-established in 1948/50 as the "Deutsche Werkstätten Fertigungsgesellschaft" in Kassel, later in Munich as well, and as "De-We-Tex" in Wolfratshausen.

DEUTSCHE WERKSTÄTTEN TEXTILGESELLSCHAFT M.B.H. (DE-WE-TEX)

Founded in 1923 in association with the textile firm Gottlob Wunderlich of Waldkirchen-Zschopenthal, which had been supplying fabrics and curtains based upon artists' designs to the Dresden sales outlet since 1902. The hand-weaving division took shape after 1900; first products included linen curtain materials with patterns by Richard Riemerschmid and hand-printed fabrics (model prints). Beginning in 1909, most orders for fabrics were received from the Deutsche Werkstätten. The firm first exhibited at the Leipzig Trade Fair in 1923. Sole proprietor Dr. Carl Emmerich was also the largest shareholder in the Deutsche Werkstätten. The characteristic style of De-We-Tex fabrics was shaped primarily by L. and K. Bertsch, F. P. Blum, J. Hillerbrand, A. Niemeyer, B. Senestréy, R. H. Geyer-Raack. Developments in production techniques included the use of Indanthren dyes and the mechanization of hand-printing proces-

ses. The Bauhaus weaving department regularly supplied the Deutsche Werkstätten with weaving patterns. Following Dr. Emmerich's death in 1952, the company was administered by the state until 1960, when it was fully nationalized.

Lit.:
Arnold, Klaus-Peter, *Vom Sofakissen zum Städtebau; Die Geschichte der deutschen Werkstätten und der Gartenstadt Hellerau* (Dresden, Basel: Verlag der Kunst, 1993).
Gunta Stölzl: Weberei am Bauhaus und aus eigener Werkstatt, edited by Magdalena Droste for the Bauhaus-Archiv (Berlin: Kupfergraben, 1987), p. 132.
Wichmann, Hans (ed.), *Deutsche Werkstätten und WK-Verband: 1898–1990; Aufbruch zum Neuen Wohnen,* issued by the WK-Institut für Wohnkultur (Munich: Prestel, 1992).

VEREINIGTE WERKSTÄTTEN (WW)

Founded in Munich in 1898 as an association of several different artists, among them R. Riemerschmid, B. Pankok, Karl Bertsch and the painter F. A. O. Krüger, who served as the first managing director. Bruno Paul joined the group during the same year. The private limited company was reincorporated as a joint-stock company in 1907. Strong demand for elaborate, finely crafted furnishings for entire rooms and interior settings fostered the development of a diverse range of furniture, textiles and lamps. In quest of a new furniture program designed for low-income groups, the Vereinigte Werkstätten introduced their modular furniture system in 1908. The firm operated factories in Munich and Bremen (furnishings for luxury liners); produced a wide variety of fabric patterns designed by such artists as F. A. Breuhaus, with his "F. A. B." fabrics collection, P. László, E. Engelbrecht, A. and M. May and E. Zweybrück. These textiles included sprayed and printed weaves, damasks and gobelin materials. The Vereinigte Werkstätten received the contract to furnish the ocean liner "Bremen" in 1929. A member of the Deutscher Werkbund, the Vereinigte Werkstätten remained in business until the 1980s.

Lit.:
DK, 31. Vols., 1927–28, pp. 111–151, 281–290.
DKuD, Vol. 63, Oct. 1928–March 1929, pp. 53, 428 bis 435.
DKuD, Vol. 64, April 1929–Sept. 1929, pp. 127 to 131.
DKuD, Vol. 65, Oct. 1929–March 1930, pp. 111–144, 343 to 350.
Wichmann, Hans (ed.), *Von Morris bis Memphis: Textilien der Neuen Sammlung; Ende 19. bis Ende 20. Jahrhundert* (Basel, Boston, Berlin: Birkhäuser, 1990); (*collection catalogue* Neue Sammlung, Vol. 3), p. 460.

WIENER WERKSTÄTTE (WW)

Founded as a production cooperative by a group of artisans under the artistic direction of Josef Hoffmann and Koloman Moser in 1903. Built and furnished the Purkersdorf sanatorium near Vienna in 1904–1906; built and furnished the Palais Stoclet in Brussels, 1905–1911. A furniture division was established under the direction of Eduard Wimmer-Wisgrill in 1910, and textile production began the same year. Designs for fabrics were supplied during the 1920s primarily by such designers as Josef Hoffmann, Dagobert Peche (a total of 113 fabric patterns), Maria Likarz (200 patterns), Felice Rix, Mathilde Flögl and Max Snischek, who became director of the furniture division in 1922. Textile designs were produced at a number of different textile print works, including Teltscher, Ziegler in Vienna and surrounding areas. The sober, functional style favored by Hoffmann and Moser provided new impulses for the Werkbund and the Bauhaus; the decorative designs of Peche and Wimmer influenced French Art Déco. The Wiener Werkstätte exhibited fashion and textile designs at the Frankfurt International Trade Fair in 1920 and was represented at the Exposition Internationale des Arts Décoratifs et Industriels Modernes Paris in 1925. The WW was one of the most important centers of the craft industry in the early 20th century; member of the Austrian and the German Werkbund. The dissolution of the Wiener Werkstätte began in 1931.

Lit.:

Fahr-Becker, Gabriele, *Wiener Werkstätte 1903–1932* (Cologne: Benedikt Taschen, 1994).

Anna, S. (ed.), *Textilien der Wiener Werkstätte*, Städtische Kunstsammlungen Chemnitz (Stuttgart: Daco-Verlag Bläse, 1994).

Völker, Angela, *Die Stoffe der Wiener Werkstätte 1910–1932*, issued by the Österreichisches Museum für angewandte Kunst Wien (Vienna: Brandstätter, 1990).

SCHOOLS

BAUHAUS, WEIMAR AND DESSAU

Founded as the "Staatliches Bauhaus in Weimar" in 1919 under its first director, Walter Gropius. Goal and program of the school: Artists and craftsmen were to join in erecting the "building of the future." Bauhaus instructors included Johannes Itten, Paul Klee, Oskar Schlemmer, Wassily Kandinsky, Gerhard Marcks, Lyonel Feininger, Georg Muche, László Moholy-Nagy and many others, who laid the foundations for the development of modern design. All workshops were equipped and furnished by 1921: metals, furniture, ceramics, glass and mural painting, wood and stone sculpture, bookbinding, graphic printing. A textiles curriculum was established in 1920 and expanded to include weaving. Georg Muche served as weaving form master from 1920 to 1927. The most gifted of the department's students were Gunta Stölzl and Benita Otte. A total of 183 textiles articles such as cloths, pillows, shawls, carpets, draperies, gobelin materials, runners, feather beds, etc. were produced by 1925. Staff members were employed in the textiles workshop to fill direct orders (productive workshop). Involvement with the engineering and industrial sectors intensified following the move to Dessau and eventually culminated in the transition to industrial design. Gunta Stölzl was appointed director of the textiles department. She was youth master for weaving in 1927 and instructed students in weaving technique and material sciences. The three-year course of training in the teaching workshop and later in the experimental and model workshop where students completed their journeyman's examination, ended with the award of the Bauhaus diploma. The Bauhaus-Polytex contract and the agreement for the delivery of weaving patterns to De-We-Tex GmbH Dresden and the Mechanische Weberei Pausa/Stuttgart were signed under Gunta Stölzl's directorship in 1930. Hans Meyer served as Bauhaus director from 1928 to 1930. He was succeeded by Mies van der Rohe (1930–1932). The Bauhaus moved to Berlin in 1932 and was dissolved in 1933.

Lit.:

Gunta Stölzl: Meisterin am Bauhaus Dessau; Textilien, Textilentwürfe und freie Arbeiten 1915–1983, issued by the Stiftung Bauhaus Dessau (Ostfildern: Hatje Verlag, 1997).

Gunta Stölzl: Weberei am Bauhaus und aus eigener Werkstatt, edited by Magdalena Droste for the Bauhaus-Archiv (Berlin: Kupfergraben, 1987).

Droste, Magdalena, *Bauhaus 1919–1933*, issued by the Bauhaus-Archiv, Museum für Gestaltung (Berlin, Cologne: Benedikt Taschen, 1993).

SCHULE REIMANN, BERLIN

Private school of arts and crafts
Founded by Albert Reimann (9 November 1874, Gnese–5 June 1976, London) as the "Schülerwerkstätten für Kleinplastik" on 1 April 1902. Associated workshops for metal crafts and wood-carving were added. The workshop curriculum was later expanded to include workshops for bookbinding, tailoring, handicrafts and batik (1908). (Albert Reimann invented a batik stick in 1907 with which the width of the line could be varied and the line segmented.) Courses offered covered all areas of free and applied art as well as training in theory. A fashion curriculum was established in 1910, followed somewhat later by a workshop for women's fashions. The school assumed the designation "Kunst- und Gewerbeschule" in 1913. The publication entitled *Mitteilungen an die Schüler der Schule Reimann* was first issued in 1916 and later *Farbe und Form*. A "Höhere Fachschule für Dekorationskunst" was integrated into the Schule Reimann in 1911, followed by a "Höhere Fachschule für Theaterdekoration" in 1913. The painter Maria May became director of the textiles department in 1922. Courses in textile art, design and decorative painting (textile painting, textile printing, spray printing, template printing, batik) were developed.

The school was repeatedly represented at Grassi expositions with metals designs, batik pieces, painted and sprayed fabrics and other hand-crafted objects. The exhibition presented in celebration of the school's 25th anniversary was shown at the Textil- und Kunstgewerbesammlung in Chemnitz in 1927. The architect Hugo Häring became director of the school following Albert Reimann's emigration in 1935 and held the position until 1943.

Lit.:

Farbe und Form: Monatsschrift für Kunst und Kunstgewerbe (Berlin: Verlag Schule Reimann, 1916–34).

TKI, 1917, No. 6, p. 185.

TKI, 1918, No. 1, p. 15.

WERKSTÄTTEN DER STADT HALLE – STAATLICH STÄDTISCHE KUNSTGEWERBESCHULE BURG GIEBICHENSTEIN

Founded in 1879 as a commercial school of drawing and crafts. Renamed as the "Handwerkerschule der Stadt Halle" in 1902. Appointed director in 1915, Paul Thiersch significantly influenced the school's development until 1928. His achievements included the establishment and expansion of the teaching workshops beginning in 1915. Maria Likarz initiated the development of a "Fachklasse für kunstgewerbliche Frauenarbeiten" in 1916. The school was accredited as the "Handwerker- und Kunstgewerbeschule der Stadt Halle" in 1918. A textiles workshop was added in 1919, followed by a fabric printing shop (1919–1923) and dying facility, of which Johanna Wolff (Schütz-Wolff) was appointed director in 1920, and a weaving studio in 1922. Woven articles included upholstery and clothing materials with simple stripe patterns as well as floor and wall carpets. The school regularly took part in the Grassi expositions beginning in 1920. From 1922 to 1934 it operated under the name "Werkstätten der Stadt Halle – Staatlich städtische Kunstgewerbeschule Burg Giebichenstein." Benita Otte (Koch-Otte), deputy director of the Bauhaus weaving division, directed the hand-weaving department from 1925 to 1933. She contributed her Bauhaus experience and expanded the weaving workshop to include the production of interior textiles in 1927/28. Edith Eberhardt was teaching weaving techniques from 1927. In the same year the weaving workshop supplied all the textiles for two apartments in Peter Behrens' house at the Stuttgart Werkbund exhibition "Die Wohnung": curtains, upholstery fabrics, carpets and draperies. Following the dismissal of Benita Otte, Edith Eberhardt became director of the weaving workshop. The school was renamed "Burg Giebichenstein – Hochschule für Kunst und Design Halle" in 1990. Training in textile arts is conducted in the Design department.

Lit.:

Burg Giebichenstein; Die hallesche Kunstschule von den Anfängen bis zur Gegenwart, issued by Staatliche Galerie Moritzburg Halle, Badisches Landesmuseum Karlsruhe and Burg Giebichenstein – Hochschule für Kunst und Design Halle (Halle, 1993).

Liane Sachs

LAMÉ

General designation for a variety of fabrics interwoven wholly or partially with gold or silver tinsel filling threads.

MERCERIZING

A method developed by John Mercer (1751–1866) in 1850 to improve the appearance and quality of fabrics. The process gives textiles a washable shine. Strength and absorbency are increased, while flexibility and resistance to abrasion are reduced.

MOLD PRINTING

Manual printing using molds (relief plates). One plate is used for each color in the pattern.

MOQUETTE

General description for velvety, pile-woven furniture fabrics, i.e. pile-woven textiles with cut pile loops. They are usually produced with multiple warps and appear in high-quality fabrics known as wire plushes.

OMBRÉ PATTERN

Designation for a pattern of stripes with graduated degrees of darkness running towards the edges of a fabric.

PLUSH

Designation for pile-woven fabrics used for furniture coverings. Unlike Turkish toweling, the loops in this pile fabric are not all closed; instead, some of them are cut, according to the pattern design, producing an appealing surface structure composed of cut and uncut piles.

RAPPORT

The smallest regularly recurring pattern unit in a printed fabric.

SILK

Fibers harvested from the cocoons of silk-spinning insects. The most important of the silkworms is the mulberry spinner, which has been bred in China and Japan for centuries. The outstanding qualities of silk are its high absorbency, strength and resistance to abrasion.

STENCIL PRINTING

The application of dye to fabric using stencils. In spray printing, the liquid dye is sprayed onto the uncovered areas of the fabric with a dye atomizer. This technique is well suited for designs covering large areas of fabric and makes it possible to achieve very subtle color transitions and artistic effects.

TURKISH TOWELING

Designation for pile-woven fabrics used for furniture coverings. In contrast to plush fabrics, the pile threads, i.e. the loops created during weaving, are not cut in this type of fabric.

TUSSAH SILK

Fibers harvested from the cocoons of saturnid moths. The silk thread is not uniform in thickness, and it is harder and more rigid than that produced by the mulberry silkworm. After the removal of bast fibers it takes on a glassy sheen. (see Silk)

VELOUR

(French: *velours:* velvet)
French term for velvet. Velours are cloths with short, upright piles (pile weaves).

VISCOSE RAYON

Viscose fabric is made from regenerated cellulose fibers. It was first produced using a process developed by Christian Friedrich Schönbein in 1845; viscose synthetic silk was commercially available as early as 1903 and has been produced on an industrial scale since 1919. The material's high absorbency, strength and resistance to abrasion contributed to its widespread use.

WARP

The term is used to designate the entire warp thread (warp system) in weaving. The warp generally runs in straight, parallel lines over the length of the weave. The warp is set up on the loom prior to the beginning of the weaving process.

WARP OR CHAIN GOBELIN, FILLING GOBELIN

Designation for a weave technique with multiple warp and filling systems in Jacquard weaving. Depending upon whether the pattern is to appear on the front side of the warp or the filling, the fabric is referred to as warp or filling Gobelin.

WEAVE

The fabric structure in which two thread systems – the warp and the filling (also known as woof or weft) – are joined. In addition to the three basic weaves – linen, twill and atlas – a number of derivatives and variations with multiple thread systems have also been developed.

WOOL

Fibers from the fleece of sheep. Types of wool are classified according to the harvesting method used. Characteristic qualities of wool are slow absorption, high elasticity and excellent insulating properties. Wool tends to felt under the influence of moisture, heat and pressure.

Allgemeines Lexikon der Bildenden Künstler, ed. by Ulrich Thieme and Felix Becker, Leipzig: Seemann, 1908–1950, Vol. 1–37.

Allgemeines Lexikon der Bildenden Künstler des 20. Jahrhunderts, ed. by Hans Vollmer, Leipzig: Seemann, 1953–1962, Vol. 1–6.

Ausstellung Europäisches Kunstgewerbe '1927, issued by Städtisches Kunstgewerbe-Museum zu Leipzig, Grassi Museum, Leipzig: Rudolf Schick & Co., 1927.

Ausstellung Moderne Bildwirkereien 1930, Dessau, 1930.

Arnold, Klaus-Peter, *Vom Sofakissen zum Städtebau; Die Geschichte der deutschen Werkstätten und der Garten-stadt Hellerau,* Dresden, Basel: Verlag der Kunst, 1993.

Art et Décoration: Revue Mensuelle D'Art Moderne, Paris: Éditions Albert Lévy Librairie Centrale des Beaux-Arts, 1897–1939.

bauhaus: vierteljahr-zeitschrift für gestaltung, ed. by hannes meyer, bauhaus dessau, april–june 1929.

Bauhaus 1919–1933: Meister- und Schülerarbeiten, Weimar – Dessau – Berlin, issued by the Museum für Gestaltung Zurich, 1988.

Bauhaus 7, issued by the Galerie am Sachsenplatz, Gisela and Hans-Peter Schulz, Leipzig, 1991.

Battersby, Martin, *The decorative twenties,* London: Philippe Garner, 1969 (John Calmann and King Ltd., 1988).

Bruno Paul: Deutsche Raumkunst und Architektur zwischen Jugendstil und Moderne, ed. by Alfred Ziffer, Munich: Klinkhardt & Biermann, 1992.

Burg Giebichenstein; Die hallesche Kunstschule von den Anfängen bis zur Gegenwart, issued by Staatliche Galerie Moritzburg Halle, Badisches Landesmuseum Karlsruhe, Burg Giebichenstein – Hochschule für Kunst und Design Halle, Halle, 1993.

Das neue Kunsthandwerk in Deutschland und Oester-reich: unter Berücksichtigung der Deutschen Gewerbe-schau München 1922, ed. by Alexander Koch, Darm-stadt: Alexander Koch, 1923.

Delaunay, Sonia: *Tapis et Tissus,* Paris: Éditions d'Art Charles Moreau, no publication date (1929, L'Art International D'Aujourd'hui, Vol. 15.).

Die Überwindung der Utilität: Dagobert Peche und die Wiener Werkstätte, ed. by Peter Noever, Ostfildern: Hatje, 1998.

Deutsche Werkstätten und WK-Verband: 1898–1990; Aufbruch zum Neuen Wohnen, issued by WK-Institut für Wohnkultur, Hans Wichmann, Munich: Prestel, 1992.

DK, *Dekorative Kunst: eine illustrierte Zeitschrift für angewandte Kunst,* Munich, 1897–1929.

DKuD, *Deutsche Kunst und Dekoration: illustrierte Monatshefte für moderne Malerei, Plastik, Architektur, Wohnungskunst und künstlerische Frauenarbeiten,* Darmstadt, 1897–1934.

Eisler, Max, *Dagobert Peche,* Vienna: Gerlach und Wiedling, 1925.

Europäisches Kunstgewerbe: Berichte über die Ausstellung 1927, issued by Städtisches Kunstgewerbe-Museum zu Leipzig, Leipzig: Seemann, 1928.

Exposition des Arts Décoratifs Paris 1925: Etoffes & Tapis Etrangers (Introduction M. P.-Verneuil), Paris: Éditions Albert Lévy Librairie Centrale des Beaux-Arts, no publication date (1926).

Fanelli, Giovanni and Rosalia, *Il Tessuto Art Déco e Anni Trenta,* Florence: Cantini, 1986.

Farbe und Form: Monatsschrift für Kunst und Kunstge-werbe, Berlin: Verlag Schule Reimann, 1916–34.

From East to West; Textiles from G. P. & J. Baker, issued by G. P. & J. Baker Ltd., Victoria & Albert Museum London, London, 1984.

Fuchs-Belhamri, Elisabeth, *Wenzel Hablik: Textilkunst und Mode,* Heide: Boyens & Co., 1993.

Großes Textilhandbuch: Ein Lehr- und Nachschlagewerk für das gesamte Textil- und Bekleidungsfach, ed. by Benno Marcus, Nordhausen: Heinrich Killinger

Gunta Stölzl: Meisterin am Bauhaus Dessau – Textilien, Textilentwürfe und freie Arbeiten 1915–1983, issued by the Stiftung Bauhaus Dessau, Dessau: Hatje, 1997.

Gunta Stölzl: Weberei am Bauhaus und aus eigener Werkstatt, ed. by Magdalena Droste for the Bauhaus-Archiv, Berlin: Kupfergraben, 1987.

HdK, *Handbuch des Kunstmarktes: Kunstadressbuch für das deutsche Reich, Danzig und Deutsch-Österreich,* Berlin: Kalkoff, 1926.

Hunton, W. Gordon, *English Decorative Textiles; Tapestry and Chintz,* London: John Tiranti & Comp., 1930.

ID, *Innendekoration: die gesamte Wohnungskunst in Bild und Wort,* Darmstadt, 1890–1945.

Lewis, F., *British Textiles,* London: Leigh-on-Sea: F. Lewis Publishers Ltd., 1951.

Marangoni, Guido, *Enciclopedia delle Moderne Arti decorative Italiane: V. Le Stoffe d'Arte e l'arredamento della casa,* Milan: Casa Editrice Ceschine, 1928.

Mendes, Valerie, *The Victoria & Albert Museum's Textile Collection: British Textiles from 1900 to 1937,* London: V & A Museum, 1992.

Osma, Guillermo de, *Fortuny: The Life and Work of Mariano Fortuny,* New York: Rizzoli, 1980.

Paulson Townsend, W. G., *Modern Decorative Art in England: Its Development & Characteristics (Woven & Printed Fabrics, Wall-Papers, Lace, Embroidery; Volume 1),* London: Batsford, 1922.

Polytex-Stoffe für Möbel und Dekorationen, issued by Polytextil GmbH Berlin, Wilhelmstr. 107 (company catalogue), Berlin, no publication date.

Saur Allgemeines Künstlerlexikon: Die Bildenden Künst-ler aller Zeiten und Völker, ed. by. Günter Meissner, Munich, Leipzig: Saur, 1992, Vol. 1–19.

Schoeser, Mary, and Dejardin, Kathleen, *French Tex-tiles from 1760 to the Present,* London: Laurence King Ltd., 1991.

Schoeser, Mary, and Rufey, Celia, *English and Ameri-can Textiles: from 1790 to the present,* New York: Tha-mes and Hudson, 1989.

Textilien der Wiener Werkstätte, Städtische Kunstsamm-lungen Chemnitz, ed. by S. Anna, Stuttgart: Daco-Verlag Bläse, 1994.

Textilkunde: Ein Hand- und Nachschlagebuch für die Praxis des Textilkaufmannes und für alle Zweige des Textilfaches, ed. by A. Jaumann, Nordhausen: Heinrich Killinger, 1938.

Textil-Lexikon: Handwörterbuch der gesamten Textilkun-de, ed. by Hugo Glafey, Stuttgart, Berlin: Deutsche Verlagsanstalt, 1937.

The Studio Year-Book of decorative Art: a review of the latest developments in the artistic construction decoration and furnishing of the house, London: The Studio, 1906–1932.

TKI, *Textile Kunst und Industrie: illustrierte Monats-hefte für die künstlerischen Interessen der gesamten Textilindustrie,* ed. by Oskar Haebler, 1908–1922.

Völker, Angela, *Die Stoffe der Wiener Werkstätte 1910–1932,* issued by the Österreichisches Museum für angewandte Kunst, Vienna: Brandstätter, 1990.

Von Morris bis Memphis: Textilien der Neuen Samm-lung; Ende 19. bis Ende 20. Jahrhundert, ed. by Hans Wichmann, Basel, Boston, Berlin: Birkhäuser, 1990 (collection catalogue Neue Sammlung, Vol. 3).

Werkbund-Ausstellung "Die Wohnung": Kleiner Führer durch die Werkbund-Siedlung Weissenhof, Stuttgart, 1927.

Wortmann Weltge, Sigrid, *Bauhaus-Textilien, Kunst und Künstlerinnen der Webwerkstatt,* Schaffhausen: Edition Stemmle, 1993.

75 Jahre Burg Giebichenstein 1915–1990: Beiträge zur Geschichte, issued by Burg Giebichenstein – Hochschu-le für Kunst und Design Halle, Halle, 1990.

Translation of the German texts by John S. Southard
Translation of the texts in the plate section by Peter Thomas Hill
Editorial direction by Hubert Bächler, Andreas Ritter and Sara Schindler
Layout by Alexandra Weller
Printed by Kündig Druck AG, Baar/Zug, Switzerland
Bound by Buchbinderei Burkhardt AG, Mönchaltorf/Zurich, Switzerland

ISBN 3-908161-61-4

Photography: May Vogt, Chemnitz, Germany
Nos. 94–98: PUNCTUM/Bertram Kober, Leipzig, Germany